3112

THE CHRISTIAN CONSUMER

THE CHRISTIAN CONSUMER

Living Faithfully in a Fragile World

Laura M. Hartman

OXFORD
UNIVERSITY PRESS

OXFORD
UNIVERSITY PRESS

Oxford University Press, Inc., publishes works that further
Oxford University's objective of excellence
in research, scholarship, and education.

Oxford   New York
Auckland   Cape Town   Dar es Salaam   Hong Kong   Karachi
Kuala Lumpur   Madrid   Melbourne   Mexico City   Nairobi
New Delhi   Shanghai   Taipei   Toronto

With offices in
Argentina   Austria   Brazil   Chile   Czech Republic   France   Greece
Guatemala   Hungary   Italy   Japan   Poland   Portugal   Singapore
South Korea   Switzerland   Thailand   Turkey   Ukraine   Vietnam

Published by Oxford University Press, Inc.
198 Madison Avenue, New York, New York 10016

www.oup.com

Oxford is a registered trademark of Oxford University Press

Library of Congress Cataloging-in-Publication Data
Hartman, Laura M.
The Christian consumer : living faithfully in a fragile world / Laura M. Hartman.
p.   cm.
ISBN 978-0-19-974642-2
1. Consumption (Economics)—Religious aspects—Christianity.
2. Christian life.   I. Title.
BR115.C67H37 2011
241'.68—dc22   2011007842

1 3 5 7 9 8 6 4 2

Printed in the United States of America
on fifty percent recycled paper

To my son, Theodore,
who has taught me about the depths
of desire and the importance of "stuff."

CONTENTS

CONTENTS

ACKNOWLEDGMENTS

With great pleasure, I wish to acknowledge the sources of some of my interest in consumption, and to thank the many people who've helped me to write this book. My interest in this topic was formed in college, thanks to eye-opening courses from Richard Wilk, David Haberman, and Michael Smith, and it was further nourished in the year I spent working at New American Dream, a nonprofit based in Takoma Park, MD, which urges Americans to change the way we consume for environmental, social-justice, and quality-of-life reasons. My interest in cooperatives arises from my experiences founding, running, and living in a coop, CHÜVA (Cooperative Housing at the University of Virginia), whose residents continue to be an inspiration.

This book began as a dissertation. Thanks are due to my dissertation committee at the University of Virginia: Jim Childress, Margaret Mohrmann, Chuck Mathewes, and Katya Makarova. Jim and Margaret offered golden, career-altering advice and I am grateful for their mentorship. Thanks are also due to colleagues who helped with the process, especially Catherine Griffith, Willis Jenkins, Daniel Weiss, and John Bugbee. Special thanks to Ross

Martinie Eiler for introducing me to John Woolman and for living out his own version of Dorothy Day's call, and to Jim Jones of NASCO (North American Students of Cooperation) for suggesting I read the work of Toyohiko Kagawa. During the dissertation stage, I benefited from the generous support of Brown Residential College and St. Paul's Memorial Episcopal Church, with special thanks to David McIlhiney for sharing an office with me.

I'm grateful to Augustana College in Rock Island, IL, both for gainful employment and for supporting research and scholarship. Thanks to my colleagues in the religion department for their encouragement and enthusiasm, with special thanks to Dan Lee and Kristy Nabhan-Warren for their mentorship. I am grateful also to my students, who continually challenge and inspire me. I've presented parts of chapter 5 at conferences of the Society of Christian Ethics and the American Academy of Religion, and I am grateful for the collegial feedback and suggestions I received from the audience at these sessions.

Thanks are due for the frank and helpful feedback from the anonymous reviewers who read this manuscript for Oxford University Press. Thanks also to Cynthia Read, for her enthusiasm for the project and her accommodating aid, to Gwen Colvin for her able work as production editor, to Rene Leath for the excellent copyediting, and to Sasha Grossman and Woody Gilmartin for their good work at Oxford. I also wish to thank those who helped create this book through their labor in factories that produced the paper and ink, printed the pages and cover, and created the finished book.

On a personal note, I thank my family for their constant encouragement from my earliest days—my sisters and parents, who taught me to read and never doubted my ability to achieve academically. All of them offered support and sympathy along the way; all have, in their own way, modeled lives of mental

engagement and practical application. I also thank my family for schooling me in thrift, savoring, and celebration.

I especially thank Anne Dickey, whose amazing insights, steadfast support, and nourishing love continue to fill me with awe and gratitude that know no bounds. Through her efforts, I've had the time and mental space to transform this dissertation into a book. Her critical thinking skills, knowledge, and willingness to painstakingly edit the entire book have vastly improved its contents, though all remaining errors are entirely my own. Finally, I thank God, the source and support of every blessing listed above, and the force that continually draws me forward into new thoughts and new work.

THE CHRISTIAN CONSUMER

Chapter 1

Introduction

Consumption Matters

At times I find shopping to be just short of oppressive. In stores, narrow aisles with hundreds of brightly colored products loom over me as if they are about to collapse under the weight of the choices they represent. Long after others have grabbed their selections and moved on, I might stand in front of the vegetables lost in thought, my mind looping through environmental factors, the family budget, and the claims of my community as I choose among produce that might be local, mid-range, or international; organic, low-spray, or conventional; fresh, frozen, dried, or canned; nutrient dense and gourmet or quotidian yet still nutritionally sound. After I make the selection, I might still wander the store, trying to determine whether to settle on the less-than-ideal item in my hand or to search for an organic, fair trade, less expensive, or locally made version elsewhere, already anticipating my buyer's remorse before I'm through the checkout line. Is it really so simple for those other shoppers I see in the store, filling their baskets and moving on with their evening plans?

I suspect that for all of us who attempt to consume carefully, shopping is fraught with similar difficulties. Buddhist scholar Stephanie Kaza, for instance, describes her own consumer paralysis, "staring at the bounty on the shelves, lost in thoughts of fair trade, farmworkers, and food security."[1] When shopping, she finds herself "barraged not only by a daunting array of goods but also by virtually nonstop moralistic thoughts," as she seeks to avoid child labor, toxic chemicals, resource depletion, over-farming, and un-Buddhist vanity.[2] Yet consumption is not exclusively distressing: those who attempt to consume responsibly may also truly enjoy the things they consume. As John Kavanaugh, a Jesuit writer and philosopher, acknowledges, "Lovely clothes, a beautiful home, diverse cuisines, stirring art and play are, at their finest, the splendid embodiment and expression of personhood [, viz., fulfilled human life rather than commodified materiality]."[3] I relish coming home to a warm house with a full larder and useful belongings. I savor the pleasures of good quality paper and pens and of homemade blueberry pie. Though I sometimes feel burdened by the "stuff" in my life, I also take great pleasure in it; it contributes to the joy and richness of living.

Those of us who both love material things and worry about the moral dimension of their production, use, and disposal naturally notice our consumption. However, consumption demands attention even from those who ignore the things they use or who do not focus on the moral dimension of life. The flow of physical materials in and through human lives is morally and theologically complex whether consumers are aware of the complexity or not. From fair trade coffee to foreign oil, from steak at home to a veggie burger at the drive-through, every act of consumption creates rippling effects, positive and negative, on humans, on other sentient beings, and on what the Book of Common Prayer calls "this fragile earth, our island home."[4] These effects are unavoidable, because all creatures must consume: without consuming, we die. Their moral import is likewise unavoidable, and for this reason consumption bears serious ethical reflection.

Though few have undertaken a sustained, thorough investigation of the moral dimensions of consumption on a conceptual level, I expect that most of us have an implicit, operative sense of what constitutes ethically defensible consumption, and express that sense in our daily, lived practice. In this book, I look to the Christian tradition, broadly construed, for historical and contemporary resources that may aid the search for an effective and explicit practical ethics of consumption. I have found in this tradition voices that indicate a variety of ethical stances, and these voices sing forth in four groups in the chapters that follow. These four groups of Christian voices form a chorus of perspectives on consumption, which then speaks as a sort of Greek chorus to offer insights into real-world ethical questions. I hope that the reflections and strategies for Christian consumption discussed here may both strengthen and inform those who have an implicit sense of ethical consumption and also offer resources for conscious ethical construction to those who prefer more structured thought.

This is not a book about how Christians *do* consume, in the aggregate, using surveys and statistics and sociological data. It is about how Christians *should* consume, using historical exemplars, major theological concepts, and some fundamental ethical ideas. I begin this chapter by discussing consumerism and consumption, clarifying the parameters of my definition of consumption. Using the example of a cup of coffee, I explore the moral ramifications of simple acts of consumption. Finally, I offer an overview of the chapters that follow this introduction and conclude with notes on my own assumptions, methods, and the book's intended audience.

CONSUMERISM DISTINGUISHED FROM CONSUMPTION

When I describe this book to my colleagues, most conclude initially that my topic is consumerism. After all, consumerism is not only a popular topic for academic scholarship in recent decades but it is also a very real problem impacting most industrial societies around the globe. And, in fact, I must first explore what consumerism is and why it is a problem before it is clear why I believe that *consumption*, rather than *consumerism*, is the proper starting point for addressing some of the problems articulated by scholars of consumerism.

While there is some variety in the way consumerism is defined, many writers agree on its fundamental meaning. In agreement with many others, I define consumerism as an ethos—a collection of attitudes, values, and cultural constructs—that places great value on shopping and consumption, such that consumption defines the parameters of the good life and the ultimate goals of the human, and a concomitant lack of attention to the moral dimension of consumption.[5]

Many Christian writers who address consumerism offer criticisms using moral language, calling it either idolatry or greed. Some see consumerism as a separate, competing religion;[6] others are concerned about consumerism's effects on Christianity, in the commodification of religion;[7] others are concerned about greed, gluttony, and the effects of advertising on Christian desires.[8] Many agree that Christian churches fail to address consumerism and related issues sufficiently.[9] Critics of consumerism often call for a "return" to a less consumerist age through strengthened communities, more robust valuation of work and production, restricted advertising, and simple living.

Ecotheologian Sallie McFague echoes many other Christians who lament the rise of consumerism when she writes, "We have become consumers—not citizens, or children of God, or lovers of the world, but *consumers*."[10] The contrast between consumer and citizen is a potent critique of consumerism. British sociologist Alan Aldridge explains that "citizenship expresses a fundamental equality, while consumerism generates and feeds on inequality.... Citizens engage in collective action to make society better, whereas consumers are preoccupied with improving their own individual lot."[11] He notes, however, that this is a stereotyped and polarized view, neglecting the ways in which adequate consumption may equip people to exercise their citizen duties, or indeed that consumers may exercise citizenship *through* consumption.

Historian Lizabeth Cohen, in *A Consumers' Republic: The Politics of Mass Consumption in Postwar America*, does not see citizen and consumer as competing identities but rather traces their integration in the historical development of the "citizen consumer" and the "purchaser as citizen" in twentieth-century North America.[12] Cohen would categorize this book as an example of an early twenty-first-century perspective on ethical consumption as a form of good "citizenship"; more specifically, how good consumers can be good Christians. British cultural critic Jo Littler would agree. In *Radical Consumption: Shopping for Change in Contemporary Culture*, she writes, "'ethical consumers' use [ethical] forms of consumption to style the self."[13] In other words, books like this that seek to coach Christians in ethical consumption are products of their time—purveyors of an ethos that says "buy the right things and you can be a good Christian."

While the book you are reading now is inescapably a product of its time, it is not a catalog of the proper items to buy in order to make our consumption "Christian." Rather, it offers an alternate ethos to that of consumerism, asserting that consumption is not a morally neutral tool to fulfill our desires or to identify with a chosen group, but rather is much more ethically nuanced. Consuming in ways that express and reinforce my ethical views is desirable, but displaying this fact is not. Jesus warns his followers to avoid conspicuous (non-)consumption: "when you fast, put oil on your head and wash your face, so that your fasting may be seen not by others but by your Father who is in secret; and your Father who sees in secret will reward you" (Matthew 6:17–18). Consuming in order to demonstrate to others my ethical status shows pride and a false faith in the opinions of others. Many Christians, including myself, would assert that consuming as a Christian does not mean "styling the self" in a Christian way by buying Christian-approved products, so much as it means subjecting our purchasing to considerations such as the needs of our neighbors, the gifts of God, and our own yearning for holiness and virtue.

It is easy to identify the ways that sociological treatments of Christian consumption are discordant with Christian understandings of how consumption and Christian identity interact. However, even among Christian writers who denounce consumerism, few articulate a constructive alternative either to the practice of consumerism or to sociological explanations thereof. If one accepts Christian criticisms that consumerism places excessive value on consumption, encourages greed, and attaches idolatrous weight to the social value of conspicuous consumption, this raises a more basic question: what constitutes good, Christian consumption? To criticize consumerism without first evaluating consumption is analogous to a Christian author denouncing militarism before clearly articulating what is right or wrong about war. Such a hypothetical situation seems absurd: how can one denounce militarism without at least implicitly relying on an ethical analysis of war? Christians writing about consumerism often reflect a simplistic, negative view of consumption without fully examining the validity of this stance. This book, then, takes a step back from most contemporary Christian criticisms of consumerism, important though they may be, in order to ask: what is consumption, and what is right or wrong about it? What and how shall we consume?

CONSUMPTION: BEYOND SOCIOLOGY

First we have to be clear about the definition of consumption. As with consumerism, many contested definitions exist in the literature on the subject. The definition I seek needs to be as workable in today's society, where consumption has been magnified and distorted to become consumerism, as it is applicable to the ancient world, where the most closely related concept was *use*.[14] The definition most appropriate for this project focuses on the physical: consumption is the physical throughput of materials and goods in human lives. I use the word *throughput*, a metaphor derived from industry and ecology, to denote the flow of materials used and waste discarded.[15] In industry, raw materials enter the factory and both waste and products exit it; the mass of physical "stuff" is the throughput. In ecology, the throughput of an organism refers to the materials the organism takes in (water, nutrients, food) and the materials it puts out (waste).[16] It may sound crass, but it is not inaccurate: humans, too, have a throughput of physical material in our lives. Consumption is not the same as shopping. It can occur even when no money changes hands: in picking and eating wild blackberries, for example, there exists throughput of materials in human lives, and thus, by this definition, consumption.

Perhaps it is surprising that *this* aspect of consumption, the physical realm, takes precedence in a book about religion and ethics. A sociologist might ask, are not the social, interpersonal, market, and meaning-making aspects of consumption more important? Sociologists, who with historians created the contemporary field of scholarly literature about consumption and consumerism, frequently refer to the meaning of consumption as its most important attribute. In fact, many sociologists and anthropologists argue that the goods themselves matter less than the meaning we attach to them.[17]

I agree up to a point. Yes, consumption has meaning, and this meaning is important. This explains why it is deeply upsetting to discover that an act of consumption that intends one meaning (the beauty, expensiveness, and prestige of my grandmother's mink coat, for example) also carries an unintended and undesired meaning (the suffering and death of approximately fifty small mammals, the exploitation of an ecosystem). But the fact that consumption has meaning is not integral to the definition of what qualifies as consumption. A dietary example may clarify: even though what I eat, and how I eat it, and with whom, carries a lot of meaning, nevertheless the definition of *eating* remains the act of taking food into my body for digestion. Similarly, even though the social circumstances of consumption carry meaning and rich cultural context, nevertheless *consumption* remains the physical throughput of materials through human lives. (Clearly, eating is one example of consumption, by this definition.)

Though this book hews to a more concrete understanding of consumption than most sociological treatments, sociologists of consumption, consumerism, and consumer capitalism might find this book to be a good example of a specific category of meaning that attends consumption: religious and moral meaning. Peace activist and member of the Church of the Brethren Arthur Gish has written, "There cannot be justice for all as long as anyone consumes more than one needs.... Overconsumption is theft."[18] Following this line of thought, certain types of consumption can render consumers accomplices to injustice and theft. Consumption, then, not only has meaning for *social* status, but it can also confer *moral* status on those who are successfully conscientious, or it can reveal the moral detriment of those who fail. For example, my discount-store blue jeans aren't simply *socially* suspect because their lower quality or lower-brow fashion place me in a nondominant social class or telegraph something about the relationships that

I form, but they are *morally* suspect because they mean I patronized a store that (allegedly) exploits its own workers and destroys community businesses, a store that buys those jeans from suppliers who run sweatshops and who source their cotton from pesticide-intensive farms. On this view, then, my act of consumption may confer both low social status and low moral status.

But the goal of Christian ethical reflection is not achieving the proper status; the point is to discern what is right. The moral meaning of consumption cannot be reduced to status, and cannot be divorced from the physical qualities of the item consumed. Too many discussions of consumption abstract the meaning (social status, style, group identity) from the object itself. Anthropologist Mary Douglas influentially advised, "Forget that commodities are good for eating, clothing, and shelter; forget their usefulness and try instead the idea that commodities are good for thinking; treat them as a nonverbal medium for the human creative faculty."[19] By contrast, my concerns about the moral import of consumption are intimately tied to the physicality of the item: its extraction, production, and transportation, and the environmental and social impact that accompanies it. I am also concerned about how buying, having, or using the item may impact one's spiritual state and one's relationships with others. These concerns are often minimized or completely ignored by sociological treatments of consumption, but I argue they are paramount to consumption's true meaning, and to the moral judgments we make about it.

REFINING THE DEFINITION

This book addresses consumption broadly defined. Many of the examples in the following chapters will be food related, as eating is perhaps the most obvious instance of human consumption.

Clothing and transportation also arise as examples. Other kinds of consumption—housing, energy use, and electronics—are less frequently discussed in the pages that follow. I recognize that, phenomenologically, there are major differences between the experience of consuming food and the experience of consuming electronics (for example). Food consumption is often motivated by physical hunger; electronics infrequently fill a physical need, though they may meet intense social or economic needs. (Medical and adaptive devices are notable exceptions of electronics that do meet physical needs.) Food consumption can be less commercial, produced among garden, kitchen, and plate; electronics are almost never grown or constructed at home, requiring instead a market interaction in a store, likely as a result of advertising. Although meaningful, even profound differences do exist among the individual acts that I classify as consumption; they are all subject to a common ethical consideration, be it a quick snack at a gas station or a deliberate purchase of a vacuum cleaner.

Further, consumption as I have defined it is not limited in scale. It could refer to an individual's consumption or the throughput of materials in an entire country. On small, medium, and large scales, consumption is morally relevant. The scope of this book only allows for a focus on individual- and household-level consumption, but the conclusions reached will, I hope, offer insights for questions of larger-scale consumption as well.

My definition purposely includes the term "human": my interest is only in human consumption. Consumption by animals, substantively free from human influence, is amoral. Given the definition of consumption as throughput, all creatures do consume. In certain situations, influenced by humans, there may even be morally relevant dimensions to nonhuman consumption (e.g., ought household pets be given "organic" food?). But for the most part, nonhuman consumption happens in an amoral

context, independent of human agency. Who can blame a bur-
geoning deer population for overgrazing their forest? They are
simply behaving according to their nature, not making a moral
choice.

Humans, like animals, consume due to natural hungers. If
humans consume excessively, eating themselves out of house
and home in the same way that overpopulated deer do, perhaps
this behavior is inherent in our animal natures. It may be argued
that humans, like deer, simply need to have our population
curbed, so we do not devour our habitat into desolation. This
emphasis on population, rather than consumption, has been a
common position in American environmentalism in the twentieth century, but the emphasis has since shifted to consumption. As journalist Fred Pearce puts it, "Any analysis of the damage
being caused today by rising population and rising consumption
must conclude that consumption is the greater peril."[20] Controlling
population growth is important, but controlling consumption is
even more important.

For better and worse, humans are animals who are capable of
moral appraisal and acting on convictions. As Wendell Berry writes,
"Whereas animals are usually restrained by the limits of physical
appetites, humans have mental appetites that can be far more
gross and capacious than physical ones. Only humans squander
and hoard, murder and pillage because of notions."[21] We are not
doomed to overgrazing; unlike deer, we can make conscious
choices. We differ from most nonhuman animals in our propensity
to consume beyond basic animal needs.[22] But we also can choose
not to do so. Human consumption originates in our personal and
collective choices, which derive both from our various appetites
and the norms established within society: culturally determined
standards, advertising, religious ideas, technological innovation,
and so forth. The human ability to ethically assess and then control

our levels and types of consumption is what makes consumption ethics possible.

Not all humans enjoy the same level of choice in consumption. In an extremely impoverished situation, for example, humans have scarcely more choice than animals in terms of food consumption. We, too, must eat to live. It is inappropriate to tell malnourished Haitians that eating animals is cruel and therefore forbidden when their crops have baked in the ground and goats are their only edible option. In such circumstances, surely, moral judgments about meat consumption ease, and attention shifts to treatment of the animal while living and the use of its flesh once slaughtered. But among affluent members of the first world, consumption is engaged in by choice and with significant room for moral appraisal and critique. We may all feel constrained by our needs, wants, and social norms; we may hardly feel liberated by the excessive choices and barrage of advertisements that characterize life in a consumerist age; but unlike someone who is in brutal fact poor, our consumption contains significant elements of voluntary choice and therefore of moral import.

The term "consumption," when used to denote a human activity rather than tuberculosis, is of relatively recent origin.[23] However, consumption as I have defined it—a throughput of physical materials through human lives—has occurred as long as humanity has existed. Still, this definition may seem to be too broad: surely there are relevant, even vital, differences between prehistoric consumption, ancient consumption, medieval consumption, my great-grandparents' consumption, and mine today. Observers of consumerism recognize that contemporary society, particularly in the first world, has undergone an unprecedented change in the ethos of consumption. This means the constant bombardment of advertising, geared at creating new desires for new kinds of objects and at disrupting the satisfaction one might have felt with what one currently possesses, now that newer versions are available. This means continual product innovation and development, planned obsolescence, and other strategies on the part of producers to entice consumers to purchase more products. Thanks to innovation, global trade, and relatively cheap energy sources, my purchasing options are much broader and more varied than that of my great-grandparents, let alone that of more ancient historical persons,[24] some of whom appear in this book.

This does not, however, change what consumption is. In this book, I draw on many historical texts in which the term "consumption" does not appear. Even thinkers who do not explicitly address consumption have something to contribute to a Christian ethics of consumption. In their treatment of concepts such as use, harvest, eating, construction, trade, celebration, market, and asceticism, these writers indicate a moral stance toward human use of the material world. Consumption ethics is, at bottom, a species of stewardship ethics, asking questions such as: what does God intend for humans in their interactions with the material world? What is creation, and what are humans to do with it? How are humans to relate well to one another concerning the proper use of the material conditions of life? By examining these questions and their historical and contemporary answers, it is possible to construct a consumer ethic in consonance with them, an ethic of consumption that draws on and is faithful to the Christian tradition.

I recognize that my definition of consumption, and the way I use it, risks oversimplification and anachronism. I discuss this broad concept across different periods of history, bracketing the specific historical contexts in which it has existed. Sociologists and historians may disapprove, but I do this with good reason. My purpose is not to analyze contemporary consumption in light of its departure from past patterns (many excellent works of history and sociology already do this).[25] Instead, I aim to find themes, attitudes, and insights from the Christian tradition that might, irrespective of their origin, inform authentic Christian responses to contemporary questions about consumption. Though I try to pay due attention to the historical and social location of these sources, this sort of cross-contextual work cannot completely import these writers' worlds along with their thoughts. Though it may seem anachronistic, this is what Christians, and Christian ethicists, do: we look to ancient and historical sources for insights into the present. The historical or social context certainly affects our understanding of these resources, but the emphasis here is on ethics, not on history or sociology.

THE MORAL IMPORT OF CONSUMPTION

To truly comprehend the consequences of contemporary human consumption falls somewhere between daunting and impossible. To trace the ramifications of one purchase requires extensive research and an advanced understanding of international trade, geography, economics, ecology, and politics. The complexity and opacity of global political and economic systems means that a multitude of moral problems may arise in relation to human consumption, yet consumers remain completely unaware of them. One act of consumption may have morally relevant effects on the nonhuman biosphere, on other humans, and on consumers themselves.

Stephanie Kaza begins her discussion of Buddhism and consumption with what is becoming the classic example: coffee. She traces the environmental impact of North American coffee consumption, moves on to the impact of other food items, and concludes, darkly, that "the consumer class is responsible for most of the environmental impact on the planet."[26] To elaborate on Kaza's coffee example, there are four distinct realms in which coffee consumption (and, arguably, all consumption) has an ethical impact. Most immediately, it impacts the consumer himself or herself: drinking coffee affects the health, well-being, and financial status of the consumer. Some consumed substances could be unhealthy or self-destructive and therefore ethically suspect (e.g., crystal meth); others may be salutary and commendable (e.g., multivitamins). Most, like coffee, offer a mixed collection of attributes: it tastes good and gives pleasure to the consumer; the caffeine may be either beneficial or detrimental, depending on the situation and the health of the consumer; if consumed hot, it may help us tolerate a cold environment, and vice versa; if dressed with large amounts of cream and sugar it may diminish the consumer's health; and so forth.

The second realm of impact is immediate and social. Coffee consumption (and all consumption) affects other people, people known to the consumer. A regular patron at a coffee shop knows the workers and other customers. Consuming that coffee involves interacting with others and, in the case of the coffee shop employees, financially supporting them in their employment. Having consumed the coffee may affect others known to the consumer—for example, business associates she meets later who appreciate her chipper, alert manner thanks to the caffeine if her consumption is moderate, or her family, whose budget may be strained by a daily habit of overpriced drinks if her consumption is not so moderate. Again, both positive and negative effects may result from this act of consumption.

Third, coffee consumption (and all consumption) affects people the consumer does not know, people she can barely imagine. Her purchase is part of the bottom line closely watched by regional managers and executives who run the coffee company and is added to the marketing data that shapes the experience future consumers have of the company. It also, somewhat indirectly, affects those who grow, process, and ship the coffee. By adding, even in a small increment, to the demand for this particular kind of coffee, the consumer affects the shape of global trade. The advent of brands billed as "fair trade" brings into focus the ethical impact of a coffee purchase on growers and farm workers across the world. Fair trade companies intend to aid struggling farmers by offering a higher price for their coffee. They achieve this by enticing consumers to pay more by appealing to their consciences, offering a guarantee that this coffee purchase supports a company that features ecological scruples and well-treated workers. Choosing the fair trade coffee, ostensibly, supports an adequate livelihood for growers across the globe. The same is true, to a greater or lesser degree, for most other acts of consumption.

Finally, coffee consumption (and all consumption) has an impact on the nonhuman natural world. Kaza names many of the devastating effects visited by the demand for coffee, concluding that "thousands of acres of biologically rich tropical forest have been cleared to support the North American boom in espresso shops."[27] Since fair trade coffee programs often require growers to engage in certain environmentally sensitive farming practices, purchasing this coffee arguably supports a healthy environment. Once harvested, the coffee must be roasted, packaged, and shipped. Each stage of production and distribution contributes significantly to the environmental impact of one coffee purchase, particularly its energy consumption and greenhouse gas emissions, or carbon footprint. In myriad ways, consumption of coffee or other materials typically impacts not just humans but also the biosphere.

Consumption, then, is an act with ethical implications on multiple levels. How then to make sense of the moral pull associated with this complex, difficult to pinpoint subject? One approach is demonstrated by philosopher David Schwartz in *Consuming Choices*. Schwartz scrupulously makes the case for the moral import of every consumer purchase, though he does so with some trepidation: "if consumers bear even a small degree of culpability for wrongdoing associated with products they purchase, then the act of going shopping can quickly become an ethical minefield."[28] Schwartz argues that the consequences of our purchases, though exceedingly difficult to track, are nevertheless significant: they bring about changes in production, which in turn affect the well-being of workers and the environment. Deriving benefit from unethical production practices, Schwartz demonstrates, constitutes complicity. Schwartz uses the tools of philosophical ethics to carefully examine the ethics of consumer purchases, concluding that whether it is approached through consequentialist or deontological ethics, consumers do in fact bear culpability for the wrongdoing associated with their purchases.[29]

This means, according to Schwartz, that none of us is free of ethical taint; but "unclean hands are better than filthy hands," and it is incumbent upon consumers to attempt to make purchases that are as ethically defensible as possible.[30] He writes, "The burden of living an ethical consumer life is in many ways an epistemological burden, a burden of knowledge."[31] Consumers have a duty to educate themselves as best they can; Schwartz also advocates better product labeling so that the carbon footprint of a product, for example, would be visible to the end consumer.[32] Schwartz denounces "culpable ignorance," that is, "willfully avoiding knowledge that might help one avoid acting immorally," but admits that consumers have "a vested interest" in finding our favorite products to be "morally permissible": there are some things we would rather not know.[33] Nevertheless, Schwartz charges consumers to take on the responsibility of knowledge and ethical action.

Daniel Goleman, in *Ecological Intelligence: How Knowing the Hidden Impacts of What We Buy Can Change Everything*, agrees with Schwartz about consumer knowledge. Goleman enthusiastically describes recent advances in the field of industrial ecology: experts can now track the environmental, health, and social impacts of various products, creating a life cycle assessment for each item on the supermarket shelf.[34] Various rating tools then allow consumers to selectively purchase items based on their ethical import, in addition to their price or quality. Goleman asserts that leveling the "information asymmetry" that has existed in the marketplace until now will allow a "radical transparency" in purchasing decisions.[35] Ultimately, consumers will no longer have to guess at the impacts of their consumption, and can use their purchasing power to direct companies toward better and better practices.[36] Goleman is right: greater information about products is an incredible boon to conscientious consumers, and the more transparency the better. I applaud the tools and rating systems he profiles as a major step in a good direction. But information is no cure-all: even with thorough knowledge of the products, it still falls to individual consumers to make conscientious choices and flex their citizen-consumer power in the proper direction. Goleman somewhat naively assumes that consumers are rational agents desiring a better world through wise purchasing decisions, but the consumer psyche is more complex than he acknowledges.

There is another way to approach the ethical implications of consumption as they play out in these multiple levels. I do not take the approach of Goleman, with his "radical transparency," which offers consumers the tools they need to calculate the ethical impact of their purchases, and I do not take the approach of Schwartz, who seems to expect consumers to calculate the consequences, or to formulate consumer rules that make for the greatest chance of avoiding complicity in undesirable production practices.

Rather, I take an approach that looks to a particular body of accumulated wisdom, the Christian tradition, for guidance. By exploring the thoughts and actions of virtuous exemplars, and by describing the dispositions of thought and action that lead to fruitful deliberation about consumption, consumers may be guided toward ethical habits and choices. Though consumption's impacts can seem overwhelming, consumers need not be experts or omniscient. We need, I contend, to be aware of our consumption and interested in its impacts, but also rooted in the insights of tradition and willing to integrate its wisdom into our choices.

FOUR CONSIDERATIONS

Christian perspectives on consumption tend to emphasize one or more of four primary considerations. These four considerations are not mutually exclusive, though they highlight very different concerns. In response to the question "What does good Christian consumption look like?" Christians answer in four ways: it avoids sin, it embraces creation, it loves the neighbor, and it envisions the future. Each of these four considerations is introduced, in brief, below; a fuller explanation and analysis of each makes up the next four chapters of this book.

To Avoid Sin

A strong ascetic strain within the Christian tradition views consumption with skepticism, as rife with temptation and overindulgence. Many Christian thinkers through the ages have counseled temperance and discipline in the consumption of food and accumulation of wealth. Contemporary Christians tackling problems relating to consumption and overconsumption often take a similar approach. Some are concerned for the well-being of individual Christians, for whom overconsumption constitutes a temptation to sin in the form of greed or gluttony.[37] Process theologian Jay McDaniel echoes many other Christian writers concerned about the spiritual effects of consumption when he writes, "The very possession of an excessive stock of material goods, paralleled by the habits of consumption that usually accompany such possession, obstructs one's capacity to be in creative harmony with the world"—and thus one's capacity to relate to God.[38] Others are concerned for the well-being of the poor, whose lack seems a direct consequence of the thoughtless overconsumption of others. "Few among us gives the poor an amount equal to what we spend on beach homes, or even fancy coffees," reproves Christian ethicist Jaydee Hanson in a representative article of this type.[39]

Increasingly, Christian pleas for a limit to consumption come situated in ecological reasoning. As Methodist environmental writer Bill McKibben sees it, "The American way of life, insofar as it revolves around consumption, drives our environmental problems."[40] Several contemporary Christian authors, in response to problems posed by overconsumption, have gestured toward a "theology of enough" (Schut), an ethic of "sufficiency" (Gibson), and the virtues of "poverty" (Foley) and "frugality" (Nash).[41] Christians who take this perspective find themselves withdrawing or stepping back from consumption. The primary theological concern here is sin: specifically, the desire to avoid both personal sin and participation in social sin.

To Embrace Creation

The Christian tradition is not entirely ascetic, however. While some view consumption with skepticism, others accept it as an integral part of a Christian life, and even embrace it as a form of participation in God's grace and blessing. Most Christian writers addressing consumption today do acknowledge the potential harms to people and the environment resulting from excessive levels of consumption. But some take pains to demonstrate that consumption still can be a positive activity. As Reformed writer David Schelhaas describes it, "Nothing is inherently wrong with making things, wanting things, buying things, and enjoying them. In fact, it is good and natural for us to do so."[42]

Few go as far as Jewish scholar Tsvi Blanchard, who describes "sacred consumption";[43] nonetheless, particularly among Christian writers with an environmental interest, it is common to see a call for greater love for, and joyful consumption of, the world, rather than a stricter renunciation of it. Wendell Berry writes,

> Apparently because our age is so manifestly unconcerned for the life of the spirit, many people conclude that it places an undue value on material things. But that cannot be so, for people who valued material things would take care of them and would care for the sources of them. We could argue that an age that *properly* valued and cared for material things would be an age properly spiritual.[44]

For Berry and others, caring for and embracing the material world can be a way to pursue a spiritual life. Christians who emphasize this consideration are characterized by a sense of forward motion and embrace as they welcome God's blessings and the earth's bounty. Their primary theological concern is creation: how to honor and celebrate creation, and how to respond properly to creation's abundance.

To Love the Neighbor

Many thinkers invoke relationships as a Christian value to guide decisions about consumption, with special attention given to categories such as neighbor-love and the common good. As Mennonite missionary and pastor Erwin Wiens puts it, "Any action, therefore, which does not have as its ultimate objective the building of right relationships, cannot be a part of Christian life-style."[45] A call for right relationships and an affirmation of relationality and community-mindedness are common features of contemporary Christian critiques of consumerism and excessive consumption.[46] Good consumption, as Catholic theologian William T. Cavanaugh affirms, is that which "increases the chances of relationship and accountability"—such as "buying things that are locally produced, and at stores that are locally owned."[47] The primary theological concern here is love, including self-love but particularly love of the neighbor. This consideration also raises the question of who counts as neighbors, as faraway sweatshop workers and even the nonhuman natural world may be relevant to the decisions of those seeking to enact neighbor-love in their consumption.

To Envision the Future

Finally, some Christians take a broader perspective on consumption, seeking to create an economic vision in line with God's will for the future of the world, using the fruits of an eschatological imagination to inform practical economic choices. These views of the eschaton vary greatly but regardless of their specifics, they are built around a sense of God's desire for the world's fulfillment as a supreme value and as a guide for economic systems and practices. Two Christian practices are particularly apt for illustrating this consideration: Sabbath keeping and the Eucharist. Christians who take this perspective look forward, orienting themselves toward a richly imagined goal, and rejecting consumption that does not move toward this same goal. The primary theological theme here is the reign of God, and requirements for human behavior in anticipation of its coming.

The four considerations represent four nodes of theological reflection: sin, creation, love, and the reign of God. The potential for these four voices to work in harmony with one another, or in counterpoint to one another, is explored in chapter 6.

METHODS, PERSPECTIVE, AND AUDIENCE

Christians conceive their sources of authority differently, but many concur with the formulation known as the Wesleyan Quadrilateral. According to the Wesleyan Quadrilateral, Christians appeal to four sources of authority: scripture, tradition, reason, and experience. Some Christian groups emphasize one source more than the others, but all have a certain amount of validity and weight for Christian thought. In this book, I emphasize tradition, and I understand the Christian tradition in very broad terms. "Christian," as I use it, includes Catholic, Protestant, and Eastern Orthodox traditions, groups with small populations such as the Religious Society of Friends, and more recently created groups such as the Seventh-day Adventists or prosperity theologians. It includes Christians from all parts of the political spectrum, from evangelical Christianity to the United Church of Christ. "Tradition," as I use it, includes but is not limited to official church statements, the writings of theological and ethical thinkers, and the witness of saints and other holy people. Though I emphasize tradition, scripture is hardly absent in this book. When Christians reflect on consumption, stories from the Bible inevitably arise, from Adam and Eve's consumption of the forbidden fruit in Genesis to Jesus' institution of the Eucharist, from Ezekiel's bread to the cities of gold in Revelation. This is not a book of biblical scholarship, however: the Bible appears as a foundation of tradition, and as interpreted by particular Christians. I choose to focus on the Christian tradition in this book because of my own background and training, and because it offers a beautiful, complex body of insight that is continually deepening and evolving.

In using the Christian tradition, I organize my findings into four categories, which constitute a typology.[48] Typologies have their detractors, and for good reason; James Gustafson points out that one must often exaggerate differences, simplify positions, and assume an artificial objectivity and critical distance in order to make a typology work.[49] And yet, he admits, "such work is extremely useful both as a way of managing divergent materials, and as a way of highlighting crucial distinctions and issues."[50] John Howard Yoder writes, in his critique of H. Richard Niebuhr's *Christ and Culture*, "A typology, when properly discerned, lies in the logic of a problem, and is not imported arbitrarily by the historian."[51] Niebuhr's typology, on Yoder's view, has exaggerated and oversimplified various Christian viewpoints in order to fit them into his preconceived system. No typology fits the data perfectly, and the following chapters contain some of the squeezing and truncating that Yoder and Gustafson lament. Perhaps this is the inevitable cost of a typology: it loses some of the nuanced, contextual nature of each source that it categorizes. I hope that the benefits of this typology, the clarity that it brings to a confusing subject and the constructive ethics that I can build with it, prove to be worth that cost.

But these four considerations also go beyond the function of a typology, in that together they can build a Christian ethics of consumption and can guide ethical reflection. In this sense, they function similarly to the principles in Beauchamp and Childress's *Principles of Biomedical Ethics.*[52] Sometimes referred to as "Principlism," Beauchamp and Childress offer a list of principles as prima facie guidance—ideally, all the obligations implied by the principles would be fulfilled—and an orderly way to discern which may be overridden, when, and why. The consumption ethics I propose is not nearly as comprehensive or directive as Beauchamp and Childress's biomedical ethics, but the idea is a similar one: four major considerations to bear in mind when making these difficult decisions, and a sense of how they may play out in real-world situations.

The underlying logic of the consumption ethics described in this book, however, is not Principlism. The four considerations are not principles; rather, they are actions that produce virtues. To consume ethically is to acquire laudable habits of thought and action, excellences of character, morally valuable traits. If we are in the habit of avoiding sin, we have acquired the virtues of purity, temperance, and self-control. If we find appropriate ways to embrace creation, this shows the virtues of gratitude, humility, joy, and stewardship. Remembering the neighbor in our consumption is a habit of love—compassion, solidarity, justice, and sacrifice for the common good. And envisioning the future through our consumption inculcates dispositions of hope, contentment, self-control, and faith. These four considerations, then, are also a school of virtue: a set of attitudes and dispositions that inform the craft of living a good life. In keeping with the modalities of virtue ethics, the following chapters contain stories of several wise Christians who have learned to embody these virtues in particularly striking ways. These exemplars, I hope, demonstrate ways to live out the truly conscientious consumption I am attempting to describe.

In this book, then, I am using a blend of methods: I elaborate a typology that extends beyond its usual descriptive function, explaining how each major consideration contributes to an integrated view of Christian consumption. In each chapter, I describe the consideration at hand and explain its contribution to the goal of ethically defensible consumption. These considerations do function somewhat like principles, but my approach is not fundamentally the same as Principlism; rather, I use these four considerations as diverse lenses on one holistic vision of virtuous consumption. In the final chapter, I use examples to illuminate this notion of virtue in consumer life.

Just as it is important to situate my work academically, I feel it is important to be honest about my own social location and that of my intended audience. The following details may be relevant to my perspective on this topic: I was born and raised in the United States, though I spent two pre-college years in England and France. I am a well-educated, middle-class white woman. My religious background has taken me through Methodism, the writings of Matthew Fox, Catholicism, Episcopalianism, and Lutheranism. I teach at a small Lutheran liberal arts college in the midwestern United States. My interest in consumption emerged from deep-seated environmental concern coupled with discouragement at the powerlessness of individual efforts. Large corporations and other systems seem to trap consumers into complicity with ecological destruction, and this angers and frustrates me. I spent a year as an intern at New American Dream, a nonprofit that addresses consumption issues.[53] My training in Christian ethics came primarily from applied ethicists, and their method of taking a broad view of a field and identifying categories for understanding that field is one that I have adopted in this book.

While I hope this book is widely read, it is aimed primarily at my fellow consumers who are affluent enough to have abundant choices in what we consume. So when I speak of "we" or "us" in the pages that follow, I typically intend North American consumers such as myself. I also sometimes address Christians, broadly construed, since this book is written with an emphasis on Christian ideas, beliefs, and practices. However, since the primary thrust of this book is toward constructing a method of reflecting on consumption choices, it should be useful to many who are not specifically addressed in its pages.

Chapter 2

To Avoid Sin

In the film *What Would Jesus Buy?* a preacher in a white leisure suit leads a be-robed gospel choir through a shopping mall. "Stop shopping!" they sing as he passionately shouts this refrain. The preacher is actor Bill Talen, in character as the Reverend Billy, and his choir constitutes the charter membership of a growing parody religion, the Church of Life After Shopping.[1] Part performance, part political protest, and part religious service, Reverend Billy and his church are hard to categorize. Talen takes his choir and his "camera-ready" hair to stage venues and churches as well as to Starbucks, Walmart, and anywhere else he feels the forces of consumerism are particularly strong.[2] Performing exorcisms on cash registers and eliciting a hearty "Change-a-lujah!" from his audiences, Talen spreads a strong anticonsumption message, in a stirring format that comes from his own Baptist upbringing.[3] In his crusade against consumerism, he charges his audience to "take your hand away from the product," and to bravely endure the "Bright Unclaimed Space" that opens up as a result.[4] By refusing to consume something, consumers reveal not a vacuum or a frightening void, but rather the "Fabulous Unknown." Former consumers can then enter the sacred state of "Buylessness," Reverend Billy's term for simplified, less commercial, more community-rich living.[5]

Reverend Billy's audience typically responds with an energy not far removed from religious fervor, while the employees and patrons of the stores he storms are less enthusiastic. His work has attracted a steady following, and fans of the Reverend Billy attend performances and listen with enthusiasm and interest to his message as he urges them to consume less for the sake of their souls and their communities. While Talen is not a qualified Christian minister (indeed, he seems not to use a Christian perspective, at least not formally),[6] his message against consumption resounds with many from the Christian tradition who renounce consumption, censure its ill effects, and maintain that reducing our consumption is the best way to be holy, virtuous people, which is in fact their primary goal.

This first consideration—how to avoid sinning in consumption—is exemplified by many Christian thinkers throughout the tradition.[7] For this chapter, I rely upon three voices to express the issue at stake and its complexities. These three, Francis of Assisi, John Woolman, and Ronald Sider, also represent some of the diversity of the Christian tradition, which lends credence to the views they have in common. If a medieval saint, a Quaker abolitionist, and a contemporary evangelical leader agree that avoiding sin is the primary consideration when judging consumption, perhaps Christians should heed what they say. Each thinker holds a more complex position than I am able to acknowledge within the space of this project; nonetheless, the existence of their complex and well-developed positions on consumption supports my claim that the avoidance of sin in consuming is a primary consideration within the Christian tradition.

This may come as no surprise to those familiar with the ascetic tradition within Christianity. In fact, when scholars and lay Christians first consider consumption, they commonly expect the tradition to say no, to encourage frugality, self-denial, cutting back, and other variations on the theme of asceticism. Consumptive self-denial for the sake of holiness is a familiar story. From Jesus' fasting in the desert to Anabaptist plain clothing, ascetic practice helps believers avoid sin and cultivate purity or holiness.

Asceticism, however, is much more complex than this simple view may indicate. As Maria Antonaccio writes, asceticism, derived from the Greek word *askesis* or discipline, is not only "a renunciatory practice aimed at mortification of the flesh and restriction of bodily pleasures," it is also "the acquisition of a skill, the practice of an art or *techne*, the education of desire in the constructive aim of living well." *Askesis*, then, is "the practice of forming and educating human desire."[8] In this sense, all four of the considerations covered in this book are ascetic, because all seek to reform or redirect consumptive desires. All four ask Christians to reconsider their consumption and to curb or reorient it, but in different directions and for different reasons. This first consideration, to avoid sin, is perhaps the most well-known reason for Christian asceticism. But as we shall see in subsequent chapters, Christians may also take care with their consumption in the name of greater joy and gratitude, in the name of neighbor-love, or for the sake of their visions of the future.

In this chapter, I draw on three Christian figures to highlight this first consideration of consumption. Francis, Woolman, and Sider share common themes and intentions, though they lived in different times and places. As this chapter describes, all three are clearly ascetic, eschewing excess consumption and pursuing poverty and simplicity. Their goal is purity, holiness, and freedom from sin. Sin is conceived not simply as gluttony or greed, but also as complicity in the suffering of others. Avoiding these sins means attention, self-control, and, when needed, careful restitution for the wrongs wrought by destructive consumption. In this chapter's conclusion, I discuss the contribution of this consideration—to avoid sin in consuming—to the broader project of a comprehensive Christian ethics of consumption.

CONSUMPTION PRACTICES OF FRANCIS, WOOLMAN, AND SIDER

A brief introduction to each man will help to illuminate who they are, and why their consumption practices are so instructive.

Francis of Assisi (1182–1226) initiated a movement of radically poor religious whose practices of poverty and piety both inspired and shocked their contemporaries. Francis, his *fratello* ("little brothers"), and the related women's order founded by Clare of Assisi arose in response to, and in interaction with, the events of their time. It was a time of economic change, with an increase in trade and a related rise of the middle class. This era also saw religious upheaval in the form of radical religious movements seeking to curtail laxity in the church.[9] Francis had a conversion experience, forsook his former self-indulgent life, and devoted himself to prayer, preaching, and poverty. Francis's status shifted from that of a young, popular, fashionable son of a cloth merchant, to a poor, often ill, but nevertheless charismatic holy beggar. From the beginning of his life in poverty, Francis walked on controversial ground, because poverty itself was controversial: were they beggars and thieves, according to the stereotypes of the time? Or were they holier than the rich, as implied by some radical movements of voluntary poverty and some scriptures highlighting the status of the poor?[10] The latter view was not a popular notion among the elites of society, including some church authorities.[11] Francis remained on the right side of church approval during his lifetime, but his followers encountered trouble soon after his death, when denunciation outweighed admiration. By 1323, within a century of his death, one of Francis's central claims—that Christ and his followers were poor and owned no possessions—was declared false by Pope John XXII.[12] Nevertheless, Francis remains a saint and much-beloved figure in Christian history.

His consumption practices, in particular, are worthy of note. Francis ate moderately and often fasted. This same austerity was present in his clothing choices. Francis's conversion experience involved a reading of Matthew 10:7–9, "As you go, proclaim the good news, 'The kingdom of heaven has come near.' Cure the sick, raise the dead, cleanse the lepers, cast out demons. You received without payment; give without payment. Take no gold, or silver, or copper in your belts." Francis felt himself called to follow the gospel passage to the letter, casting aside his belt and sandals, tying a rope around his one tunic.[13] This simple clothing became a very powerful symbol for the Franciscan order. "All the friars must wear poor clothes and they can patch them with pieces of sackcloth and other material, with God's blessing," Francis writes.[14] After Francis's death, four Franciscans were burned by the Inquisition in 1318 after refusing to alter their clothing in accordance with papal decree.[15] Francis's holy poverty was a strong and inspirational ideal for his followers.

John Woolman (1720–72) is widely regarded as a central figure in faith and social reform for the Religious Society of Friends, or Quakers, in eighteenth-century North America. Woolman began his career as a shopkeeper in New Jersey but soon gave up the business and devoted his life to the abolitionist cause. It is largely thanks to his efforts that Quakers became "the first significant group in America to emancipate their slaves."[16] The development of Woolman's theology and ethics—and his views about consumption and its complicity with slavery—can be traced in his *Journal*, published posthumously in 1774.[17]

Woolman, in keeping with the Quaker Testimony of Simplicity, advocated moderate consumption and the avoidance of luxury. In particular, he was concerned about consuming items that would make him complicit in slavery, which he considered an evil practice. Woolman's witness against slavery was singularly effective.

His preaching was persuasive, but the way he embodied his ethical concerns—arriving at a Friend's house on foot in protest of the mistreatment of post-carriage horses, and refusing to use silver during the meal because of its link to the slave trade, for example—added strength and integrity to his message.[18] "During a market revolution that swept the Atlantic world," writes historian Thomas P. Slaughter, "Woolman was an outspoken critic of consumption and the accumulation of wealth."[19]

Ronald Sider (b. 1939) wrote *Rich Christians in an Age of Hunger*, which stirred intense discussion among evangelicals when it was first released in 1977 and is still in print, five editions later. Craig Blomberg calls it "one of the most influential catalysts among British and North American evangelicals to help them finally come to grips with global poverty."[20] It is among *Christianity Today*'s "Top 100 Religious Books of the Century."[21] Sider has been a leader among American evangelicals, helping to found Evangelicals for Social Action in 1978, a group that continues to foster a broad range of related activities, including the work of the Evangelical Environmental Network.[22]

In *Rich Christians*, Sider offers both personal testimony and biblical interpretations to support his contention that affluent Christians should simplify their lives in order to mobilize significant sums of money to aid the hungry poor. Sider's testimony and suggestions are startlingly specific: live communally, buy secondhand clothing, and fast occasionally.[23] These are all ways to tighten the family budget, in order to free up excess money to help those in need. Sider even offers the algorithm by which he and his wife decided how much money, beyond 10 percent of their income, to put into their "tithe." Sider believes that participation in a strong and active Christian fellowship is necessary to help contemporary individuals to adequately resist the temptations of a ubiquitous and encroaching consumerism, and Christian communities should proactively provide this countercultural support to their members.[24]

ASCETICISM, POVERTY, AND SIMPLICITY

For these three Christian voices, good consumption avoids sin and embraces virtue. This may mean voluntary poverty, a life of simplicity, or some combination of poverty and simplicity. Many of the more ascetic voices in the tradition agree with this; Kierkegaard, for example, wrote: "With respect to the earthly, one needs little, and to the degree that one needs less, the more perfect one is."[25] Consuming less, for many Christians, leads to perfection.

For Francis of Assisi, voluntary poverty was a virtue to be embraced. Early in Francis's religious life, he and two companions identified three passages that formed the core of the Franciscan way of life: "Go, sell what you own, and give the money to the poor, and you will have treasure in heaven; then come, follow me"; "Take nothing for your journey, no staff, nor bag, nor bread, nor money—not even an extra tunic"; and "If any want to become my followers, let them deny themselves and take up their cross and follow me" (Mark 10:21; Luke 9:3; Matthew 16:24).[26] These passages established an ascetic tone for Francis's ministry.

Francis himself maintained an extreme of poverty and asceticism, which his biographers did not hesitate to extol. Thomas of Celano writes enthusiastically of Francis's observance:

> With all zeal, with all solicitude, he guarded holy Lady Poverty, not permitting any vessel of any kind to be in the house, lest it lead to superfluous things, when he could in some way avoid being subject to extreme necessity without it. For, he used to say, it is possible to satisfy necessity and not give in to pleasure.

Cooked foods he permitted himself scarcely at all or very rarely; and if he did allow them, he mixed them with ashes or destroyed their flavor with cold water.[27]

The extremes of this practice are shocking to contemporary sensibilities. Francis himself recognized that his asceticism may have gone too far, confessing on his deathbed that he had sinned against "brother body."[28] But Leonardo Boff defends Francis's bodily mortification as "the activity of putting to death the overflowing of the passions so that their creative power may be directed toward holiness and humanization."[29]

If Francis went too far, he did so in avoidance of sin and in pursuit of virtue. Lady Poverty was, by all accounts, Francis's moral muse, and his desire for her and for the holiness she entailed balanced his negative emphasis on the rejection of material goods. Francis's devotion to poverty was also inspired by his desire to embrace another figure, that of Christ as a poor man (as well as Mary, his mother). In his *Rule* of 1221 he counsels:

> The friars should be delighted to follow the lowliness and poverty of our Lord Jesus Christ, remembering that of the whole world we must own nothing; *but having food and sufficient clothing, with these let us be content* (1 Tim 6:38).... [Jesus] was poor and he had no home of his own and he lived on alms, he and the Blessed Virgin and his disciples.[30]

Francis's friars lived as austerely as he did. According to the monastic rule Francis wrote in 1221, those who wished to join his order were required to sell all their worldly possessions and give the money to the poor.[31] On becoming full members of the order, "The friars are to appropriate nothing for themselves, neither a house, nor a place, nor anything else," according to the rule.[32] Francis and his brothers were to live very simply, touch no money, and subsist on in-kind donations of food and other goods, which they acquired through begging.[33]

Francis's praise of poverty may seem idealized, but Francis and his brothers did experience the hardship of deprivation first-hand. Still, Francis distinguished between the voluntary, though real, poverty of him and his fellow formerly affluent renunciates and the involuntary poverty of the poor and indigent they encountered. While Francis was strict with himself and his brothers, he was kind to the poor. He is said to have remarked that if he were to ever take more than he needed he would be robbing from the poor.[34] On one occasion, giving his cloak to an elderly poor man, he remarked that he simply wanted to return what was rightly his.[35] This kindness may have been cultivated by Francis's ascetic practices, as Boff explains:

> Poverty is a way of being by which the individual lets things be what they are; one refuses to dominate them, subjugate them, or make them objects of the will to power. One refuses to be over them in order to be with them. This demands an immense asceticism of the renunciation of the instinct to power, to the dominion over things, and to the satisfaction of human desires.[36]

Poverty, then, may become a path to a holy nonattachment to possessions and a gentle renunciation of dominance over others.

Francis pursued poverty qua poverty, but John Woolman followed the classic Quaker ideal of simplicity. Although *simplicity* in current North American popular culture sometimes is used by advertisers and magazines to denote a "lifestyle" that values a minimalist aesthetic without challenging the prevailing consumerist ethos, that is not what the Quakers mean by the word. The Quaker "Testimony of Simplicity" refers to a practice of humble plainness in dress and other displays and a spiritually grounded detachment from possessions.[37] It is in the same continuum as, but less extreme than, Francis's practice of voluntary poverty. In Woolman's time, this took the form of strict dress codes and boundaries on consumption, but these were more observed in letter than in spirit. As Ross Martinie Eiler describes it:

> Many outsiders recognized that, though plain in style, Quaker clothing was made from the most expensive materials available. People would have recognized such Friends as luxuriously enjoying unnecessarily costly items, and yet they would be violating no written code of discipline and participating in no explicitly condemned behavior.[38]

The mid-1700s was a time of reformation for Quakers, in response to a growing affluence and a growing ambiguity about the difference between simplicity and luxury. Woolman joined other reformers of his time in condemning the relaxation of strict Quaker codes of simplicity, particularly when Friends overstepped the line into luxury by owning slaves.

As Woolman uses it, the term "luxury" denotes consumer practices determined by desire for comfort and current fashion, rather than need. Woolman's main concern is not moral decadence or superfluous vanity (though he acknowledges these ethical entrapments, as well). For Woolman, to consume in excess, to indulge in luxury, is to contradict God's will for the world, and disrupt "a certain harmony in the universe."[39] By indulging in luxury, we "depart from that use of the creatures which the Creator of all things intended for them" and appropriate "an increase of labor which extends beyond what our Heavenly Father intends for us."[40]

Luxury is sinful because it transgresses God's plan for a harmonious world.

Woolman has no trouble linking luxury and evil: "Every degree of luxury hath some connection with evil," he insists, even when that connection is not immediately obvious.[41] Luxury can only be obtained by *over*use of human labor, slavery being the main case in point. Even overworking ourselves goes against God's plan, according to Woolman.[42] But none of this exploitation is necessary.

> Were all superfluities and the desire of outward greatness laid aside and the right use of things universally attended to, such a number of people might be employed in things useful that moderate labor with the blessing of heaven would answer all good purposes relating to people and their animals, and a sufficient number have leisure to attend on proper affairs of civil society.[43]

If our needs are sufficiently simple, moderate labor will fill them amply, according to Woolman. God could not possibly have created a world of such scarcity that we have no choice but to overwork and exploit one another.[44] If all luxury is enjoyed at some poor laborer's expense, and being involved in this exploitation is sinful, then consuming well means avoiding luxury and pursuing humble simplicity.

Ronald Sider would agree. He, too, is concerned about luxury and exploitation, and he, too, feels that the excesses of the rich are essentially robbing the poor. Sider begins *Rich Christians in an Age of Hunger* with a survey of world poverty and hunger, designed to shock and outrage his readers, followed by a critical look at affluent U.S. lifestyles and patterns of charitable giving, with special attention given to the role of advertising in promoting excessive consumption. Global economic inequality is his main concern, and he expects Christians to share his righteous indignation at the severity and scope of this worldwide problem.

Sider then surveys the Bible, finding and interpreting passages that speak to issues of poverty and riches. There is no shortage of biblical support for Sider's position. God identifies with the poor, according to Sider, and more affluent Christians neglect them at their souls' peril.[45] If Christians would truly act on what is written in the Bible, Sider believes, they would divest themselves of their own affluence and treat the poor differently. Christians who fail to do this must be reading the Bible from a corrupt perspective, he contends: "Have we allowed our economic self-interest to distort our interpretation of Scripture? Undoubtedly we have. But precisely to the extent that our affirmation of scriptural authority is sincere, we will permit painful texts to correct our thinking."[46]

Sider strongly indicts his fellow evangelical Christians who turn a blind eye to these issues. He provocatively calls them "liberal" if they live at the same level of affluence as everyone else in contemporary society:

> In an Age of Hunger most Christians, regardless of theological label, will be severely tempted to succumb to the liberal heresy of following current cultural and societal values rather than biblical truth. Society will offer demonically convincing justification for enjoying our affluence and forgetting about a billion hungry neighbors.[47]

Not only does he accuse them of liberal laxity and corrupt Bible readings but he also diagnoses covetousness and idolatry in many Christians' economic attitudes and practices. Sider recommends "church discipline" for covetous or greedy persons, just as Paul did (1 Corinthians 5:11).[48] For Sider, the world's economic inequalities are about sin. "If God's Word is true," he writes, "then all of us who dwell in affluent nations are trapped in sin."

> Thank God we can repent. God is merciful. God forgives. But only if we repent. And biblical repentance involves more than a hasty tear and a weekly prayer of confession. Biblical repentance involves conversion. It involves a whole new lifestyle. The One who stands ready to forgive us for our sinful involvement in economic injustice offers us his grace to begin living a generous new lifestyle that empowers the poor and oppressed.[49]

In describing that "generous new lifestyle," Sider begins to describe good Christian consumption. Like Woolman, he urges Christians to shun luxury. Like Francis, he praises poverty. But unlike Francis, and in a more nuanced way than Woolman, Sider recognizes two levels of sin in consumption: there are the individual sins against God and neighbor, and then there are the structural sins that support the systems of poverty and oppression. These cannot simply be solved by pursuing poverty or simplicity. They require collective repentance, forgiveness, and transformation.

COMPLICITY IN CONSUMPTION

Sider's discussion of structural evil introduced an idea that was, at the time, a new concept for evangelical audiences.[50] The complex social structures that serve to keep the poor in poverty and keep the rich oblivious to the world's injustice are, according to Sider, sinful. The sin of these structures, he contends, is palpable and serious, regardless of the intentions of the people involved in them.[51] As theologian Michelle Gonzalez writes, in agreement with Sider but in language that Woolman would appreciate, "Through our consumerism we participate in global slavery, whether we admit it or not."[52]

Participation in structural evil does not convey the same clear guilt that a chosen, personal-level sin does. Still, Sider will not let affluent Christians claim complete innocence or ignorance when it comes to structural sin. Those who benefit from it, know it to be wrong, and do nothing to combat it have committed a genuine sin. "We have profited from systematic injustice," he laments, "sometimes only half-knowing, sometimes only half-caring and always half-hoping not to know. We are guilty of sin against God and neighbor."[53] The mind-boggling complexities of the system are no excuse. Most of the time, he argues, "people living in and benefiting from unjust structures know something—albeit not everything—about their evil. In fact, very often we know enough to choose not to learn more lest we feel guilty."[54] To choose such culpable ignorance is in Sider's view a choice to sin. Sider's ethic, then, involves a demanding moral epistemology: Christians are asked to face the injustices they would rather not see, and to take action to avoid complicity in them.

Sider does not idealize poverty: he recognizes that it arises from many factors, including personal sin on the part of poor people (alcoholism, unwise choices) and structural sin on the part of society (racism, the injustices of market systems, and a simple lack of will to redistribute wealth).[55] Sider's argument, however, is that those who are not poor can and should consume more simply and donate the excess to help the poor. Insofar as we neglect this imperative to redistribute, and other work that seeks to rectify the structural evils of poverty, we sin. Sider prescribes profound conversion, repentance, and turning away from both personal and structural sin. On this issue, he writes, faithful Christians need to experience a "deep inner anguish that leads to a new way of living."[56]

Woolman, too, was painfully aware of sinfulness in complicity of consumption, particularly slavery and its products. He maintained a "close and laborious inquiry" into his own habits, asking himself whether any of his actions benefited from or fomented war or other violence, at home or in Africa; he desired, rather, to "live and walk in the plainness and simplicity of a sincere follower of Christ."[57] Woolman engaged in many personal boycotts: traveling on foot to avoid complicity with the maltreatment of post-horses, insulting hosts by refusing to touch silver (which came from the slave trade), and taking medicine only if it came through trustworthy channels.[58] He carefully avoided sugar and molasses from the West Indies, because of news he had heard of the slaves' bad treatment there.[59]

Woolman acknowledges how small the effects of such a boycott would be, in terms of affecting market forces and changing conditions for the slaves, because "the number of those who decline the use of the West India produce on account of the hard usage of the slaves who raise it appears small, even amongst people truly pious."[60] His reasoning, then, is based on a concern to avoid complicity rather than on the political effectiveness of this abstention. His dogged avoidance of complicity was, largely, a pursuit of purity: Woolman felt that "personal purity was of value for its own sake."[61]

But in addition to his boycotts, Woolman also crusaded against slavery and made consumption choices that expressed his concern for the neighbor—particularly the poor and the enslaved.[62] Slaughter describes Woolman's willingness to accept culpability: "Like the Old Testament prophets upon whom he modeled his ministry, Woolman identified with the moral failings of his people. He addressed Quaker slaveholders compassionately, believing that their sin was also his."[63] By sharing the slaveholders' guilt and the slaves' suffering, Woolman's compassion and purity made his message to the slaveholders particularly convincing.

THE ECONOMY OF AVOIDING SIN

When an older Woolman reflected on his work as a young shop-keeper, he recognized the degree to which his business partici-pated in the oppression of slaves.

> I once, some years ago, retailed rum, sugar, and molasses, the fruits of the labor of slaves, but then had not much concern about them.... But of late years being further informed respecting the oppressions too generally exercised in these islands [viz., slavery in the West Indies],... it hath appeared that the small gain I got by this branch of trade should be applied in promoting righteousness in the earth.[64]

This passage shows that Woolman had some sense of the amount of money he made at slaves' expense, and he resolved to dedicate that money—and his life's labors—to the cause of abolition. Woolman essentially chose to make financial restitution for the wrongs in which he participated. As his journal narrates, he fre-quently used a kind of moral accounting to rectify his complicity with slavery.

Woolman traveled frequently, due to his leadership duties for the Society of Friends, and also for the express purpose of con-vincing slave-owning Friends to free their slaves. "His sense of obligation," according to Phillips Moulton, "was twofold: insofar as possible, to avoid complicity with evil, and to urge others to do likewise, individually and collectively."[65] Thus, when Woolman would stay at the houses of Friends who kept slaves, enjoying the free hospitality that Quakers gave to one another, he felt this two-fold obligation. Woolman engaged in earnest discussion with his slave-holding hosts, attempting to persuade them to free their slaves; however, to receive their hospitality represented complicity with the evil of slavery. As narrated in his *Journal*, after much anguished prayer, Woolman resolved to leave money (in essence, paying for his stays at the slave-keeping Friends' houses), often giving that money directly to the household slaves.[66] In so doing, he was not treating them as slaves, but as hired servants—and therefore his conscience was assuaged.

Sider, too, uses careful financial calculations as a way to salve the conscience of the complicit Christian. He notes with approval that some early Christian communities, as described in the book of Acts, lived in an attitude of "sweeping liability for and availability to each other," generously sacrificing to meet one another's needs. He continues, "If the need was greater than current cash reserves, they sold property. They simply gave until the needs were met. The needs of the sister and brother, not legal property rights or future financial security, were the deciding factors."[67] When early Christians did this, in Sider's interpretation, their numbers increased and the church grew in faith and scope. For this reason, Sider recommends radical, worldwide economic sharing among Christians in richer and poorer countries. Not only would this redress the scandal of hunger and poverty in the world, he suggests, but it would also prove an effective tool for evangelization. To see Christian churches doing this would make more people want to become Christian, an important goal for all Christians, and particularly for evangelicals.[68]

Sider proposes that Christians follow his lead in offering a "graduated tithe." He narrates the process whereby he and his wife calculated the bare minimum amount of money they needed to live on. They then tallied their tithe by adding (a) 10 percent of this minimum to (b) an even larger percentage, increasing with each thousand dollars, of whatever they earned above the minimum.[69] So, for example, using the chart he created in 1997, I calculate that someone with an income of $30,000 should give away approximately $6,300 in tithe. This makes for a tithing rate of 21 percent and an effective income of $23,700. This model may not work for everyone, Sider says, but it is a good place to start.[70]

"The proposal," he admits, "is probably so modest that it verges on unfaithfulness to Saint Paul [and his teachings about being a 'cheerful giver' in 1 Corinthians 9:7]. But it is also sufficiently radical that its implementation would revolutionize the ministry and life of the church."[71] The purpose of this tithe, as Sider clearly states, is to facilitate a redistribution of financial resources. Living simply is of little use if one simply keeps the money one has saved in the bank: Sider's assumption is that the "extra" income is to be donated to worthy charities, and he coaches his readers on the criteria they might use to discern which organizations should receive their donations.[72]

The essence of Sider's message is about measurement: "Will we dare to measure our living standards by the needs of the poor rather than by the lifestyle of our neighbors?" he asks.[73] The standard should not be society's continually escalating consumerism but the biblical vision of enough for all, what Quaker author Adam Finnerty calls a "Just World Standard of Living"—an idealized reckoning of how each human ought to live, if the world's resources were distributed equitably.[74] Sider's inclusion of an income chart in his book of popular theology may seem out of place. But Sider maintains that everything, even economics, is subject to religious scrutiny and biblical ethics. As Sider says, "The God of the poor is Lord of economics—Lord even of interest rates."[75]

Francis, too, prayed to the God of the poor and found his own way to be freed from sin: a strategy that was less calculated but no less economic. Francis and his early biographers believed that to lose a luxury in this world is to gain treasure in heaven, and to gain a luxury in this world is to lose treasure in heaven.[76] Following this reasoning, the extreme asceticism of the Friars Minor was seen as a sign of their blessedness—testimony to the rich treasures they were amassing in heaven.

This medieval Christian perspective saw a vast exchange of merit and good works at play in the world. People who gave alms secured merit in God's eyes, not only by losing earthly goods but also by helping the poor. Francis's brothers were able to use this concept to set up a mutually advantageous system between the religious order and local lay communities. The brothers received spiritual benefit from humbly begging; local villagers received spiritual benefit from giving food and in-kind donations to the brothers. Also, in the process, the brothers were able to feed themselves without recourse to touching money (which was strictly forbidden).[77] As Francis understood it, the world needed the example of the brothers' humility and poverty: it was a service they offered to the world. So long as they kept this up faithfully, the world would reward them by seeing to it that they got the food and other items they needed to survive.[78] God, the generous source of all that exists, is the ultimate almsgiver in this system.[79]

Some contemporary Christians may disagree with this worldview for the material/spiritual and religious/lay split it entails, but there is a deeper insight to be gained from this example. Francis got his bread in a way that benefited both him and the giver. His order created a mutually supportive relationship with the people in his community, an economy that liberally mixed grace and goods, to meet a variety of needs. The transfer of goods, in this case, conferred blessing in both directions, and (presumably) strengthened community ties. Woolman paying the slaves for their service, or Sider's simple living and careful tithing are similar: all offer a glimpse of the generative, communal side of ascetic practice. Beyond avoiding sin, it can create new possibilities for human flourishing.

THE IMPORTANCE OF AVOIDING SIN IN CONSUMPTION

As Maria Antonaccio writes, asceticism is not self-denial pursued for its own sake: true self-discipline does not stifle natural desires but rather transforms them in order to pursue a greater, spiritual good. She understands

> *askesis* as reorienting human desires through practices that seem to run counter to what one normally understands as "flourishing." In such practices, conventional notions of what constitutes human fulfillment are shattered by the insight that true fulfillment is of a different order than what one had thought.[80]

In this way, Christian ascetic practices reenvision the nature of human flourishing and fulfillment: though Francis of Assisi is thin and ill, his fasting brings him into a better life of holiness; though John Woolman's conscience is tortured with his every economic decision, his attention brings him the zeal of spiritual strength; and though Ronald Sider's family tightens their belts and toils in their garden, they rest easy knowing their excess is being fairly distributed to those in need. In the Christian ascetic tradition, saying no to one's desires is saying yes to something better. In the case of the examples featured in this chapter, a no to excess consumption means a yes to purity, holiness, or freedom from sin. By pursuing poverty and simplicity, and by divesting from sinful systems while redirecting the money toward just causes, Christians may pursue the deeper flourishing that freedom from sin allows.

Avoiding sin in consuming is a vital first step in understanding Christian views on consumption. The negative effects of consumption on the consumer, on near and distant others, and on the planet are dire: this consideration is discussed first not only because it is the most common but also because it is truly essential to a Christian understanding of consumption. Christians taking this consideration to heart are in good company, and their concerns are faithful to the Bible and to core Christian concepts. This first consideration, then, to avoid sin in consuming, is necessary to a comprehensive Christian ethics of consumption. It is necessary, but it is not sufficient.

Avoiding sin is not the only consideration of Christian consumption ethics, and the thinkers used in this chapter are not without their critics. For example, Francis has received criticism for his position with respect to the involuntarily poor people of Assisi. Kenneth Baxter Wolf, in his book *The Poverty of Riches: St. Francis of Assisi Reconsidered*, contends that Francis loved his own holiness more than he did his neighbors, and may indeed have harmed, more than helped, the poor of his time. Because of the power and prestige that his poverty conferred upon him, according to Wolf, Francis's holy, voluntary poverty bore almost no resemblance to secular, involuntary poverty. He points out:

> It required a considerable amount of effort on Francis's part
> to maintain the kind of poverty and humility that he had set
> out to embrace [because people impressed with his holiness

were continually showering him with gifts]....Needless to say, no truly poor person ever had to work this hard to earn the disdain of his community.[81]

But Francis and his brothers called themselves poor, and begged for alms, among the poor. On Wolf's view, they competed with the other poor for a limited supply of alms. A person of means, wondering which beggars truly deserved their alms, would choose Francis and his friars over other beggars, because of their spotless reputation for virtue and holiness.[82]

The ordinary poor could hardly hope to achieve that level of trust and respectability, Wolf claims, because Francis's model of holy poverty really only applied to the rich. It required a person of means to turn a corner in life, giving up everything and renouncing possessions. A poor person had nothing to renounce: even if she decided to take a renunciative, detached attitude toward her few possessions, no one would be the wiser. There was no outer sign of conversion, and thus no social benefits or edge in the pursuit of alms.[83]

Even if Francis did not offer to the involuntary poor a vision of holiness that they could embrace and benefit from socially, he did offer them alms, occasionally—but, according to Wolf, not enough. Francis and his brothers were so strict about avoiding any commerce in money that their ability to help the poor was limited. The strictness about money came from a fear of greed and pride that might develop from such transactions.[84] "Charitable distribution," he notes, "was clearly ancillary to the Franciscan spiritual program," which emphasized living in poverty over helping those in poverty.[85]

Wolf's arguments, concerned almost exclusively with the social status and material succor of the poor, neglect questions of spiritual benefit. Whether or not Francis was able to materially help the poor of his time, he was, according to his early hagiographers, an extraordinarily holy man who brought inspiration and blessing to all he encountered, including many of the poor. Wolf's sympathy with the lack of drama associated with the conversion and renunciation of a genuinely poor person is too narrow: if the person experienced an important spiritual renewal, surely the value of this experience outweighed the lack of interest from the almsgivers and gossips of Assisi. Medieval views of poverty varied widely, and while Francis may have provided an excuse for some to neglect the "unholy" poor, his ministry may also have provided an inspiration for others to aid *all* of the poor, holy and unholy alike. Franciscans, though their legacy of extreme poverty has been cushioned over time, continue to live among and work with the poor.

Nonetheless, Wolf correctly perceives that Francis's message was primarily intended for those of his own social class, though his contention that Francis harmed the poor may be an overstatement. Wolf's book speaks to a larger concern about Christians who renounce consumption in order to avoid sin: is this a position that speaks to, and makes sense for, anyone besides the relatively affluent? Does this position materially aid the poor, or is it simply a self-focused pursuit of holiness? Would Woolman, for example, have expected a hungry poor person to adopt his standards and avoid foods deriving from slavery? This position would be impossible to maintain for a slave—the poorest of the poor in Woolman's time—who herself would likely have nothing to eat that was not produced by slaves. And does avoiding the products of slave labor really make life better for the slaves? Uncertainties abound.

Notably, the slaves' African American descendants are largely absent from the group of Christians who advocate this position in considering consumption; other considerations are much more emphasized by African American Christians, as demonstrated in the next chapters. One exception is Martin Luther King Jr., whose later writings sharply criticize the consumerism he saw developing in mid-twentieth-century America. King wrote, "We're prone to judge success by the index of our salaries or the size of our automobiles, rather than by the quality of our service and relationship to humanity—thus capitalism can lead to a practical materialism that is as pernicious as the materialism taught by communism."[86] Still, the suspicion of consumption espoused by King and his followers is eclipsed by the embrace of prosperity theology, as described in the next chapter.

Less affluent Christians may well benefit from Sider's attempts at monetary redistribution, but it takes something else entirely—the experience of being *too* well-off, of overloaded consumption—to make the practice of renunciation and austerity seem attractive in and of itself. Antonaccio speaks to the experience of those who have consumed to excess and have experienced its associated spiritual lethargy when she writes that disciplined austerity can lead to a deeper fulfillment than the pleasures associated with the satiated life.[87] She notes that those promoting asceticism must persuade their audiences that this deeper fulfillment is worthwhile, but she does not address *why* this persuasion can be difficult or acknowledge that for those struggling with the basics, renunciation looks less like fulfillment than satiation does. And abundance, from the perspective of involuntary poverty, looks like flourishing, grace, and blessing.

"Take your hand away from the product!" preaches Reverend Billy. This is an essential first step in the process of considering consumption. But, as the next chapter shows, Christian ethical consideration of consumption must go beyond simply renouncing it.

Chapter 3

To Embrace Creation

The ascetic strain of Christianity avoids sin by avoiding sinful consumption. When Francis felt hungry, he reckoned it part of his purification for God. When Woolman desired sugar, he reminded himself of the slave labor that created it, and renounced his desire. When Sider wishes for indulgent food, he contents himself with beans and rice, or fasting, adding to his donation to a microlending enterprise in India.

But this is not the only Christian response to a feeling of hunger. Listen to L. Shannon Jung, a contemporary Reformed theologian:

> [We read] in Psalm 34:8: "O, taste and see that the Lord is good!" Sometimes we think these imperatives—taste, see— are only figurative. We only taste or see in a metaphorical sense. We don't really taste the goodness of God.
>
> What would it mean if we took them somewhat more literally? Can we indeed taste the goodness of God in the food we eat?
>
> I think so.[1]

Where some Christians renounce consumption, others accept, affirm, and embrace it. This chapter draws upon influential voices and schools of thought in support of this embrace; well-respected voices such as Thomas Aquinas and Clement of Alexandria are joined by unconventional contemporary voices, including prosperity theologians. Throughout the chapter I note instances where I disagree with some of these individuals and schools of thought; however, I include them because such popular, widespread arguments should be addressed, and because the more legitimate aspects are helpful to my thesis. Prosperity theology, represented in this chapter primarily by Creflo A. Dollar Jr., is justifiably criticized but also contains grains of truth and influences much of contemporary U.S. Christian culture. Similarly, John Schneider's controversial defense of middle-class life contains valid points, and many North American Christians, explicitly or implicitly, agree with him. And although Matthew Fox has been criticized for an overly positive theology of creation, I am not assessing the efficacy of his theology; he is included for his enthusiasm about creation and the joys of consumption.

This diverse collection of Christian voices agrees: the most important consideration when judging consumption is not sin, but blessing. Good consumption, they say, is consumption that gratefully embraces the blessings of God's creation. This chapter is organized thematically, with sections that outline the general contours of this second Christian position on consumption: creation is fruitful; hunger is not sinful; consuming with gratitude, savoring, and sharing is holy; wealth may be virtuous; we are God's beloved children; and we should steward our blessings well.

THE EARTH IS FRUITFUL AND BLESSINGS ABOUND

The Bible begins by declaring the fruitfulness of God's created world. The unfettered bounty and human enjoyment in the original garden of Genesis seem to represent the ideal human-earth relationship. As contemporary Reformed theologian John Schneider writes, "We are fashioned from the earth to live upon the earth, to dominate, cultivate, and care for the earth—*and* to use and *enjoy* the fruits of the earth."[2] Schneider's use of the word *dominate* may sound harsh in an environmentally conscious age, but he understands proper dominion (from the Latin "ruler of the house") to include careful stewardship of the planet.[3] Above all, Schneider sees the earth as fruitful, a place of bounty and blessing, and we insult God, the source of that bounty, by failing to enjoy it.

Reformed ecotheologian L. Shannon Jung (whose books focus upon eating within the broader topic of consumption) agrees with Schneider on this point. He writes, "There is a feast laid out for us, and we cheat ourselves and God out of enjoying it. God (the hostess) has outdone herself and created a marvel, and we are blind to it."[4] Our duty as created beings is to do justice to God's banquet by enjoying it. To truly enjoy food—to give thanks for it and feast on it in a God-centered manner—is a skill set that Jung believes has been lost; his books seek to teach Christians to engage in the practice of truly enjoying their food.[5]

In Jung's view, food of all kinds consists of God's abundant, overflowing blessing, and when consumed with appreciation it connects eaters with the rest of creation. "The forces of the universe sometimes line up in the pecan pie or the pasta. They become not only concrete and tangible; they are also succulent!"[6] Eating connects humans and the earth, in the words of Wendell Berry: "Eating with the fullest pleasure—pleasure, that is, that does not depend on ignorance—is perhaps the profoundest enactment of our connection with the world."[7] Good consumption of food, then, becomes a means of praising and expressing gratefulness to God. Jung writes, "With joy as a foundation, we learn to eat as a response to God's goodness, and we realize that this is the way things are supposed to be—the way we were created."[8]

Prosperity theology also proclaims God's promise of abundance to believers. Prosperity theology is the scholarly term for a loose collection of pastors and congregations influenced by the "Word of Faith movement," which teaches that believers may gain health, wealth, and prosperity through practices such as "positive confession" (results-oriented prayer) and "seed-faith" (targeted giving to the church).[9] This movement's major message to believers is that God wishes to grant them prosperity. Pointing to the Hebrew Bible ("a land flowing with milk and honey" [Exodus 3:8]) and the New Testament ("I came that they may have life, and have it abundantly" [John 10:10]), prosperity theologians make the case that God's blessings may take the form of material prosperity derived from the earth's abundance, and they defend these blessings as well deserved and worthy to be embraced.

Creflo A. Dollar Jr. (his real name) is a prosperity preacher based in Atlanta, Georgia. His World Changers Church International (WCCI), founded in 1986, "serves nearly 30,000 members," and has given rise to "a host of satellite churches," from Los Angeles to New York City.[10] His television shows air on half a dozen networks, including Black Entertainment Television and the Trinity Broadcasting Network.[11] World Changers Church International's ministry broadcasts Dollar's *Changing Your World* programs in Australia ("serving the Asia-Pacific region"), South Africa, Nigeria, and the United Kingdom. He received an honorary doctorate of divinity from Oral Roberts University in 1998 and has authored several books.[12] Dollar and his wife, Taffi, engage in ministry together, and their churches are booming. Worship services at WCCI in Atlanta feature security guards, partly to watch over the donations, which can total as much as $85,000 on any given Sunday.[13] The abundance of financial wealth that flows through Dollar's ministry has given rise to a congressional investigation into the organization's financial practices. Far from staining Dollar's reputation, this seems to have had "the effect of rallying the faithful and heightening Creflo and Taffi Dollar's allure and mystique."[14]

Dollar preaches that God wants believers to be prosperous, which he defines broadly to include money, health, love, and good family relationships.[15] Above all, for Dollar, prosperity means control: "Biblical prosperity is the ability to be in control of every circumstance and situation that occurs in your life. No matter what happens, whether financial, social, physical, marital, spiritual, or emotional, this type of prosperity enables you to maintain control in every situation."[16] Gaining this control is like ascending to the throne of one's own life: I, not my circumstances, determine the course of my days.

From Dollar's perspective, prosperity granted by God knows no boundaries. Dollar's own fortunes have skyrocketed along with his expanding ministry. "He wears tailor-made suits and owns two Rolls Royces and two private jets," notes one article in the *London Times*.[17] The jets are used to commute weekly between his Atlanta and New York congregations.[18] The *Times* article quotes a low-wage member of the congregation who is not disturbed by Dollar's conspicuous consumption; much of Dollar's wealth came in the form of gifts, and this seems to valorize his luxurious lifestyle. Indeed, "Dr. Dollar was given his two cars by students and followers," the article notes, adding drily, "he received one Rolls-Royce on Pastor Appreciation Day—a holiday of his own creation."[19] Dollar is not the only religious leader to live richly thanks to the offerings of the faithful, but his lifestyle raises the question: is he appropriately celebrating creation's abundance and God's generosity? It is perhaps no wonder that his ministry has been the subject of a congressional investigation: Dollar seems to be taking the justified practice of enjoying God's abundant blessing to an unjustified extreme.

HUMAN HUNGERS ARE NOT SINFUL

Something seems too simple in that formulation; surely human hungers have an inescapably sinful element, something akin to greed, gluttony, envy, or materialism. John of the Cross, for example, writes that Christians must "be vigilant over your will and desires, for these are the corrupt forces that dwell within, and keep you from living free."[20] But other Christian voices disagree. Perhaps the most illustrious of them, Thomas Aquinas (1225–74), explains in his *Summa Theologia* that everything in nature, including hungers and genuine needs, is good, because God created them good. Even before the Fall, the first humans living without sin ate, presumably in response to hunger.[21] Indeed, *not* to have eaten would have been a sin, because in Genesis 2:16, God expressly commanded humans to eat of all the trees in the garden (with the exception of the one forbidden tree) (I.97.3). God created humans to need food, to be hungry, and to consume. For Aquinas, human consumption in response to needs and hungers is good because humans were created by God in such a way that makes consumption necessary, and because consuming keeps people alive. Staying alive, in turn, is a good because it allows humans to pursue virtue and to love God.

There are boundaries on Aquinas's approbation of hungers and desires, however. In his discussion of gluttony, he makes a distinction between "any desire of eating and drinking" and "an *inordinate* desire" (II–II.148.1, emphasis mine). The former, the "natural appetite," is without sin, while the latter, the "sensitive appetite," is subject to concupiscence and hence gluttony (ibid.).[22]

The natural appetite, then, can and should be satiated without sin. Aquinas makes a parallel argument with other external goods such as clothing, furniture, and other items.[23] These things help humans in their quest to stay alive and to act in virtuous service to others (II–II.83.6). God made humans hungry, because God has desires too—desires for communion with humans, and the fulfillment of human hungers is a way to achieve this spiritual communion.

John Schneider agrees. He could easily be paraphrasing Aquinas when he says, "We human beings are designed by God to enjoy material things—in the right way, of course . . . [and] there is a right way."[24] By rooting his discussion in Genesis and Exodus, in which God creates humans for abundant living and liberates the Israelites out of bondage and into the bountiful promised land, Schneider can argue that rich, delightful consumption "is God's intent from the beginning, and is thus the end that he has in view for humanity forever."[25] If this is God's plan, it cannot be sinful. On the contrary, it must be blessed. Jung supports this. "Hunger is a clue to genuine desire and to God-given appetites," he posits. "God creates in such a way that all beings are given food."[26] Jung's is a creation-focused ethic, declaring practices right and good because God made humans to need or desire certain things. Jung believes humans are created with appetites, with bodies that respond positively to the stimulus of food, because God has purposely created us this way.

But humans aren't simply hungry for food or desirous of life's necessities. We also want comfort, stability, and social respect. For those who are deprived of these benefits, prosperity theology is particularly attractive. Writing of African American prosperity theology, scholar Stephanie Mitchem describes a sense of "longing, [which] has always been a significant component of black American spirituality."[27] Prosperity theology taps into and answers this longing—for freedom from poverty, for meaningful and fairly compensated work, for a sense of control over life circumstances.[28] Prosperity theology defends these desires and longings, channeling them into particular practices and expectations. Because human desires for prosperity are so highly valued and unquestioned in this system, however, there is little room to evaluate the rightness of those desires.[29] Still, in affirming desire, prosperity theology joins other Christian theologies in affirming creation.

WE SHOULD CONSUME WITH GRATITUDE, SAVORING, AND SHARING

For these writers who hold that our desires are not sinful and that what we desire is abundant, three conclusions have emerged: we should consume with a sense of gratitude, with savoring, and with sharing.

Schneider discusses the importance of gratitude for God's blessing in this passage from *Godly Materialism*:

> The other evening I sat on my newly built cedar deck. I looked around at the giant oaks standing surrounding the house. I watched as my children played innocently and safely....As I enjoyed the smells and tastes of the summer barbecue I was moved to feel sheer gratitude to God and to those before me who made this life possible. I was overwhelmed with the thought that life is indeed good, a gift from God.[30]

In describing this evening, Schneider says he knows that some (such as Ronald Sider, to whom he responds directly) might see his lifestyle as "profoundly wrong," but he simply shakes his head: how could that be, when to him it seems so clearly to consist of

God-given blessing?[31] If we are grateful for our blessings, and share them appropriately (as discussed below), we are consuming well, according to Schneider.

Jung agrees that gratitude is important. He describes saying grace before a meal as one of the "master practices" of Christian spirituality. This expression of gratitude before a meal, he believes, is "anything but innocuous or simple."[32] Expressing gratitude is "spiritually formative," shaping our characters.[33] Gratitude gives rise to humility: "when we say grace we acknowledge our dependence on a power beyond ourselves."[34] And gratitude helps extend the range of appreciation, bringing attention to the people and creatures whose labor brought the food to the table. Jung writes, "We are expressing our gratitude to God for all the ways the world is arranged so as to bring food and sustenance to our table."[35]

Gratitude is only the beginning. Gratitude in action often leads to savoring, an activity of lingering over and taking delight in our consumption. As ecotheologian Matthew Fox sees it, "If we savored more, we would buy less. We would be less compulsive, less unsatisfied.... If we savored more, we would communicate more deeply, relate more fully, compete less regularly, and celebrate more authentically."[36] Savoring our consumption can become a meditative practice, as we fully enter into the physical practices and actions that bring material goodness into our lives. This, too, is creation affirming, milking the experience for its spiritual essence and practicing attentiveness to the created world that we consume. Emerging church theologian Brian MacLaren echoes Fox's position on savoring. "The consumer is right," he asserts, "there is pleasure to be had in good things, sacred and almost unspeakable pleasure," but this pleasure comes not from increased possessions but "by possessing them more truly through grateful contemplation."[37] Grateful contemplation, or savoring, deepens the experience of consumption, allowing us to be truly satisfied rather than hungry for more.

While Francis reportedly stirred ashes and cold water into his food to dampen its sinfully tempting qualities, Jung commends the joys of consuming food in mouth-watering prose. "Something is wrong if we fail to enjoy food," he writes. "Eating is so enjoyable, so much a part of God's intentions, that its underappreciation is almost a crime!"[38] To this end, Jung offers eating advice: "Slow down. Before we devour our food, let us think just a moment about what we are doing. Smell the food, look at it, alert our senses to what this is. We might think about what it took to get this to our table.... During the meal...try to savor the food and continue to give thanks *by* enjoying the meal."[39] This describes an explicit connection between savoring and gratitude.

Both gratitude and savoring imply a certain detachment from the thing itself. To be grateful is to recognize the blessing as a gift that was gratuitously given, not as something earned, something we can count on. And to savor is, paradoxically, also to detach. Though it is attentive to and embraces the created world, savoring brings about a certain spiritual fulfillment that helps humans detach from an idolatry of "stuff" and attend to what really matters. Hence Fox's intuition that better savoring would lead to less materialism and more genuineness.

WEALTH MAY BE VIRTUOUS

Grateful, savored consumption may be an aesthetic and spiritual experience, but abundant consumption rarely comes free. Is it possible to be wealthy without sin? Francis's example notwithstanding, a life of poverty is not the only way to holiness and virtue. In fact, God may desire wealth for the faithful. As Schneider notes, in

Exodus, God grants the Israelites a land "'flowing with milk and honey.'... [God] liberated them into a life of luxurious productivity and excess."[40] God wants delight and abundance for God's people. God may condone consuming richly and living prosperously.

Prosperity theology supports this conclusion. High-quality possessions are called "blessings"; nice things are well deserved in the hands of God's beloved children. Prosperity preachers John Avanzini and Frederick K. C. Price defend a life that includes rich possessions by appealing to a particular interpretation of Jesus' life: "Jesus had a nice house, a big house—big enough to have company stay the night."[41] "Jesus was handling big money."[42] "John 19 tells us that Jesus wore designer clothes...the kind of garment that kings and rich merchants wore."[43] "That's the reason why I drive a Rolls Royce. I'm following Jesus's steps."[44]

Similarly, Schneider, too, asserts that Jesus was not poor, but rather had a middle-class background. This is significant, not only because Jesus' life is a model for Christian living but also because Jesus was the incarnation of God. This meant his incarnational social location was no accident, but rather a deliberate, divine choice. He could have come as a poor man, or as a rich ruler, but instead, Jesus was a craftsman (or, as Schneider puts it, "a builder and a businessman").[45] Thus, to desire a safe and healthy middle-class life for one's children is not reprehensible: God's son received comparable luxuries.[46]

Not all Christians agree, of course. Jesus' wealth status has been debated throughout Christian history, and so has the status of wealthy Christians. In light of Bible passages that seem to condemn the rich, many have discerned a pastoral need: what does God wish for rich Christians? As Schneider contends, "there is a gospel of liberation and affirmation for Christians with money."[47] In direct opposition to Sider, he is less worried about the ill effects of a rich lifestyle on the well-being of the world's poor than he is concerned about how absurdly unjust and spiritually devastating it may be for the rich to be told that they ought to feel responsible for these suffering poor. New Testament scholar Craig Blomberg may be correct that "the number of affluent Christians imposing a false guilt on themselves" is probably "far smaller than he imagines," in light of the low rates of charitable giving among American Christians.[48] Still, Schneider addresses a genuine pastoral problem.

The earliest pastoral document addressing the salvation of the wealthy comes from Clement of Alexandria (ca. 150–ca. 215). His "Who Is the Rich Man That Shall Be Saved?" argues that, despite biblical statements to the contrary, it is possible for the rich Christian to be saved. Clement begins his treatise by condemning those who flatter the rich, when what the rich really need is help in working out their salvation.[49] The other extreme, however, to scorn the rich and deny them the hope of salvation (because Jesus said that a camel shall pass through the eye of a needle more easily than a rich man shall enter heaven [Mark 10:23–27]) is equally damaging ("Rich Man," 2). Clement urges the rich not to despair: salvation is possible for them. But it will take much disciplined work, like the training of an athlete; the rich cannot simply buy their way into the privilege of eternal life ("Rich Man," 3). All Christians, rich and poor, are expected to behave virtuously and follow Christian teaching.

Clement uses an allegorical interpretation to understand the story from Mark about the rich young man who fails to follow Jesus after Jesus told him to sell his possessions. Clement explains:

> He does not, as some conceive off-hand, bid him throw away the substance he possessed, and abandon his property; but bids him banish from his soul his notions about wealth, his excitement and morbid feeling about it, the anxieties, which are the thorns of existence, which choke the seed of life. ("Rich Man," 11)

The passions of the soul, not one's worldly possessions, determine one's salvation, according to Clement (and the Stoic philosophers who influenced his thinking) ("Rich Man," 18).[50] In his *Instructor*, Clement compares wealth to a snake: an untrained or inexperienced grasp will lead to injury.[51] But with proper guidance and discipline, rich Christians can achieve a completely detached attitude toward wealth.

Clement has, to some extent, a false "reputation as toady to the rich": on some interpretations, he offers them a loophole, a way to be virtuous Christians without having to change the material aspects of their lives.[52] But this is not Clement's intention, and neither is it Schneider's. In discussing Amos, Schneider draws a distinction between the righteous and the unrighteous rich. Amos, he believes, condemns unrighteousness, not riches. "It takes real depth, wisdom and spiritual discernment to know the difference between true delight and demonic narcissism.... I do not wish to say that the evil is only spiritual and not a matter of lifestyle," Schneider claims, but, fundamentally, "the rich must be liberated, not from riches, but from the mind of the serpent."[53]

It is not being wealthy that threatens one's soul—it is being so attached to these riches that one's purpose and virtue becomes clouded. In fact, God may desire to bestow wealth on us; as God's beloved children, perhaps we have a right to abundance.

WE ARE GOD'S BELOVED CHILDREN

An anthropology of abundance underlies the perspectives we have read so far in this chapter: we are royal persons, loved by God and created in such a way that we can and should embrace the blessings God bestows. Though the soul's salvation, in a spiritual sense, may be the most important aspect of this blessing, God grants material abundance too.

Matthew Fox's encouraging, empowering theology uses the terminology of royalty: Christ "calls people to the kingdom/queendom of God; that is, he invites all people to be royal persons. He calls them to their dignity as images of God." Fox clarifies that with this dignity comes responsibility "for justice-making and preserving creation."[54] There is also a strong theme of royalty in Schneider's thought, which helps him define human agency.[55] He uses the term "majesty" to describe the way God created humans to live.[56] Rich people have a particular kind of God-given responsibility, as Schneider sees it. "For people who have good reason to believe that God has blessed and entrusted them with wealth and the ability to create it, creative and productive economic living is both a mandate and a blessing."[57] We are monarchs of individual kingdoms, in Schneider's view: "The message, I believe, is to enlarge and to dignify whatever realm God has given us. We should go about our work with royal pride and dignity."[58]

Prosperity theology affirms a similarly positive view of believers. Though it has a wide appeal throughout American society (and increasingly abroad), prosperity theology is particularly popular among populations who are deprived of social affirmation in the workplace or other arenas of life. Perhaps this is because of its strongly positive, uplifting anthropology.

Dollar guides his faithful toward prosperity through the practice of *positive confession*. This means, in the words of Black Church social ethicist Jonathan Walton, that "believers articulate their trust in God, and tangentially themselves, through verbal expression."[59] They are to pray with confidence, out loud, for the thing they want. Speaking aloud has potency, according to Dollar: God created the world through the power of speech, and we, in God's image, have a similar power.[60] A doctrine of human deification is at work here. Dollar tells his congregation: "you are gods, little g. You came from God and you are gods."[61] Therefore, humans can create, as God does, through speech. As multicultural sociologist David Pilgrim explains the concept, believers should pray for specific items: "modes of transportation (cars, vans, trucks, even 2-seat planes), homes, furniture, and large bank accounts."[62] Dollar urges his readers to think big: limited expectations limit God.[63]

Dollar "relentlessly attacks the idea that Christians should limit material possessions."[64] God's royal children deserve the best. Barbara Ehrenreich and Dedrick Muhammad describe Dollar's congregation repeating the affirmation: "I want my stuff—right now!"[65] In his writing, Dollar mixes conspicuous consumption with positive thinking, counseling his readers to start immediately behaving as if they had achieved their goal of prosperity:

> You can't walk around wearing that same old polyester dress and shopping at Thrift Town....Men, stop wearing that supermarket cologne and get the real deal, even if it's a small bottle....You might not see anything wrong with buying cheap stuff, but as long as you do that, you will have a discount mentality. If you are ever going to receive God's best, you're going to have to break through your wall of containment and think big.[66]

Dollar decries a "discount mentality" or a "poverty spirit." As Walton describes it, "A poverty spirit encourages low self-esteem and deceives people into believing that they do not deserve infinite health and wealth."[67] This is antithetical to prosperity theology.

While there is indeed power in positive thinking, and God does esteem and love God's people, prosperity theology conveys the troubling implication that being poor is one's own fault, due to a lack of faith. Walton writes, "People are poor, according to Pastor Dollar, because they do not have enough faith that God wants them to be rich. Poverty is essentially in one's mind."[68] This teaching offends many Christians who see the poor as uniquely beloved of God.

Some Christians are also troubled by the way that prosperity theology seems to limit God's power. "God sits there," according to Dollar, "with your blessing and your prosperity until you position yourself to receive. Once you get in place, God winds up and releases prosperity toward you."[69] To receive blessing, then, is less a matter of trusting God than it is exerting the right kind of prayer-pressure on God. "Whatever you're believing God for [sic], put as much pressure on it as you can," Dollar advises.[70] In this scenario, human empowerment has been taken too far, and God is "reduced to a kind of 'cosmic bellhop,' attending to the needs and desires of his creation"; serious theological problems result.[71] Rather than a message of unearned grace, the prosperity message is one of reward in response to proper prayers and behavior.[72] Dollar's definition of prosperity as control of one's life shows the importance of human power: power over one's own life, and even over God as the source of all prosperity. "A striking illustration ... can be found in the simple act of saying grace at mealtime. [Robert] Tilton [another prosperity preacher] has said that he no longer thanks God for his food. Instead he takes on the divine prerogative of speaking to the food itself and pronouncing a blessing on it."[73] Contrast this with the position of Jung, Fox, and Schneider on gratitude.

Still, prosperity theology cannot simply be rejected out of hand. While many aspects are troubling, there are elements of truth in this teaching. Like liberation theology, prosperity theology tells the poor that God wishes for an end to their suffering, and helps them gain dignity as children of God. As British theologian Geoffrey Grogan observes, "In fact, in Israel's experience, liberation and prosperity were the two sides of the same coin, for the God who brought them out—from Egyptian bondage—also brought them in—to a land flowing with milk and honey."[74] Liberation through economic advancement is a powerful message in prosperity theology, though there is disagreement about whether it truly appeals to those who are destitute or to the newly affluent who feel guilt for having left poverty, and their poor neighbors, behind.[75] Regardless, prosperity theology correctly asserts that every human, even the poorest, is of great dignity in God's eyes. Activities, including consumption, that undermine that dignity are unworthy of Christian endorsement. Dollar decries a "discount mentality," and he is right: consuming meagerly can show an unseemly depreciation of the self, inconsistent with God's own esteem for God's beloved children.

The Dollars and the Francises of the world, in fact, agree: God wants what's best for us. But they disagree about the meaning of "what's best for us." Francis's God offers grace to believers who engage in ascetic practice; Dollar's God offers grace to believers who enjoy the finer things in life. Are these two Gods mutually exclusive? Perhaps not.

GOOD STEWARDSHIP OF BLESSINGS

All the authors mentioned in this chapter, from Aquinas to Dollar, from Jung to Schneider, say that the key to enjoying Christian consumption is good stewardship of God's blessings. Though they embrace what seems to be a more hedonistic attitude toward consumption, most Christians who emphasize enjoying creation also impose boundaries on this enjoyment. Those boundaries, together with the affirmation of enjoying consumption, create a complete picture of good stewardship.

Moderation Is Essential to Proper Enjoyment of Blessings

Aquinas, who defends the goodness of human hungers, also carefully articulates their limits. To exceed the boundaries of right and proper desires is to sin against oneself (immoderate desires are unfitting, violating one's natural integrity) and one's neighbor (since superfluous property must, in his view, be gotten at the expense of someone else) (II–II.118.1).[76] Both covetousness and gluttony may become mortal sins if they edge out love of God and love of neighbor (II–II.118.4; II–II.148.2). To avoid these sins means, in Thomist ethicist Jame Schaefer's words, "to use only what is needed to sustain human life and not what is desired beyond the necessities of life."[77]

Aquinas, however, defines the necessities of life more generously than Francis or Woolman might define them. He first acknowledges two ways to define "necessary": "that without which a thing cannot be at all" and "something without which a thing cannot be becomingly" (II–II.141.6). In discussing this second sense of necessity, Aquinas acknowledges the requirements of one's station in life and the decorum necessary for "good conduct" (ibid.). While Francis simply renounced his station in life, and Woolman cared less for good conduct than good conscience, Aquinas is more accepting of the social status quo when it comes to wealth and consumption. He simply urges moderation, "according to the demands of place and time, and in keeping with those among whom one dwells" (ibid.).

Clothing consumption offers a specific example: Aquinas urges moderation in keeping with local customs, and moderation in pleasure associated with clothing. He also defends the costly apparel of those in high church offices: their dress is "not for their own glory, but to indicate the excellence of their office or of the Divine worship" (II–II.169.1). Food consumption is also instructive. This requires the virtue of temperance, which "moderates the affections of the soul."[78] The task of the temperate person is to "use the power of reason to bridle their impulses and the feelings of pleasure that attend them."[79] Even fasting should occur in moderation, according to Aquinas, who finds a place of moderation between the church-sanctioned practice and the world-denying stance that its extremes can entail (II–II.147).

Clement articulates a similar sense of moderation, using the idea of the poor Christ as his exemplar:

> I affirm that truckle-beds afford no worse repose than the ivory couch; and the goatskin coverlet being amply sufficient to spread on the bed, there is no need of purple or scarlet coverings.... See. The Lord ate from a common bowl, and made the disciples recline on the grass on the ground, and washed their feet, girded with a linen towel—He, the lowly-minded God, and Lord of the universe. He did not bring down a silver foot-bath from heaven. He asked to drink of the Samaritan woman, who drew the water from the well in an earthenware vessel, not seeking regal gold, but teaching us how to quench thirst easily. For He made use, not extravagance, his aim. (*Instructor*, 2.3)

Though he seems austere in this passage, Clement makes room for certain concessions: "the wearing of gold and the use of softer clothing is not to be entirely prohibited. But irrational impulses must be curbed" (ibid., 3.9). He accepts some rich consumption, concerned more for the inner passions of the soul than an external standard of riches or poverty. Both Clement and Aquinas allow certain concessions to comfort or to social circumstances: good stewardship means moderation, not austerity.

The Wealthy Should Be Detached, and Share with Those in Need

Christians' wealth is often defended by highlighting the duty to be charitable toward those in need. If no one were wealthy, who would give alms? Though Clement approves of rich Christians, he expects them to be so detached from their possessions that they are willing to give freely and generously to those in need. The rich are to actively seek out those who need their help and to give generously regardless of whether the recipient seems deserving ("Rich Man," 31, 33). Possessing wealth means owning the power to help others: Clement recognizes the potential for good that resides in riches. He hopes that some of his rich congregants, with proper spiritual training, will be able to use that power well, rather than succumb to its temptations.

Scholar Barry Gordon, writing in the late 1980s, attributes a view to Clement that resembles the "trickle-down economics" of the late twentieth century: he says that Clement believes the rich cannot robustly help others if they are destitute themselves, or even if they are barely scraping by; when the rich have a thick enough financial cushion to allow for entrepreneurship, they are most able to be creative and productive in ways that help others.[80] Gordon attributes a keen understanding of capital and entrepreneurship to the worldly Clement, who may have absorbed his business sense through conversations with merchants in the cosmopolitan city of Alexandria.[81] Gordon correctly notes Clement's belief that rich Christians can "participate freely in the process of accumulating capital, provided that they are prepared to use that capital as if its ownership is common."[82] The rich Christians who can be saved, then, are those who are spiritually advanced enough to be good stewards of their property, using it to help others.

Prosperity theology also teaches that the rich should be detached and help others generously. In addition to the blend of prayer and positive thinking prescribed by prosperity preachers, most also instruct their followers to practice "seed-faith," a way of "giving in order to get." This idea stems from biblical sources such as Galatians 6:7 ("you reap whatever you sow").[83] "Financial offerings," explains Walton, "are considered sown seed: like any seeds that are planted, they will produce a recurring harvest."[84] If a believer gives to worthy causes (usually the church), he or she will then reap similar generosity in return—often with a tenfold or hundredfold increase.[85] Robert Tilton vividly describes how giving away leads to getting: "I started noticing good things showing up around me. I gave away a pair of shoes, then I noticed three or four pairs came back. I kept giving watches away, then I noticed a very expensive Rolex watch jumped onto my wrist."[86]

But to receive prosperity requires a certain discipline of giving and delayed gratification. "Continue to plant your seed," counsels Dollar, "until you reach the destination that the Word of God has promised. Don't eat your seed. Keep sowing. God wants you to live a prosperous life."[87] As Dollar warns his followers, there is a difference between multiplied seed (initial returns on generosity) and harvest (success in the goal of prosperity). To "eat the seed" prematurely is to prevent further growth from happening.[88]

Generous giving, or sowing the seed, is foundational to prosperity theology. In contrast with Sider, who discusses, at length, which organizations should receive a Christian's tithe, Dollar emphasizes the giver, not the recipient. As Mitchem writes:

The tithe is given to Jesus, Creflo Dollar states, not to "some man." The preacher may be the one collecting the tithes, but you have placed your dedicated thing before the throne of God. If someone chooses to do something stupid with your tithe after you've presented it, that's between that man and God.[89]

If tithes are used to enrich an already wealthy man rather than to help the poor, that does not undercut the spiritual effectiveness of the tithe, in Dollar's view. Sider would probably disagree. But he would have to concede that among Dollar's faithful (and many other prosperity congregations), the rate of giving is admirably strong: security guards watch over the offertory every Sunday.[90] While congregants who have become rich may indulge in the blessings of designer clothes and Rolls-Royces, they are also required to tithe a full 10 percent of their pre-tax earnings.[91]

Though it teaches discipline and generosity, prosperity theology has been rightly criticized as being prone to exploitation and as overly self-focused. It is not uncommon for poor congregants who can barely afford to pay their bills to donate large sums of money to the pastor and to the church. Though believers hold that such sacrifices will pay off with proper faith, outsiders worry about the exploitation of gullible congregants by profiteering pastors. Regardless, it is a self-focused generosity. Baptist ethicist David Jones notes, "Whereas Jesus taught His disciples to 'give, hoping for nothing in return,' prosperity theologians teach their disciples to give *because* they will get a great return."[92] For a Christian theology that concerns itself with economics, there is an astonishing dearth of concern for or solidarity with the poor. Mitchem condemns prosperity theology's unwillingness to challenge economic systems that create poverty. She questions "the solid connection between Word of Faith and politically conservative groups who support ideas and activities that are not actually for the benefit of poor black people," concluding, "this preaching cannot stand in solidarity with the poor."[93] Walton shares her insight but not her condemnation as he writes, "Accommodating to macro systems [e.g., economic systems that perpetuate poverty] in order to carve out a space of micro achievement is a long-standing tradition of African-American response to social injustice."[94]

In defense of prosperity theology, however, African American cultural commentator Milmon Harrison writes:

> There is more to the teaching of prosperity than mere money-grubbing.... The people are being taught that it is God's desire to "prosper" them and meet their financial needs *in order to make them channels of those same financial blessings toward those who are still in need.*[95]

While many prosperity churches urge members to give offerings primarily to the church, others encourage unmediated financial support between members as needed.[96] These churches are hardly different from Clement's—congregants are taught that the rich may be virtuous to the degree that they are willing to give to others. The practice of seed-faith requires detachment, just as Clement's wealthy spiritual athlete does. Both are enjoined to donate generously and trust in God. In fact, the donations given by believers in Dollar's church may not be so different from the alms given to Francis by the people of Assisi. Both systems create a mutually beneficial economy in which giving away riches accomplishes a good for both the giver and the recipient.[97]

It Can Be Acceptable to Enjoy Consumption
Even while Others Suffer Deprivation

If well-off Christians have a responsibility to help others, how, then, can anyone enjoy some measure of richness—monetary wealth and delightful consumption—when others are in need? Until all are provided for, are we not indulging at others' expense?

Jung, in his reflections on food and feasting, has pondered this very point. Sharing and joy need not be mutually exclusive, since sharing food with others, on Jung's interpretation, is just as much an inherent source of joy as eating it, and to do both is doubly joyful.[98] Again, Jung appeals to human nature, the way God created us, as the source of his assertion: "Christians consider sharing to be a joy *because* relating to others enters into our very constitution."[99] Jung discusses the joys of sharing other things, but returns to food as the most obvious (and "most enjoyable!") example.[100] Jung links his jovial interest in delicious food with a genuine concern for poverty, particularly the problem of hunger: "I see the obscenity of world hunger and our own underappreciation of eating as linked phenomena. If we truly enjoyed eating more, we would want to share more."[101] Jung knows the temptation to overeat is strong; he dedicates *Sharing Food* to "all those, like me, who fight being overweight because they love sharing food."[102] North American eaters are "caught in systems that are pleasurable and unjust at the same time."[103] Jung considers it sinful to consume greedily and without true appreciation. Similarly, he considers it sinful to fail to acknowledge or transform unjust food systems. Redemption comes when eaters become aware of their sin, ask for God's forgiveness, and surrender to the "transformational attitudes" of contentment and generosity.[104] "We are encouraged and encourage each other to resist evil and complicity, as well as to delight and share. We learn to live in the tension of being justified, but still sinners."[105] Despite the reality of food-related sin, it remains virtuous to savor, appreciate, enjoy, and express gratitude for the bounty we consume.

Where Jung grants centrality to our responsibility to share food, Schneider places limits on sharing. Schneider recognizes that the rich Christian has a call to serve God by using wealth for good, as Joanna and other patrons did in the time of Jesus and the early church.[106] But he cannot accept Sider's concept of structural sin and collective culpability, arguing that even rich people cannot be held responsible for entire evil systems. God, mercifully, "judges us within boundaries."[107]

Schneider, creatively echoing the Catholic principle of subsidiarity, imagines a "principle of moral proximity... [which] states simply that our moral obligations in economic life are greater or lesser in proportion to their moral proximity to us."[108] This is a commonsense principle that plays out in many lives: most of us feel most responsible for those nearby, either from family ties, shared community identity, or emotional connection.[109] The principle of moral proximity, he writes, makes "the demands of morality in economic life reasonable, bearable, and humane." Without it, a conscientious person would be unable to accept God's blessings; without it, "the Israelites could not have affirmed the vision [of abundance and delight in the promised land] that God had for them."[110] The force of God's promise of abundant material blessing orients Schneider's reading of the biblical texts about hungry neighbors and the righteous poor.

For Schneider and for many North American Christians, having a nice single-family home with a deck and a yard, and eating food barbecued on one's own grill, is an acceptable level of consumption. Schneider defends his lifestyle against imagined criticisms from Sider and others, who might question him about the sustainability of the wood for his deck, or why he does not share his ample home with others in need. These are legitimate questions, highlighting the somewhat walled-off defensiveness that characterizes Schneider's position. While Jung is always aware of sin while he's consuming with pleasure, Schneider seems defended from such awareness.

Nevertheless, Schneider admirably articulates an important defense of upper- and middle-class living. Though Christian theologians rarely articulate such a defense, perhaps they should, since it represents the tacit position of many upper- and middle-class Christian believers. His practice of assuming boundaried responsibilities has merit: surely it is more practical to set achievable goals than to expect the impossible. As Schneider sees it, we risk becoming overwhelmed—and idolatrous—if we inflate God's humble, reasonable mission for rich Christians into a call on a "messianic" scale. Am I, myself, called to transform the entire unjust economic system? Surely God only calls me to effect a certain blessed liberation within the bounds of my power, not beyond it. I should help the poor in my neighborhood, and support schools and programs for the elderly, but I should not attempt to save the world. Schneider counsels rich Christians to ask themselves in any given instance: "What is my realm of dominion?"[111] From this, they can ascertain their responsibilities. The needy within my realm are my responsibility; the others should be helped by someone else. If I have fulfilled my responsibilities, I can comfortably consume with gratitude and joy.

The reality of living with an open conscience, though, is that the needs of others threaten the scruples of carefree consumers, and concerns about the environment impinge on the enjoyment of creation's fruitfulness. Wendell Berry puts it best:

> To live we must daily break the body and shed the blood of
> creation. When we do this knowingly, lovingly, skillfully and

reverently it is a sacrament. When we do it ignorantly, greedily and destructively it is a desecration. In such a desecration, we condemn ourselves to spiritual and moral loneliness and others to want.[112]

When does our consumption desecrate creation and when does it revere it? Berry has pinpointed a paradox: though improper use of creation is horrific, not all death and destruction is evil. Christians recognize the salvific quality of (some) suffering and sacrifice. Although we mourn the creatures that become our food, we also recognize that eating is essential for life.

Jung speaks of consumption in liturgical terms. "Could it be that all eating is sacramental?" he asks, and answers that yes, it can be: "*Food itself is a means of revelation. Through eating together we taste the goodness of God.*"[113] Not all consumption is sacramental, for these writers—certain ethical criteria are required. Wendell Berry is concerned about his food and where it comes from, and is particularly interested in food that has a good ecological and social impact.[114] Jung, too, has implicit criteria for what qualifies as sacramental eating. He inveighs against both personal "eating disorders" (greed, gluttony, sloth) and social, ecological, and economic "eating disorders" (ecologically unsound food production, a consumerist system, the presence of both hunger and obesity).[115] For eating to be sacramental, according to Jung, not only should the food be consumed and produced in a way that is free of such eating disorders but also it should be characterized by genuine enjoyment in community with others.[116]

Aquinas, too, has guidelines for an acceptable degree of ecological destruction relating to the consumption we enjoy. Aquinas indicates that a modest amount of superfluous consumption is acceptable, provided those blessed with wealth are not fleecing the poor or abusing creation. A moderate use of the natural world must be ordered toward the true good for all persons (in other words, humans must exercise proper dominion, not in excess), and at the same time, creatures do possess an intrinsic goodness apart from all natural usefulness.[117] Use of creation for the physical benefit of people is acceptable, even blessed, but is limited by considerations of justice to other humans, temperance in desires, and devotion to God in the form of responsible stewardship. Thus, human consumption, while good, should be curbed in light of its effect on creation and on human dignity.

CONSUMPTION AND CREATION

The voices we hear in this chapter appear to be consistently aware of those of the previous chapter. At every turn, the goodness of consumption is defended against those who primarily associate it with sin. This chapter began with the notion that creation is fruitful and filled with blessings. Then, Christian voices affirmed that human hungers and desires are not sinful, and that in fact their fulfillment can be spiritually edifying; that good consumption is performed in gratitude, savored, and shared; that properly used wealth may in fact be virtuous; and that as God's beloved children we deserve what is good. But the concerns of the previous chapter cannot be banished. To embrace creation, then, means to consume as a good steward. Three prominent features of good stewardship emerge: to consume joyfully but in moderation, avoiding sins associated with excess consumption; to consume with a detached attitude and readiness to share, avoiding idolatry or greed; and to consume in a way that is aware of the ethical challenges of enjoyment in an imperfect world, avoiding a denial of others in need or of the good of creation.

Finally, Christians from a variety of perspectives—Catholic and Reformed, capital-centered and creation-centered—agree that enjoying consumption as a good steward entails enjoying creation and the creator. Jung quotes the Westminster Catechism to describe "the nature and destiny of human life: to glorify God *and to enjoy* God forever!"[118] If enjoying God is essential to the human calling, as many Christians affirm, and if enjoying creation is a major way to enjoy God, then the voices in this chapter describe a valid means of fulfilling this essential Christian duty.[119]

This second consideration deepens and complexifies the conversation about consumption. Where the first consideration has little to say about blessing and fulfillment, the second consideration emphasizes such joys and encourages Christians to pursue them. The first consideration speaks to affluent Christians seeking to purify their lives, while the second consideration speaks to poorer Christians seeking to pursue abundance, blessing, and enjoyment—to attain, at times, those same blessings that affluent Christians seek to purify.

The first and second considerations seem, at first sight, to be somewhat contradictory, and there are certainly some striking differences between them. The varying emphases on God and Jesus that arise in these two chapters elucidate these differences. According to Francis, Christ and his disciples were radically poor, and Sider refers to God as Lord of the Poor. But according to Schneider, Jesus was a middle-class skilled craftsman, and prosperity preachers go further, describing him as rich. These hermeneutical differences support theological concerns and life practices so divergent that, in the case of Francis and Creflo Dollar, they may hardly be recognizable as adherents of the same religion. Schneider touches on this when he describes two accounts of Jesus present in the Gospels: he is characterized as both the austere son of man, acquainted with grief and with no place to lay his head; and as the feasting, celebratory messiah, who comes eating and drinking.[120] These models of consumption seem contradictory, and indeed, Schneider fails to truly reconcile them, simply raising and affirming the second, celebratory view of Christ.

In fact, however, the considerations elaborated in these chapters are not as contradictory as they sound. Jesus both fasted and feasted, and perhaps so should we.[121] It is rare to find a Christian who affirms austerity without tempering it with some enjoyment, or who preaches feasting without some notion of sharing or moderation. In fact, many Christians who write about consumption espouse a position that either strikes a balance between the two, or affirms them both as a profound paradox. For example, James A. Nash, in his writings on frugality, describes it as a "middle ground" between austerity and profligacy. While he primarily speaks of frugality as cutting back, he also affirms the goodness of enjoyment. "Surely," he writes, "there are even occasions for indulgence—for a festive frugality!"[122] "Frugality," he writes, "is an earth-affirming, enriching, even hedonistic norm that delights in the non- and less-consumptive joys of the mind and flesh.... At its best, therefore, frugality can be described paradoxically as hedonistic self-denial."[123] Hedonistic self-denial—enjoyable asceticism—is surely a key to ethical Christian consumption. Though this paradox is both provocative and productive, sin and creation are not the only considerations that apply to consumption. As the next two chapters show, Christians are also called to love the neighbor and envision God's reign as they consume.

Chapter 4

To Love the Neighbor

Dorothy Day's Catholic Worker Movement featured houses of hospitality that served food to the urban poor in New York City. Day placed special value on shared food because of the way shared meals express love and create community. Sitting down with others for a meal, she writes, "is the closest we can ever come to each other.... It is unbelievably, poignantly intimate."[1] Day's appreciation of food included its quality, and she enjoyed serving good food to the poor she encountered. "What a delightful thing it is," she writes, "to be boldly profligate, to ignore the price of coffee and go on serving the long line of destitute men who come to us, good coffee and the finest of bread."[2] Day enjoyed showing respect and love for her guests by offering them good-quality food to consume.

Dorothy Day founded the Catholic Worker Movement with Peter Maurin in 1933. It began as a newspaper, but the movement grew into Maurin's threefold vision of "round-table discussions, houses of hospitality and agronomic universities [farming communes]."[3] Catholic Workers sought to practice the works of mercy (feed the hungry, give drink to the thirsty, clothe the naked, etc.), motivated by love for others.[4] As biographer Mel Piehl writes, "Day always insisted that the works of mercy are neither paternalistic charity nor formal religious duty, but an opportunity for expressing the freely given love at the heart of Christian faith."[5]

Love was central for Day. Oral historian Rosalie Riegle recounts: "As someone told me, 'Dorothy Day was never too polite to speak of God's love.'"[6] "Her basic message," according to biographer James Forest, "was stunningly simple: we are called by God to love one another as He loves us."[7] One way Day showed this love of others was through her consumption choices. Not only do the Catholic Workers help the poor through hospitality and works of mercy but they also put this love into action through voluntary poverty in solidarity with those who do not have enough, consuming carefully with the poor in mind.

"Love is the measure by which we will be judged." This statement is attributed to St. John of the Cross, but Day adopted it as a maxim for her own daily life and often repeated it to other Catholic Workers.[8] Day did measure her life—including her consumption choices—by a standard of love, placing both love of God and love of the neighbor in a central position in her decisions.

In this chapter, Dorothy Day and the Catholic Worker Movement provide the foundational example for explicating exactly how love of neighbor can manifest in consumption decisions. Supporting material comes from Catholic social thought and the work of several Protestant theologians. Catholic sources are prominent in this chapter because they offer the best, most explicit examples of Christian thought that considers neighbor-love in judging consumption. However, as the use of other, non-Catholic voices shows, this is not a uniquely Catholic position.

Christians from all parts of the tradition are called to love the neighbor, and consumption choices can be one way to do so. Love for a variety of subjects can be a vital consideration in assessing ethical consumption, including love for the self, close others, somewhat distant others, place, faraway others, and God. To some extent, these represent a gradual spectrum of proximity, from self to faraway others; discrete categories are boundaries imposed by the needs of the discussion, rather than by the subject matter itself. A few of these categories, particularly love of place and love of God, transcend both scale and proximity, for both God and place can be very large or very intimate, or both.

Loving another through consumption is more complex than avoiding sin or enjoying creation. To foster reflection on that complexity, I offer fictional examples at the beginning of each section. These are designed to be heuristic: few of us live in the way described, but the examples highlight the scope and meaning of the loving consumption I wish to discuss.

WHAT IS LOVE?

Love, in the words of Jesus, constitutes the essence of the greatest commandments: loving God and loving the neighbor. Christians see neighbor-love as a paramount duty, something that should shape every action. Christian bioethicist Arthur J. Dyck speaks of "love as a test for deciding whether something is right or wrong"; "such love takes the form of sensitive discernment": "a cognitive ability to vividly imagine...how other persons feel, what they need, and how they would be affected by our actions."[9] It is therefore quite appropriate to apply the criterion of love to consumption.

What is love? Economic historian and philosopher Deirdre McCloskey sums it up well: love is "a commitment of the will to the true good of another."[10] Love as an act of will means that it is not merely a feeling, not something we spontaneously "fall into." Rather, like any virtue, it is a habit of thinking, feeling, behaving, and willing in a certain way—a way that acts on behalf of another's good. Before we may know another's good, we must be attentive to the other and ascribe value to the other's well-being. Acting in love can mean many things, including sacrificing for the beloved, offering hospitality to the beloved, acting in solidarity with the beloved, and celebrating the beloved.

In Christian thought, love and justice are intimately interrelated, though they are often placed at odds with each other, and their relationship is often debated. I do not wish to enter into this debate. For this project, I treat love and justice as two overlapping concepts, a position frequently taken by Christian thinkers.[11] "Justice is inseparable from charity," writes Benedict XVI, "and intrinsic to it."[12] The overlap between love and justice is large: both are virtues that require us to consider others' well-being. The question of whether one should "do right by" others because of love or justice is moot: regardless of the reason, the duty remains.

Love often seems weaker than justice; it seems less rigorous to say "love requires me to do X" than to say "justice requires me to do X." But this difference is based on a false definition of love: love is not a weak feeling, the product of fickle yearning. On the contrary, Christian love is an act of the will in response to a commandment. When asked the greatest commandment of all, Jesus did not answer "be just to others." He said, "You shall love the Lord your God with all your heart, and with all your soul, and with all your mind ... [and] you shall love your neighbor as yourself."[13] If it were simply a contingent, whimsical affection, it could not be required. But love *is* required of the Christian; Søren Kierkegaard rightly speaks of it as a duty, emphasizing Jesus' word *shall* as a source of moral "ought."[14] Supporting love, in this formulation, is not just the mind but the soul and the heart: it is a robust virtue requiring the engagement of the whole person.

In this chapter, I use McCloskey's definition of love as "commitment of the will to the true good of another," plus a Christian understanding that this commitment is required of Christian persons, and manifested as and through God's love. For Christians, the command to love the neighbor has purposefully broad boundaries to include enemies and the like.[15] To put love into action means concerning myself with the myriad others who touch my life, and whose lives are touched by mine. I can pretend these relationships do not exist, or are morally unimportant, but that is hardly a Christian position. In fact, as the U.S. Catholic Bishops put it, love is constitutive of my humanity: "being a person means being united to other persons in mutual love."[16] To the degree that I deny this, I undercut my own personhood.

I understand love to be a question of right relationships, and with Kathryn Tanner I recognize that this is a primary function of ethical thought: "Maintaining *relations* and establishing the nature of one's responsibilities to others—figuring out what the situation and the needs of others require from one—are the primary foci of moral concern."[17] In this chapter, I stretch love very far: from self-love to love of nonhumans to love of aggregate groups of people I'll never meet. When the discussion turns to communities or the common good or the health of the biosphere (large, abstract concepts) the reader may wonder if these considerations really qualify as love. Feminist ethicist Linda Woodhead insists that genuine love must be particular rather than vague, implying that whatever notions I have about seeking the good of "the poor" or "the planet" may be laudable, but they are not love.[18] I maintain that I can, in fact, love in this abstract way, but that the more abstract such love becomes, the more it is unstable, attenuated, and prone to error in judgment, since it relies on secondhand accounts of what "the true good of another" actually means.

The meaning of loving the neighbor through consumption varies by situation. We begin with the simplest, but nevertheless quite challenging, context: love of self.

LOVE OF SELF

Before I enter the cafeteria, I repeat to myself: "I love my body. I will choose healthy food." Dr. Gosalia had told me, at my appointment the day before, to be careful of cholesterol. I steer clear of the french fries and get myself a salad. But Kate coaxes me into eating the coconut flan: "You've had a rough morning," she argues. "A little sugar will help you feel better. Accept the blessing of delicious dessert. Don't punish yourself; live a little!" I've had this flan before—it's the speciality of one of the cafeteria workers. She is an excellent chef, and she uses copious amounts of cream, butter, eggs, and sugar to achieve this remarkable dish. The last time I ate this flan, I felt such joy and well-being, savoring the light sweetness on my tongue. Dr. Gosalia said the situation wasn't dire—yet—but I should watch what I eat to keep my cholesterol down. To deny myself the joy seems cruel, but is it really loving to put unhealthy foods into my body?

While the consumer herself is the person most immediately affected by consumption, self-love through consumption is not as simple as it may seem. The concept of self-love has been problematic for some Christian thinkers.[19] Others, however, have noted that Jesus' phrasing about neighbor-love includes self-love: one is to love one's neighbor as oneself.[20] Without self-love, this exhortation is meaningless.

To love the self is to attentively regard the self, to care for the self, and wish its well-being. This means seeking the self's pleasure and fulfillment, health and wholeness, through consumption. Balancing healthy eating with pleasurable eating, as mentioned in the example above, is a challenge familiar to many North American consumers. The criterion of self-love provides a clue to this conundrum, though it may not always solve it. This discussion connects with the "royal personhood" mentioned in chapter 3: if we are not to sell ourselves short, but to love and respect ourselves, how then shall we consume? Arguably, this may mean some indulgence, "pampering," or times of luxurious consumption in the name of self-respect and self-care.

Self-love can easily be taken too far, however. If my only considerations are my own needs and desires, then this is no different from the shallow materialism rightly criticized by many Christians in their comments on consumerism. Consumables, whatever they are, have existence and value in their own right and do not solely exist in order to fulfill my immediate needs. Though my genuine needs probably should be met, I am not the only needful person in the world: others should enter into consideration when I make consumption choices. In addition, it is a great challenge to correctly perceive my own needs. As the example of the coconut flan indicates, the difference between joyful, necessary consumption and rationalized self-indulgence is hard to discern when I am salivating over dessert in the cafeteria line. Augustine addresses this very situation, describing insightfully the way that such uncertainty may lead one's concupiscent self to offer "excuses in its own defense, glad to take advantage of the ambiguity about what temperate preservation of health requires, and cloaks its self-indulgence under the pretense that health is being prudently provided for."[21] In this situation, my own self seems to be at odds: the state of my arteries seems to demand that I not eat the flan, but my taste buds seem to long for it. If I want to love myself in this situation, should I love my arteries or my taste buds?

To complicate things further, the self as Christians understand it is not singular or individualistic. Ecotheologian John B. Cobb, writing with economist Herman Daly, criticizes mainstream economics for its incomplete anthropology, its view of *Homo economicus* as rational wealth-maximizer. Cobb and Daly describe humans as being primarily relational, as constituted by their relationships: "by their internal relations to their bodies, to the wider world of nature, and especially to other people. Apart from these relations, they do not exist at all. They are formed and informed in human communities."[22] Ecotheologian Sallie McFague affirms loving relationality as a central feature of God, which leads her to see the world as "characterized by radical relationality ordered by and to the Power in the universe, who is love."[23] Central to the worldview she promotes "is the individual-in-community: everything *is* because of relationships of interdependence."[24] Cobb and Daly agree: "Instead of *Homo economicus* as pure individual we propose *Homo economicus* as person-in-community."[25]

If individuals are constituted by their relationships, then the self's well-being is intimately tied to the well-being of the community. This can mean sacrificing my immediate wants for the sake of the common good, as later sections of this chapter show. But my gain is not necessarily another's loss, as L. Shannon Jung writes: "This hunger, this appetite to eat, to taste the gift of love that comes to us from others and allow ourselves to be transformed by that love: this is revelation. We also share food with others; we give pleasure to others; and their delight likewise transforms us."[26] While Jung acknowledges that love of needy neighbors may require eating less, he believes that sharing food with those in need does not make eating any less delightful. On the contrary, sharing food with others makes both the eating and the relationship richer.[27] Sharing does not necessarily entail renunciation or austerity; rather, it is an occasion for delight.

On the topic of self-love, Jung diagnoses personal and social "eating disorders" from which North Americans suffer. Failure to love the self can manifest as disordered consumption of food: either as gluttony or as self-loathing.

At base both are born of misdirected desire—in the case of gluttony, a drive to consume enough in order to feel good and to enjoy life; in the case of self-loathing, a desperate attempt to be enough (thin enough, pretty enough, bulky enough) to merit the acceptance of others.[28]

Those who suffer from either disorder, according to Jung, fail to adequately appreciate the blessing of food, and fail to appreciate and love themselves, as well. (Jung does not, however, place the blame for eating disorders on individuals alone: he recognizes the social factors that shape human desires and distort our thinking.[29]) Thus, for Jung, to love the self may in fact mean to consume more, though this should not preclude sharing with others.

Finally, Dorothy Day offers insights into self-love and consumption. Day sought to find a balance between her sacrificial acts on behalf of the poor and her own need to care for herself. Writing both metaphorically and literally, Day claims, "I too am hungry and thirsty for the bread of the strong. I too must nourish myself to do the work I have undertaken; I too must drink at these good springs so that I may not be an empty cistern and unable to help others."[30] Day, though living in solidarity with the poor, kept a modest apartment to herself and appreciated gifts of good food.[31] There is a certain level of healthy self-love indicated in her living habits, which were modest but did not approach self-destruction.

At bottom, loving the self means caring for the self. Often, this means consuming enough to ensure health and well-being. Extravagance may be rationalized as self-care, and this is a genuine temptation for many North Americans. Nevertheless, some level of enjoyable consumption is required for genuine self-love and in order to fill the "cistern" that Day speaks of, the reservoir that she draws upon when she does the work of loving others.

LOVE OF CLOSE OTHERS

Marian lives down the street from me. Yesterday, on my daily walk, I saw her filling her bird feeders with sunflower seed for the cardinals and chickadees, wearing her purple sweatshirt that says "Proud Grandmother" on it. She stopped me and said, "Would you like to go to the antique store? I need to get a birthday gift for my sister. She loves old jewelry." Marian doesn't drive, and though I wasn't sure I had the time, I agreed to help her by driving her to the store that afternoon.

As this example shows, much of the consumption we do relates to our love of others close to us—that is, those we care about the most. As with Marian, this often involves gifts, be it jewelry for a loved one or food for the birds. Sometimes we consume things that enhance or show off a loving relationship (like Marian's sweatshirt—she wears it every time her grandkids visit). Sometimes we consume as a way to help someone, like the car and the gasoline I used to drive Marian to the store. All of this consumption, from the birdseed to the sweatshirt to the gas to the jewelry, occurs because the consumer loves someone—someone nearby, a family member or friend or near neighbor. Pets, plants, and other nonhuman companions qualify as close others in this understanding, if we love them and consume because of that love.

Often, Christians disturbed by consumerism accuse consumers of selfishness. Theologian Michelle Gonzalez takes a common position in her book *Shopping* when she writes, "We need to stop obsessing about what we own and what we don't own and instead focus on those things that have true value in our lives."[32] But consumption isn't necessarily motivated by self-obsession. As Deirdre McCloskey rightly notes, "Much of consumption...is *on behalf* of someone not the direct purchaser or income earner. After all, in the average American family with children about 35 percent of expenditure is directed at the kids. Moms are not buying all those frozen pizzas to feed *themselves*."[33] When we love someone, we often buy things for them—as with Marian's sister, or her birds.

Loving someone also may mean offering goods for consumption in times of trouble. Some, notes Methodist pastor Shirlyn Toppin, "use food as a form of caring and pastoral concern by using it to enrich a social gathering or in order to sympathize with others in times of bereavement."[34] Toppin describes how eating together can nurture communal relations between close associates, as with the example of "soul food": "the meaning of 'soul food' cooking is clearly evident . . . 'as a way of Black people expressing their love for one another.'"[35]

The lack of this communal consumption can indicate the breakdown of social ties, as religion scholar Mary Hinton notes. She celebrates the roots and rituals of African American food traditions, positing that "Blacks were given leftovers and were treated as leftovers. That these unwanted foods could be transformed with our own hands, our own ideas, and our own cooking skills makes the food important to Black culture."[36] Over feasts of "soul food," African Americans developed a "prophetic voice of hope and energy in the midst of empiricism."[37] Community solidarity, prophetic hope, and consumption of soul food have diminished together, according to Hinton, as the culture has shifted toward "privatized religion and prosperity."[38] Hinton calls for a renewal of both soul food and African American culture, arguing that cooking and consuming food together serves a vital pedagogical and community-strengthening role.[39] The consumption of food, then, can express, form, and strengthen loving bonds between close associates.

Love of close others can also lead us to eschew consumption. Anyone who has left the last piece of pie for a friend or given up smoking for a lover or a child knows that loving someone can mean sacrificing for them. Sacrifice may be the measure of love— our greatest loves are those for whom we are most willing to sacrifice. The particularity that comes with the love of close others—family, friends, and associates—is what moves us to sacrifice: it is much harder to sacrifice for abstract causes or vague, distant others. This close love is strong love; its results are immediate and have a personal impact. The strength of love for closer others explains otherwise irrational phenomena in charitable giving. For example, I would bid more freely at a fund-raiser auction for a dear friend with cancer than at a fund-raiser auction for general cancer research. Rationally, I should give the money to cancer research, which may save many lives, rather than to support my struggling friend, who is only one person. But as Woodhead notes above, love that is particular is a stronger, more robust motivation than abstract, impersonal caring.

Sacrificing consumption for love of close others was standard practice among Dorothy Day's Catholic Workers. Day herself lived with legendary austerity.[40] Her friends and followers seem to delight in relaying details of her lifestyle of poverty. As James Forest recounts, "It wasn't a comfortable life. At the time I joined, Dorothy had a sixth-floor walk-up apartment in a tenement on Spring Street. For $25 a month she got two small rooms, a bathtub next to the kitchen sink, and a bathroom the size of a broom closet."[41] Still, an apartment to herself presented a certain luxury—Day was not utterly ascetic.

Indeed, Day felt conflicted about any small luxuries she allowed herself. Faced with the close, concrete realities of others' needs, she writes, "It is hard to comfort ourselves with the reflection that if we did not get rest and food we would not be able to do the work we do."[42] Forest recalls, "She was rejoicing over a fruit salad brought to her by her godchild, Jean Kennedy, though she had a slightly guilty conscious [sic]. 'I ate it all! How sensual I am. A glutton. Was it St. Catherine of Siena or St. Angela Foligno who wanted to tie a baked chicken around her neck and run through the streets shouting "I am a glutton"?' "[43]

Love of close others also engenders vulnerability, a vital component of loving consumption. In the example above, Marian becomes vulnerable when she gives the gift to her sister, because it reveals something about her (her taste, how much she is willing or able to spend) and about how she sees her sister (if Marian chooses something ugly, the sister may wonder, "Does she dislike me? Does she think this is something I would like?"). And receiving a gift means vulnerability as well: Marian's sister does not know whether she will like the gift; to have it thrust upon her may be an imposition if it's something she truly does not want; and she is placed in the precarious position of choosing to respond either truthfully or tactfully, if she dislikes or is offended by Marian's gift.

Loving the close neighbor through consumption means finding ways to celebrate, sacrifice for, help, and become vulnerable to, the other. It may be sharing a birthday cake with my son or eating very little so he can have more; it may be giving a gift or allowing myself to receive a gift; in all of these cases, consumption can be a way to express love for close others.

LOVE OF SOMEWHAT DISTANT OTHERS

Ben and I got our coffee. "No packaging for my food," he said. "I'll just hold it in my hand." The barista put down the paper bag and gingerly delivered a croissant into his hands, using metal tongs. "Thank you so much," Ben smiled at her. He shoved a generous tip into the jar by the cash register. "I'm worried about this coffee shop," he said as we exited. "They have a lot of competition from that chain store up the street. I try to patronize these folks whenever I can." As we walked along, I was about to pitch my apple core in a trash can, but he stopped me and pocketed it with an enigmatic smile. When I raised my eyebrows he shrugged, saying, "Compost!" He added, "Have you heard about how full the local landfill is?" I realized that's why he had asked for no packaging. A homeless man sat by the corner, and though we had a green light to cross, Ben stopped and squatted down next to him. "Hey, brother," he said, "you want half my croissant?"

In this example, Ben does not personally know the barista or the shop owners or the homeless man; he does not live near the local landfill. But he has a feeling of care and compassion—neighbor-love—for these somewhat distant others. By "somewhat distant others" I mean those with whom a person does not have a close relationship, but who, nevertheless, he or she does occasionally, or can potentially, encounter. These are people the person knows exist, and who he or she could seek out and speak to if he or she chose, but who do not count among that person's close friends or immediate acquaintances. This level of relationship is present in the story of the good Samaritan: the Samaritan and the wounded man live in the same area, but do not know each other personally, and are not members of the same ethnic group. Nevertheless, their paths cross and the Samaritan is able to show neighbor-love to the wounded man. That is love of some-what distant others.

To love these neighbors requires greater attentiveness and imagination than to love closer neighbors. In the previous example, I could hardly have ignored Marian, since she knew me and called out to me, but I could easily have ignored the barista and the homeless man (and probably would have, if I were not with someone as attentive as Ben). The Christian duty to love the neighbor seems to imply that we should be more like Ben, having the awareness and broadness of thought to remember others who play somewhat anonymous roles in the network created by our consumption. This level of neighbor-love, the somewhat distant other, is the most commonly treated topic among Christians who consider love as a criterion for ethical consumption. For that reason, this section is longer and subdivided into the following: marketplace transactions, hospitality and solidarity, care for the community, and envisioning the reign of love in economic community.

Loving Somewhat Distant Others in the Marketplace

Much consumption in a North American context occurs as purchasing: we exchange money for goods, either impersonally (online or at a vending machine) or in person, at a store or marketplace. With in-person consumption, the neighbors we encounter (those who work at, and own, the store) fit this category of somewhat distant neighbors. Though they may not be close associates, they are near enough to meet and treat with neighbor-love.

Martin Luther was prompted to write about neighbor-love in the marketplace because of the egregious practices he observed in a time when capitalism was first developing in Europe.[44] Luther rails against merchants who sell their goods at as high a price as the market can bear (a practice that has become so widespread that it is an elementary principle of market economics today):

> What else does [this practice] mean but this: I care nothing about my neighbor; so long as I have my profit and satisfy my greed, of what concern is it to me if it injures my neighbor in ten ways at once?...Because your selling is an act performed toward your neighbor, it should rather be so governed by law and conscience that you do it without harm and injury to him, your concern being directed more toward doing him no injury than toward gaining profit for yourself.[45]

Luther acknowledges a merchant's need to make a living. But he denies that charging backbreaking prices is necessary: such practices arise from greed, not necessity. He appeals to the temporal authorities to set fair prices; in the absence of such guidance, merchants should price according to their consciences (and pray for the forgiveness they will undoubtedly need, since they will probably commit some wrongs in the process).[46]

What would Luther say to consumers who wish to practice neighbor-love? It is hard to know, since his writings only address sellers, but his words imply that a virtuous consumer would be willing to pay the merchant a high enough price that he or she, and all those along the supply chain, have enough. Just as sellers should not take advantage of desperate buyers, so buyers should not take advantage of desperate sellers willing to sell at inappropriately low prices when the market is down. Analogously, perhaps, consumers should not use the showroom, free advice, and customer service of a brick-and-mortar store, only to go home and order the same item for less money on the Internet. These practices would not meet Luther's criteria because they show little compassion for the seller. As Luther might say, where is the neighbor-love in this practice?

Loving Somewhat Distant Others through Hospitality and Solidarity

Beyond the marketplace, Christians love somewhat distant neighbors through hospitality to the stranger and solidarity with those in need. Hospitality may be defined as welcoming another by sharing one's resources—offering food, a place to stay, and one's time. In the example above, Ben is exhibiting hospitality when he offers the homeless man some food. Jung names "hospitality" a central Christian practice, not only because it is a way to love the neighbor but also because humans, on his view, are made to share: "*Sharing is natural. It is natural to share because God created human beings to be in relationship.*"[47] Paul considered hospitality vital to the early church (Romans 12:13), and many Christians interpret it as a gift of the spirit.[48]

Forest describes a social worker who asked Dorothy Day how long the poor were permitted to stay at the Catholic Worker's houses of hospitality. "Forever," was her reply. "They live with us, they die with us, and we give them Christian burial. We pray for them after they are dead. Once they are taken in, they become members of the family. Or rather they always were members of the family. They are our brothers and sisters in Christ."[49] Though Day's practice seems extreme, it is well grounded in Christian thought, which teaches that all people, as children of God, are brothers and sisters and should be treated as such. Truly loving the neighbor means not only wishing them well but also being as open to their needs as to our own.

This is a difficult teaching to act on, because hospitality is challenging. Hospitality means vulnerability. But this very vulnerability can be spiritually efficacious, as it leads to a different relationship with possessions, as theologian Daniel DiDomizio explains of the Catholic Workers:

> The act of hospitality posits vulnerability, allowing others access to one's life space. When one is tied to possessions, even the most meager, one can readily become anxious for their safety.... Dorothy Day occasionally wrote of this temptation to grow attached to such objects, objects that regularly enough vanished into the pocket or bag of a guest at the House of Hospitality. Hospitality means vulnerability embraced and accepted day after day.[50]

Both the ascetic Christians of chapter 2 and the justifiably rich Christians of chapter 3 agree with this: attachment to possessions is incompatible with love of God. Martin Luther agrees that Christian vulnerability, including the willingness to be robbed, is part of Christian hospitality. As Luther writes in *Trade and Usury*:

> There are four Christian ways of exchanging external goods with others.... The first way is to let them rob or steal our property.... The second way is to give freely to anyone who needs it.... The third way is lending [expecting nothing in return].... The fourth way of exchanging goods is through buying and selling, but for hard cash or payment in kind [not credit].[51]

These are listed in order: trade is the least ideal way to exchange goods, according to Luther, because it so easily becomes theft, a sin against the neighbor.[52] He would agree with the Catholic Worker practice of being willing to be robbed, and giving freely to anyone who needs it. These are practices of hospitality, of loving the neighbor by offering material things.

For the Catholic Workers, hospitality goes hand in hand with solidarity. Solidarity, as defined by the U.S. Catholic Bishops, means standing with the poor and "taking on" their struggles by living with them and identifying with them: it consists of attentiveness (taking the perspective of the poor) and advocacy (volunteering, speaking up), and both are manifestations of proper neighbor-love.[53]

Day's solidarity with the poor took the form of voluntary poverty, and the other members of the Catholic Worker joined her in this observance. The "Aims and Means of the Catholic Worker Movement" explains voluntary poverty as follows:

> "The mystery of poverty is that by sharing in it, making ourselves poor in giving to others, we increase our knowledge and belief in love" (Dorothy Day). By embracing voluntary poverty, that is, by casting our lot freely with those whose impoverishment is not a choice, we would ask for the grace to abandon ourselves to the love of God.[54]

This model is rooted in, and enhances, love. Though such a lifestyle can be challenging, Catholic Workers insist it is theologically sound and spiritually salutary. As Day writes, "It is true that it is never easy.... But we are convinced that this is how the work should go. We are literally sharing the poverty of those we help."[55]

Expressing love for others through a life of voluntary poverty draws criticism from those who seek to defend their own less austere lifestyles. One form this criticism takes is the searching for hypocrisy. Day encountered this on a regular basis. She engaged in a good deal of travel, and frequently received questions about her spending habits: "'Where do you get all the money to travel around with?' is one of the embarrassing questions asked us when we appear on lecture platforms," she admits.[56] Her answer is that they travel as simply as possible: by bus, usually, or sometimes "a used car on its last spark plugs."[57] Day's voluntary poverty was not as unequivocally pure or spotless as Francis's practice of holy poverty, but no matter: the Catholic Worker standard is not purity, but love—love for neighbor as manifested in hospitality, vulnerability, and poverty.

Loving Somewhat Distant Others through Care for the Community

The proximate poor are not the only ones with whom one can practice solidarity. In the example above, Ben is arguably practicing solidarity both with the struggling coffee shop and with the overburdened landfill. He is "taking on" the challenges of the coffee shop owners as his own, and he is engaging in action to help them. When care and concern for somewhat distant others become collectivized and generalized, this is often referred to as concern for "the community." Ben seems to be community-minded in his practices of neighbor-love: he would probably explain that it damages the community if the locally run stores disappear and the landfill fills up.

What is a community? A community is a group of interdependent individuals who, collectively, share at least some elements of a common identity, purpose, and shared future, and who work together for their common welfare. To judge consumption decisions based on how it affects a community is to take the criterion of neighbor-love—concern for the well-being of close and somewhat distant others—and enlarge it to the aggregate scale. The U.S. Catholic Bishops echo this in *Economic Justice for All*. They write, "The obligation to 'love our neighbor' has an individual dimension, but it also requires a broader social commitment."[58]

Neighbor-love means broadening horizons beyond the personal scale to encompass not only the neighbor but also the community of which the self and the neighbor are an integral part. True communities, according to the bishops, rely on love: "Only active love of God and neighbor makes the fullness of community happen."[59]

The way to achieve this community fullness is through virtue, particularly "the virtues of citizenship," which can be seen as "an expression of Christian love." Nevertheless, these virtues transcend the personal scale, since they "grow out of a lively sense of one's dependence on the commonweal and obligations to it."[60] One example of citizenship virtue, according to Catholic scholar Jane Mansbridge, occurs as a solution to the problem of "free riders"— individuals taking unfair advantage of a shared resource.[61] The free rider problem may be solved when individuals choose to make "the good of others their own. When people see themselves in community with others, they are far less likely to free ride."[62] I define the virtue of "community-mindedness," then, as expressing Christian love through habits of good citizenship, as Ben does in the example above.

John B. Cobb has a normative definition of community: true communities should exhibit both mutual responsibility and mutual respect.[63] These qualities—responsibility and respect— are inherent in an understanding of love as commitment to another's well-being. Cobb's definition of community can and should include the nonhuman world, albeit in a "qualified sense."[64] Nonhuman nature cannot offer the same kind of respect and responsibility toward humans that one would expect among humans. But humans can and should behave with responsibility and respect toward the nonhuman world: a one-sided community relationship exists, then, between humans and the nonhuman world. Humans gain a much-needed change in perspective, Cobb and Daly contend, when we behave as if the nonhuman world were part of our community: "Once community with other living things is truly experienced and appreciated, aspects of our thinking and our way of life previously taken for granted become unacceptable. . . . The rise of this vision . . . has been one of the great advances of this generation."[65] McFague agrees with Cobb, including nonhuman creatures as members of the moral community because, she claims, they have intrinsic value and are deeply interconnected with humans.[66] A person rooted in this perspective "understands the absurdity of 'going it alone' and the injustice of trying to do so."[67]

Regardless of who precisely qualifies for membership, communities formed by love have value; community well-being should be enhanced and preserved, just as the well-being of the individual neighbor should be enhanced and preserved. Economic choices do affect communities; for this reason, the U.S. Catholic Bishops pose the following as a moral question: "Does economic life enhance or threaten our life together as a community?"[68] The bishops endorse those aspects of economic life that enhance communities, but oppose those that threaten community well-being.

Each individual is a member of several overlapping communities. In fact, Cobb and Daly see the entire globe as a network of communities. "The smallest community is the family, the next is the face-to-face community, and beyond that are towns and cities, larger regions, nations, continents, and the world."[69] He uses the phrase "communities of communities" to describe this vision.[70] This notion of nested communities brings to mind the Catholic concept of subsidiarity, a principle holding that every political issue should be addressed at the smallest, most local level possible.[71] Subsidiarity is a localizing principle that resists centralized control over political and economic enterprises. According to the principle of subsidiarity, world governance may be necessary for certain international issues such as global warming, but most problems will be best addressed by small, local communities or mid-range regional governments, depending on the nature of the task at hand. Subsidiarity may be applied, analogously, to consumption—consumers ought not consume from national or international sources if local sources would suffice.

Envisioning the Reign of Love in Economic Community

In light of the foregoing discussion of community, I wish to revisit market transactions as sites for neighbor-love. Two very different Christian voices speak in surprisingly similar terms on this topic: contemporary feminist theologian Kathryn Tanner and Japanese evangelist Toyohiko Kagawa (1888–1960). Tanner and Kagawa both prescribe community-mindedness and mutual benefit in market transactions, with specific considerations for Christian consumers.

Tanner and Kagawa both begin with God's abundant grace. Kagawa defines Christian love as superabundant, gracious "God-activity flowing through human channels," distinguishing it from romantic love in its divine origin.[72] Kagawa affirms that to love God, who is love and defines love, is to love God's creation, and this love is appropriately expressed in work on behalf of others.[73] Tanner also speaks of God's gifts. "God's purpose in giving," she writes, "is to benefit creatures, and therefore the proper return for God's giving is not so much directed back to God as directed to those creatures."[74] Any return humans try to render to God will be woefully inadequate, but to further God's purposes and keep the gifts in circulation is to join God fittingly in God's gifting work.

For both, this mandate to love others means that humans should form certain kinds of community. Tanner calls them "communities of mutual fulfillment," explaining that such communities are "dedicated to the well-being of all, without exception," and achieve this state of mutual benefit through practices of "unconditional giving."[75] In Kagawa's community vision, he advocates the work of "brotherly" love in the form of cooperative organizations: businesses owned and managed by the workers and consumers themselves, for their own mutual benefit, rather than by the government or an economically privileged few, for the sake of power or profit. (Cooperatives of this sort originated with a consumer cooperative in Rochdale, England, in 1844. Some of the guiding principles include "open, voluntary membership; one member-one vote; limited interest on capital; cash trading; reserves for education; rebates paid on purchases; [and selling items at a] market price."[76] Many common institutions in North America, such as food cooperatives, credit unions, and utility cooperatives, are organized using these Rochdale Principles.)

For Kagawa, the redemptive love of God overflows into the world through acts of love between people, including acts of consumption and production. Christianity, he writes, "calls us to purify and to make rational by conscious acts of redemptive love all economic activities which have heretofore been relegated to the sphere of undeveloped instinct" (i.e., competition rather than cooperation).[77] God's abundant love should prompt Christians to set up cooperative businesses, and indeed an entire cooperative society, making it possible to "bridge over the gap between producers and consumers with brotherly love."[78] Kagawa believes that cooperatives can offer a way for individual desires and community needs to harmonize.[79] Some degree of self-sacrifice for the sake of the community is implicit here, as well as an enlarged, collective sense of self.[80]

Tanner reaches similar conclusions. She advocates a "common possession right": by virtue of being alive and being human, everyone has a right to his or her share of God's gifts. Private property, though not abolished, should be lessened and relativized, in Tanner's view.[81] There should, therefore, be "no competition in property or possession": many things can belong to, and be used by, many people at once; other things should be equitably and peacefully shared.[82] But Tanner understands that this level of sharing only works when individuals transcend their sense of self and identify with the community. If everyone is "identifying with others in a joint pursuit of universal benefit," such that all, collectively, seek to create benefits for all, then the need for competition vanishes.[83]

This situation gives rise to an altered sense of self, in which one is "owned" by others: "One includes others, incorporates them, so to speak, within one's sense of self.... One does so out of a recognition that the life one lives is essentially constituted by relations with those others, to one's own benefit."[84] As with Day's sacrificial solidarity, Tanner asks Christians to be economically and psychologically vulnerable toward neighbors or toward the community. This utterly relational model of community underlies her economic prescriptions. Strong social relationships are vital but largely absent today, she laments, partly because of the individual economic self-sufficiency that exists in affluent countries like the United States. "You don't need that neighbor, whose friendly relations you cemented with a dinner and the loan of your lawn-mower, to jump-start your car when its battery is dead; you call your... automobile club."[85]

Following this discussion, Tanner and Kagawa would advocate consumption that is mutually beneficial. Humans should harvest, eat, buy, construct, and acquire goods in ways that benefit not only themselves but also the others with whom they are in relation: the sellers, producers, distributors, and so forth. To pay too much for an item benefits the seller but not the consumer; to pay too little may be taking advantage of the seller (or may be evidence that the seller is taking advantage of producers, as in the case of products made in sweatshops). Mutual benefit, on this reading, entails economic transactions that do not fleece consumers, and that pay sellers, producers, and others well. This is, in a sense, a call for fair wages and pricing, such that everyone involved in economic transactions can benefit appropriately. It may also go beyond wages and pricing to incorporate concerns for working conditions, quality of items bought, and other nonmonetary considerations that affect the well-being of consumers, producers, and others.

A more ecologically focused reading would also include the nonhuman players (relevant ecosystems and creatures affected) as other parties whose mutual benefit also bears consideration. Much human consumption simply destroys other creatures (how many hundreds of wheat plants' lives are dedicated to one loaf of bread?), so it may be impossible to find economic transactions that constitute mutual benefit for all, if nonhumans are included in the reckoning. Still, Tanner's criterion of mutual benefit provides a useful goal or rubric from which to evaluate consumption choices; even when no option is perfect, degrees of more or less mutual benefit are likely present, and can guide the ethical evaluation of consumption.

Kagawa writes, "The well-being of the producers' groups is a matter of concern to the consumers, and...this must be taken into account in the organization and plans of the latter."[86] In other words, consumers must consume in ways that keep the well-being of the producers in mind; in their consumption, they must act lovingly toward the producers. Kagawa urges unity between the two groups, such that "producers are consumers, and consumers are producers."[87] By forming one united community, and acknowledging the different roles one may play as both producer and consumer, Kagawa envisions producers and consumers in a kind of symbiotic relationship with each other.

Tanner and Kagawa think that when we purchase consumables, we and the producers and sellers should be part of a non-competitive community of mutual benefit. We should identify with those somewhat distant neighbors and be vulnerable to them, loving them and wishing their well-being. From care and concern between buyer and seller, to hospitality and voluntary poverty, to the virtues of community-mindedness and mutually beneficial economic relationships, Christians can show love of somewhat distant neighbors through consumption. When we are mindful of others, others we could meet but rarely do, we are broadening the scope of neighbor-love.

LOVE OF PLACE

I was waiting for the bus near the community garden when Shaunica cycled by. She stopped to chat and I saw that she wore a heavy backpack, which clanked loudly as she dismounted. "Are those your gardening tools? Why don't you drive to your garden plot?" I asked her. She smiled and said, "I know—it seems a bit silly. But I love the neighborhood around here, and on a lovely day like today I don't want to whiz through it in a car. Bike-speed lets me linger a bit." Gardening seems like a lot of effort to me, but my green thumb is somewhat lacking. "Do you get many vegetables from your plot? Is it worth the effort?" I ask her. "Some," she shrugs. "They are so precious—they taste like this place, you know: the soil we're standing on is so delicious in tomato form! Mine aren't ripe yet, but they will be next week—I should give you some. So yes, it's definitely worth the effort. It helps me to love this valley in a new way." She gets back on her bike and pedals away, but I see

her stop, partway down the road, to pick up a discarded aluminum
can from the gutter. I smile and shake my head: this isn't even her
neighborhood and she's helping to make it better for others.

Loving a place is a love that spans the spectrum of relationships
that I am establishing in this chapter. Place, in this understanding,
is the community of living and nonliving beings that constitutes a
particular location. It can be very close: loving my garden means
consuming produce whose leavings I can compost into nourishing
fertilizer to enrich my garden. It can be very distant: loving the
rain forest means avoiding South American grazed beef. But primarily, love of place resembles loving somewhat distant others. It
often involves a sense of community-mindedness and concern for
people we know exist but may not immediately encounter. It also
includes love of the ecosystem, the plants and animals, rivers,
rocks, soil, hills, valleys, and other geographic features.

"Local" is a commonly named environmental virtue. Even if it
is not organic, food that is local seems to have a small carbon footprint and supports nearby farmers, building up rural communities
and strengthening the foodshed. To love a place, then, seems to
entail favoring local businesses and local produce. Peter Maurin,
cofounder of the Catholic Worker with Dorothy Day, preferred to
consume food that was locally grown because of the connection it
afforded to the work of laborers in his own area, laborers he might
know and could join as fellow workers. The "agronomic universities" he envisioned as part of the Catholic Worker were intended,
in part, to allow people to live according to his maxim: "Eat what
you raise and raise what you eat." This meant, according to Day,
"that you ate the things indigenous to the New York climate, such
as tomatoes, not oranges; honey, not sugar, etc. We used to tease
him because he drank coffee, chocolate, or tea, but 'he ate what
was set before him.'"[88] Maurin anticipated (by several decades)

contemporary bioregionalists, local-food advocates, and others who value localized food production based in one's own region. Arguably, Maurin understood that prioritizing the local is an effective way to express love of a place.

But also, as Shaunica demonstrates, loving a place means desiring to spend time enjoying it and effort making it better. This may seem a nonconsumptive consideration, promoting civic engagement and volunteerism, but it can also entail certain consumption decisions, such as transportation and food, as the example shows. Indeed, love for a distant place can be expressed and cultivated through consumption, as when admirers of Japan seek out Japanese food, clothing, or other items representative of Japanese culture. As Hinton notes, slaves brought to North America from Africa cherished their lost homeland and reestablished their lost humanity by growing and eating foods whose seeds they had smuggled from Africa: yams, peanuts, okra, rice, and watermelon.[89] Consumption connected them with the homeland they loved.

Loving a place can also entail sacrifice. If Shaunica did not care about her place, she wouldn't bother with a community garden at all, choosing instead to buy cheap produce at the discount store, and saving herself both time and money. If she did not care about her place, she would drive more and bike less, saving herself precious time. If Ben, in the previous example, did not care about his place, he would have patronized the cheaper chain store rather than the struggling local shop, and he may not have even noticed the barista or the homeless man. He would have used and discarded the food packaging rather than bothering with the alternatives. But this is what love does: love bothers. Love sacrifices.

And such sacrifices for the sake of the place or the community are worthwhile, according to many Christian voices. In deciding between good-quality community relationships and abundant consumption, Cobb does not hesitate. "From the Christian point of view...participation in a healthy community is more important to human well-being than consumption of goods and services beyond what are essential for biological health."[90] Cobb asserts that curtailing consumption among affluent North Americans, in conjunction with careful use of technology to increase efficiency, is a necessary step in order for all people to have "the material means for a good life" without decimating the earth's resources in the process.[91] To urge this personal sacrifice, Cobb calls upon "Christian values supportive of frugality" and "the renewal of an ancient Christian virtue—the willingness to make personal sacrifices for the sake of the well-being of others," including "all the living creatures that share the earth with us."[92]

McFague advocates sacrifice as well: "We cannot love our neighbors—neither the human ones nor the earth ones—unless we drastically cut back on our consumption."[93] She appeals to the cross of Christ as a model for the appropriateness of sacrifice on behalf of others. "I believe Christian discipleship for twenty-first-century North American Christians means 'cruciform living,' an alternative notion of the abundant life, which will involve a philosophy of 'enoughness,' limitations on energy use, and sacrifice for the sake of others."[94] It will not be easy, but it is the cross that the affluent now have to bear, for the sake of other humans and for the earth. "For affluent Christians this ['enoughness'] should mean a different understanding of abundance, one that embraces the contradiction of the cross: giving up one's life to find it, limitation and diminishment, sharing and giving—indeed, sacrifice."[95]

Loving a place does not only mean sacrifice and consuming less, however. Shaunica, in fact, consumes her place, in the form of garden tomatoes. If I consume the thing I love, is that truly love? Among humans, no: consumption implies a kind of swallowing and devouring, and to do this to another human, even metaphorically, violates the other. For other creatures, it depends: loving the other means wishing for their truest good. Might this include consuming—indeed, destroying—the other? While some "fruitarians" eat only the fruits of a plant (not killing the plant itself), most Christians do devour other creatures in order to live. It is difficult to call this act "loving" toward the eaten beings, unless we believe that a carrot plant's true fulfillment lies not in growing peacefully in the sun, but rather in giving its life to be made into salad. (Some Christians, described in chapter 5, do support this position.)

Regardless, loving a place can mean consuming more, not necessarily less. It can mean richness of experience and a sense of engagement with the community. From patronizing local businesses to supporting local farmers, from planting trees to picking wild blackberries, and from urban hiking to bicycling around the neighborhood, there are many ways that consumption can express, and foster, a love of place.

LOVE OF FARAWAY OTHERS

Julio's hybrid car was plastered with bumper stickers. I saw it in the church parking lot as I approached for the Haiti mission meeting. His car bore environmental stickers like "Love your mother [with a picture of the earth]" and "When we tug on a single thing in nature we find it attached to everything else— John Muir" and "Plants & animals disappear to make room for your fat ass." But Julio also had stickers relating to his consumption decisions: "Boycott BP"; "Support Fair Trade"; and "Don't breed or buy while shelter animals die!" He and I were the first ones to arrive at the meeting. Julio poured fair trade coffee into a faded, chipped mug and handed it to me. The mug had a picture of Mother Teresa and the quote, "We cannot do great things, only small things with great love." We clinked mugs as he smiled and said, "Taste the love!" It took me a moment to realize he was quoting the slogan printed on a nearby poster featuring pictures of smiling coffee farmers, urging church members to buy the fair trade coffee we were drinking. Julio handed me an agenda for the meeting, with a provocative question on top: "How can we love our brothers and sisters in Haiti?" I noted that several agenda items included consumption: we planned to sell Haitian craft items to churchgoers in time for Christmas, and we were making plans for a fund-raising spaghetti dinner next month—with proceeds funding the next medical mission trip to Haiti.

In this example, simply by purchasing bumper stickers, Julio is declaring his care and concern for distant others: a general concern for the planet, for animals, and for workers affected by the "fair trade" movement. He seems to be making consumption decisions—boycotting British Petroleum (BP), purchasing fair trade items—that are designed to have an impact on people and creatures he will never meet personally. In this example, drinking fair trade coffee is characterized, by its marketers, as a loving choice, because workers are paid better than they are in conventional coffee plantations. The Haiti committee is encouraging members of the congregation to consume craft items and spaghetti as a way to help distant others whom they will likely never meet. They hear reports of suffering in Haiti, feel moved to compassion, and act on that compassion by consuming. This is consumption motivated by love of faraway others, who are, by definition, people we will probably never meet personally and can only envision in the abstract, such as "those suffering in Haiti" or "the workers who picked my grapes" or "the pelicans affected by the oil spill."

Concern for faraway others can prompt consumption, including bumper stickers and fair trade coffee, but the plight of faraway others can also motivate consumers to abstain from consumption, as Cobb and McFague note above, and as the writings of Ronald Sider demonstrate (chapter 2). But with this level of abstraction come certain challenges. Is it possible to love someone you never will meet and cannot know with any specificity? If everyone in the whole world, including animals and other creatures, is a potential neighbor I should love, has the concept become so generalized that it has no meaning?

The classic faraway neighbor urged upon Christians is "the poor," for whose sake we ought to consume less. But the scale and specificity varies. For Dorothy Day, the principle is direct: "'If we have less, everyone will have more.' So on this very immediate practical idea, many are helped."[96] When running a house of hospitality, as she did, there is a clear zero-sum situation: if I do not eat that extra muffin, a hungry guest can eat it. If I refrain from spending money on jewelry, there will be more money available for milk.

But in other Christian rhetoric, "the poor" can become quite generalized. The U.S. Catholic Bishops invoke the "preferential option for the poor" as economically normative, explaining it thus: "*The fulfillment of the basic needs of the poor is of the highest priority*.... This means that all of us must examine our way of living in light of the needs of the poor."[97] Sider makes a similar statement when he challenges his readers: "Will we dare to measure our living standards by the needs of the poor rather than the lifestyle of our neighbors?"[98]

The situation described by the bishops or by Sider, however, is not the clear zero-sum of the carefully run house of hospitality. If I spend less money on jewelry, the effects are multiple: there will be more money in my bank account, which I may or may not attempt to pass on to those who could benefit from it; even if I do, by sending it to a charity, I have only a vague sense of how the money is being used (though many charitable organizations admirably pursue financial transparency and donor education, the connection between my money and the good it does is still attenuated). At the same time, my jewelry boycott will have an impact on the production of jewelry, which may have good environmental effects if the jewelry is produced in a harmful way, but may also lead someone to lose her job, as the demand for jewelry drops. To focus on the job issue: I don't know whether my avoiding jewelry will cause someone to lose her job, but it might. I also don't know whether it was a good job (not all jobs are worth preserving, though the argument that consuming less might lead to job loss is often a conversation stopper). Changing employment can be stressful, but it can also be liberating; would the particular employee whose job is eliminated due to my lack of purchasing be better off, perhaps even grateful for the change? I don't know. I want to love this distant other, but how can I, not knowing what is in her best interest—or even who she is?

John Schneider solves this problem, in chapter 3, by drawing boundaries around the responsibilities of consuming Christians: we cannot, and should not, be responsible for the entire world. Julio may feel the personal call to help certain distant others, like the people of Haiti in particular—Schneider acknowledges the genuineness of this sort of call—but Julio should not expect all of us to share it. Even if our consumption decisions do have a global impact, this impact is too overwhelming for most of us to consider. Either we must draw a line, like Schneider, and disavow responsibility for those too distant, or we must attempt to consume locally, minimizing the unknowable impacts by shortening the supply lines. While local consumption is (often) laudable, it is extremely hard for North Americans to exclusively consume items produced locally. Anything electronic (telephones, radios), plastic (children's toys, medicine bottles), complex (cars, clocks), or tropical (chocolate, bananas) will likely come from faraway places. Even conscientious global consumers like Julio can only do their limited best with the information they can gain through careful research. Such consumers still draw a boundary (even if it is a boundary of ignorance) around the consumption harms that they simply cannot address.

But perhaps this discussion is too pedantic. Maybe the key is simply having the proper attitude of openness to the neighbor, without being weighed down by the details. This seems to be the strategy of communitarian ecotheologian Larry Rasmussen, who defines the neighbor expansively, as "anyone or anything we ought reasonably to think may be affected by our actions....In this sense," he writes, "neighborly responsibility is infinite in extent, with no preordained boundaries."[99] Rasmussen includes non-human entities in his definition of neighbor—so the very food we eat does count as our neighbor. Rasmussen seems not to mind the extent to which this demand might seem overwhelming; indeed, he finds it inspiring and exhilarating.

John Ruskin, a British social critic of the Victorian era, shares a similar enthusiasm for consumption's social interconnections. He writes:

Every atom of substance, of whatever kind, used or consumed, is so much human life spent; which, if it issue in the saving of present life, or gaining more, is well spent, but if not is either so much life prevented, or so much slain. In all buying, consider, first, *what condition of existence you cause in the producers of what you buy*; secondly, whether the sum you have paid is just to the producer, and in due proportion, lodged in his hands; thirdly, to how much clear use, for food, knowledge, or joy, this that you have bought can be put; and fourthly, to whom and in what way it can be most speedily and serviceably distributed.[100]

There is profound truth in this vision of the world: all are, indeed, intimately interconnected, and whatever I do affects people and creatures around the world, most of whom I will never meet. The mysticism behind this view has a certain appeal that is lacking in Schneider's pragmatic boundary drawing. The awed vision of both Rasmussen and Ruskin seems to justify abstraction in neighbor-love at this level of complexity.

Here, we speak of "the common good" as a generalized love of those we will never meet, but nonetheless care for. For example, Julio's purchase of a hybrid car probably indicates a concern for global warming, a worldwide problem that may only weakly impact his own well-being, but which is already wreaking havoc on fragile ecosystems and precarious human lives around the world. If I asked Julio why he drove that car, he probably would not say, "Because I care about Khaled living in Bangladesh, at risk of flooding if the sea levels rise." More likely, he would say, "Because it's better for the world, for everyone who is impacted by global warming." He wants to do what's "better for everyone"— what corresponds to the common good.

Gaudium et Spes, written by the Second Vatican Council in 1965, defines the common good as follows: "'the sum of those conditions of social life which allow social groups and their individual members relatively thorough and ready access to their own fulfillment.'"[101] This definition—a social good that confers well-being and access to the conditions of flourishing upon small groups and individuals—became foundational for later works of Catholic social teaching. In the U.S. Catholic Bishops' letter *Economic Justice for All*, the common good is intrinsically linked to the command of neighbor-love: "The obligation to 'love our neighbor' has an individual dimension, but it also requires a broader social commitment to the common good."[102]

Such an emphasis on the common good may properly be called *communitarian*, defined as an ethical strategy explicitly placing value on the well-being of communities or aggregate social groups (often equal to or greater than the value placed on individual well-being, though individuals and communities are symbiotically related, and pitting the good of the community over against the good of the individual usually creates a false conflict). DiDomizio describes the importance of community for Day and the Catholic Workers. "The spirit of community was, and remains, therefore, the underlying assumption of the Catholic Worker vision of social change.... Catholic Worker spirituality is profoundly communitarian."[103] "The Aims and Means of the Catholic Worker Movement" invokes Aquinas in this regard: "In contrast to what we see around us, as well as within ourselves, stands St. Thomas Aquinas' doctrine of the Common Good, a vision of a society where the good of each member is bound to the good of the whole in service to God."[104]

Does the common good include nonhuman nature? It can. Jesuit theologian Drew Christiansen speaks of the "planetary common good." This would include "the global commons: the air, water, and soil resources together with migratory stocks of fish and birds.... Likewise the safe disposal of products, such as nuclear and toxic waste, which take collective action to secure, would be part of the common good."[105] Ethicist William French agrees, citing Aquinas, whose notion of the common good is, on his reading, not merely ethical and political: "we find the concept also employed as a cosmological-ecological principle suggesting that all species, including the human, are parts which participate within the greater whole of the universe."[106]

In the name of this common good, which includes the common good for all of humanity and for nonhuman nature, Christiansen calls for

> readjustment and sacrifice on the part of those living in the affluent parts of the world, so that the global majority can enjoy a degree of development consistent with their human dignity and the sustainability of the planet. In Catholic social teaching this sacrifice is social as well as personal. Groups and nations, not just individuals, are expected to sacrifice for the sake of the universal common good.[107]

Again, it is a call to consume less, to sacrifice—for the poor, for the community, and for the common good. Love of distant others prompts us to measure our consumption by its impact on the collective whole.

This sort of love has its detractors. As Wendell Berry writes, "Love is never abstract. It does not adhere to the universe or the planet or the nation or the institution or the profession, but to the singular sparrows of the street, the lilies of the field, 'the least of these my brethren.'"[108] The more distant, collective, and abstract the focus of my love, the more fragile, attenuated, and prone to mistakes that love becomes. It is in the nature of love to adhere most strongly to the particular; I am indeed more generous to my friend with cancer than to a cancer-research charity. I care about the poverty-, earthquake-, and hurricane-stricken people of Haiti, but I do not think of them nearly as often as I think about my own son. And perhaps most strikingly, I know what my son needs and how to help him with much more certainty than I know what the Haitian people need, and how to help them. I love both and am committed to the well-being of both, but one commitment is much stronger than the other. With stronger love would seem to come stronger responsibility: I am indeed more directly responsible for my son than for the Haitians (though some responsibility exists in both cases). And the flexibility of these categories means that the bonds of love may strengthen or weaken over time. With Julio's help and several trips to Haiti, for example, I may discover that certain Haitian individuals become only somewhat-distant, rather than faraway, neighbors.

In the Gospel of Luke, one of Jesus' interlocutors, skeptical of his neighbor-love theory, asks him, "Who is my neighbor?" (10:29). Jesus' reply, the story of the good Samaritan, concludes with a different question: "Which of these three, do you think, was a neighbor to the man who fell into the hands of the robbers?" (10:36). Jesus turns the question on its head, not asking who one's neighbors are (or how close or distant they are) but instead how to *be* a neighbor *to* someone. The Samaritan deals mercifully and generously with the crime victim because he sees him (rather than crossing to "the other side" to avoid acknowledging him [10:31–32]), recognizes his relationship to him (a neighbor, which moves him to compassion [10:33]), and honors that relationship by helping him (10:34–35).

Similarly, the best question may not be "Who is my consumption-neighbor?" but "Who should I be, as a consumer-neighbor?" Tanner speaks of an altered, enlarged sense of self that arises when relationships of mutual benefit become the criterion for judging economics. Day and the Catholic Workers see themselves as transformed when they allow themselves the vulnerability of genuine solidarity with the poor. Day and Tanner both highlight an important aspect of the process of loving the neighbor through consumption: it entails vulnerability and transformation of the self. Beyond the frustrating details of an overwhelming number of economic neighbors, one may arrive at a point of openness and receptivity, a simple willingness to be transformed by the will to love, regardless of how unsuccessful the effort may be.

Love is indeed transformative, and the loving engagement in a disposition of community-mindedness can bring about a deeper sense of self. As Cobb and Daly put it, "The well-being of a community as a whole is constitutive of each person's welfare. This is because each human being is constituted by relationships to others, and this pattern of relationship is at least as important as the possession of commodities."[109] To privilege relationships over goods is to be willing to surrender the self for the good of the whole.

Ultimately, the question of how to be a loving consumer-neighbor is a question for virtue ethics. If I exercise frugality, temperance, and generosity, this will likely benefit my neighbors whether I know who they are or not. Virtues, indeed, may be a shortcut to ethical consumption in this regard—to be truly virtuous is to love myself and my neighbor through virtuous acts of moderate consumption, temperance, prudence, and generosity. Of course, the Christian tradition ranks love as the highest virtue of all (1 Corinthians 13:13).

LOVE OF GOD

I sat quietly in a pew in one of the smaller chapels flanking the great cathedral nave. I heard someone approach, sitting opposite me. Though I tried not to stare, I noted several details about the man who sat to my right. He was wearing a T-shirt that said "Real Men Love Jesus." A bracelet reading "W.W.J.D.?" graced one wrist; he had a gold cross hanging around his neck. He removed a rosary from his pocket and caressed it gently. He was about to pray, but stopped himself, getting up to place coins in

the collection box next to the bank of candles at the front of the
chapel. He lit a candle, crossed himself, and sat down. I saw him
remove a prayer book (it may have been a Bible) from another
pocket. He silently mouthed some words to himself, and then
began praying with his rosary.

What does it mean to love God? Discussions of love often privilege the neighbor's needs and wishing the good of the other. But God, surely, transcends needs and simply *is* good. Is it nonsensical to wish for God's good or to meet God's needs? Is it futile to love a God who *is* love? Perhaps not. Many Christians regard prayer as a way to love God, and if this is so, then the stranger in the example above, who uses many items directly related to prayer—Bibles, candles, prayer beads, and the like—may be consuming because he loves God, and because he wants to express or enhance his love. If Marian's "Proud Grandmother" sweatshirt, in the example about loving close others, expresses and strengthens her love for her grandchildren, so also may this man's "Real Men Love Jesus" T-shirt. However, some consumer items with Christian themes, perhaps including his bracelet, necklace, and T-shirt, may neither express nor enhance a love of God, serving rather to display the consumer's Christian identity to others, or to strengthen the consumer's sense of himself or herself as a follower of Jesus who has indeed "been there, done that, and bought the T-shirt."

There are other ways to love God through consumption. Francis loves God by fasting; Jung loves God by feasting. Both practices can be undertaken with the goal of lovingly approaching God. Loving God also means loving what God loves, which may mean embracing the loves already discussed in this chapter: loving the poor, doing well by the community, loving nonhuman creatures, and loving the self as part of God's good creation. In this way, the practices already discussed—including sacrifice, solidarity, and attentive awareness—are all ways for Christians to love God in consumption.

God is the most worthy object of Christian love; ideally, all consumption should lead to, and express, the love of God. This is a genuine challenge, however. Regretfully, in the words of theologian David Klemm, "Rare is the love of goods that remains true to love of God as the final resting place of the heart's desire."[110] Too often our human desires become distracted from their final goal, God. Klemm's apt statement echoes the thought of Augustine, who wrote, addressing God, "Anyone who loves something else along with you, but does not love it for your sake, loves you less."[111] This statement reflects the challenges that many believers face as they attempt to direct physical consumption to spiritual ends. Ideally, human encounters with the physical world would function like an icon, opening a window into the eternal, but this is not always the case. Augustine laments his own tendency to be distracted by worldly temptations, and it is in this context that he surrenders completely to God's will, writing, "Give what you command, and then command whatever you will."[112] For Augustine, the ability to dedicate physical consumption to the love of God must come from a supernatural source, because it is beyond the capacity of sinful humans to achieve this.

The love of God mobilizes and animates all the other loves described in this chapter. God who *is* love both exemplifies and inspires the caring attention to another that characterizes human love. Without grounding in a good relationship with God, human love falls short and consumption loses its depth. As Augustine concludes, "All abundance, which is not my God, is emptiness to me."[113]

ENVISIONING A BETTER LIFE FOR ALL NEIGHBORS

This third consideration, neighbor-love, constitutes an essential component of a comprehensive Christian ethics of consumption. While it is important to avoid sin and embrace creation, loving the neighbor adds a dynamic and other-regarding dimension to Christian consideration of consumption. The scope of love and the range of neighbors can be overwhelming, as described above, but the command to love remains as central to consumption ethics as it is to other modes of Christian moral thought. Yet as comprehensive as the consideration for neighbor-love may seem, it cannot replace avoiding sin or embracing creation; some sins do not reduce to violations of love, and loving creation carries a potential conflict with joyfully consuming it, as discussed above.

Notably, every thinker discussed in this chapter is reform-minded. Loving others means wanting to change the world for the better. The Catholic Worker envisions a transformed world in which all who have enough help those who do not, and engages in lobbying for policies that help the poor.[114] Cobb and Daly envision a world of healthy communities, frugal consumption, local economies, greater community accountability, shorter supply lines, and greater quality of life.[115] McFague charges the church with the ultimate countercultural mission of cruciform living.[116] Kagawa wants to see producers and consumers cooperate, and wishes for entire societies to be modeled on cooperatives.[117] Tanner measures economic behavior against her "theological vision of a universally inclusive community of mutual benefit."[118]

Love prompts such visions. The place of imagination and creative visualization in ethics is a large topic that is beyond the scope of this work; suffice it to say that the visionary Christians in this chapter seek a better world according to their ideals, of which love of the neighbor ranks highly. They judge current consumption practices with that vision as a standard. The next chapter brings together several other Christian thinkers who also judge consumption based on their vision of the future: specifically, their eschatological visions. Eschatology forms a fitting complement to this chapter's themes, as the U.S. Catholic Bishops acknowledge: "The Christian tradition recognizes, of course, that the fullness of love and community will be achieved only when God's work in Christ comes to completion in the kingdom of God."[119] It is to the vision of this kingdom, then, that we now turn.

Chapter 5

To Envision the Future

Christian eschatological belief is typically viewed with suspicion by non-Christians. It is not uncommon for environmentalists to report that Christians believe humans should "use up" the planet's resources in order to hasten the return of Christ. As Glenn Scherer writes, in a representative article of this type from the environmental magazine *Grist*,

> People under the spell of such potent prophecies cannot be expected to worry about the environment. Why care about the earth when the droughts, floods, and pestilence brought by ecological collapse are signs of the Apocalypse foretold in the Bible? Why care about global climate change when you and yours will be rescued in the Rapture? And why care about converting from oil to solar when the same God who performed the miracle of the loaves and fishes can whip up a few billion barrels of light crude with a Word?[1]

Though it makes a provocative and appealing argument, end-time prophecies are less influential on environmental behavior than Scherer might believe.[2] The most frequently quoted source for such a belief is from James G. Watt, who served as U.S. Secretary of the Interior from 1981 to 1983. Indeed, Scherer's original version of his article quoted Watt: "God gave us these things to use. After the last tree is felled, Christ will come back." But Scherer corrected the article and apologized to Watt, who denies ever holding this position and charges that the quote, which came from another source, was fabricated.[3] Watt writes, "I never said it. Never believed it. Never even thought it. I know no Christian who believes or preaches such error. The Bible commands conservation."[4] Watt also observes, correctly, that it is nearly impossible to find credible Christian voices who admit to supporting the eschatologically justified devastation of natural resources.

Most Christians will not admit such beliefs because they clearly contradict Christian teachings about stewardship and conservation. As Wendell Berry says, "There is nowhere in the Bible a single line that gives or implies a permission to 'use up' the 'natural environment.'"[5] Christians consume in an unsustainable manner not because of false beliefs but because of bad habits. If it were only a question of doctrinal error, this could be corrected easily enough. Sadly, we consume unsustainably because Christians are subject to more universal, and less easily remedied vices of shortsightedness and myopic selfishness, which lead us to prize self and convenience over other considerations. The habits and virtues associated with environmentally sound consumption may be difficult to inculcate, but such transformation is not impossible. In this chapter I argue that a proper emphasis on Christian eschatological visions can correct our distortions, inculcate wise habits, and enhance environmental sensibilities that manifest in considered, conscientious consumption. Many Christians look to such eschatological visions as an ideal, as they consider their everyday consumption.

The world to come—whether it is called the end-times, the end of the world, the return of Christ, the kingdom of God, the world as it ought to be, God's purpose for the world, or visions of what a redeemed or fulfilled world would be like—is a vital source of Christian inspiration and imagination. It is also a powerful motivation to consume in certain ways. For some Christians, the eschaton is a long-awaited event in history, over which humans have no control; for others, it is a potentiality indwelling in creation, which may be encouraged and increased through inspired human action; for still others, it contains elements of both. In this chapter, I examine how such a forward-thinking, visionary orientation can lead to certain consumption practices. Christians who prioritize visions of the future use these to justify their consumption choices in the present. Just as Christians in the third chapter embraced creation as a gift to be celebrated, so in this fifth chapter Christians turn toward the *new* creation, a fulfilled and redeemed world.

When do Christians get a glimpse of this fulfilled world? In the course of two practices relating to consumption: Sabbath keeping and the Eucharist. Both of these are practices in which Christians claim to receive a foretaste of the world to come. And both shape consumption practices in particular ways, as discussed below.

SABBATH KEEPING

So then, a sabbath rest still remains for the people of God; for those who enter God's rest also cease from their labors as God did from his. Let us therefore make every effort to enter that rest, so that no one may fall through such disobedience as theirs. (Hebrews 4:9–11)

Anybody can observe the Sabbath, but making it holy surely takes the rest of the week.[6]

What is the Sabbath?[7] In its most basic form, a Sabbath is a day of rest; the word's etymology derives from the Hebrew word for "ceasing." The concept originates from two places in the Hebrew Bible: the first story of creation in Genesis and the fourth commandment of the Decalogue. In the first Genesis account of creation, after six days of creating the world, God rests on the seventh day and hallows that day (Genesis 2:2–3). The fourth commandment of the Decalogue reads:

> Remember the sabbath day, and keep it holy. For six days you shall labor and do all your work. But the seventh day is a sabbath to the LORD your God; you shall not do any work—you, your son or your daughter, your male or female slave, your livestock, or the alien resident in your towns. (Exodus 20:8–10)[8]

Sabbath observance, this weekly day of worship and refraining from work from sundown Friday to sundown Saturday, remembers and echoes both creation (Genesis) and liberation (Exodus).

There is controversy about the Sabbath: whether it is required for Christians, when it should be observed, what activities are permitted or forbidden, and what it means.[9] In this chapter, I will not debate the proper day of observance, the optional nature of Sabbath keeping, or the details of what should or should not be allowed on the Sabbath. Rather, I examine what it means for Christians who practice Sabbath keeping, and how this impacts their consumption decisions. To this end, I use a broad understanding of the Christian Sabbath: a weekly time of spiritual observance and altered habits, primarily characterized by rest and prayer or worship. The Sabbath traditionally lasts for one day, although shorter observances may also qualify under this definition. When I refer to "Sabbath keeping" or "observing the Sabbath" in this chapter, I have this broad definition in mind.

WHO OBSERVES THE SABBATH?

As a practice associated with Judaism, Sabbath keeping is not universally observed among Christians. Christian Sabbath keeping has been inconsistent throughout history, and contested from Jesus' time. Jesus became a controversial figure partly because of his willingness to transgress the Sabbath rules established by the religious authorities. He gathered grain and healed people, two activities that were forbidden on the Sabbath (Mark 2:23–28; 3:1–6). When confronted about this, Jesus declared, "The Sabbath was made for humankind, and not humankind for the sabbath; so the Son of Man is lord even of the sabbath" (Mark 2:27–28; cf. Matthew 12:8–12). Jesus' position on Sabbath keeping took part in a religious debate of his time, regarding the proper parameters for Sabbath observance. Later rabbis ruled in partial agreement with Jesus—observing the Sabbath should not come at the expense of human well-being.[10]

Early Christians disagreed about whether, and how, to observe a Sabbath. Some kept a Jewish identity and observed a Saturday Sabbath; others felt that Jesus' resurrection made Sunday a more important day and abandoned the Saturday Sabbath in favor of Sunday observance; still others observed both. Paul urged his fellow Christians not to judge those who follow different Sabbath practices, and he refrained from endorsing any one particular Sabbath observance.[11] In 321, Constantine made Sunday a legal holiday throughout his empire; it became a day of rest and worship for all, much like the Jewish Sabbath. But it was less strict and less consistent than Jewish Sabbath observance, and over time the Christian Sabbath has seen its more observant and less observant seasons. Throughout history, various Christian groups, including the Puritans of colonial North America, have sought to renew Sabbath observance.[12] Some vestige of this is still present in communities that maintain their "blue laws," which require businesses to be closed on Sundays, or in areas that do not sell alcohol on Sundays or before noon on Sundays. In contemporary industrial societies, in which Christians often seem too busy for spiritual practice, the Sabbath concept has again become popular in devotional literature.[13]

Writings from contemporary Christian Sabbath keepers typically fall into three categories: those from Seventh-day Adventists and other Seventh-day denominations;[14] prominent devotional authors, including evangelical and "Emerging Church" voices, from Rob Bell to Marva Dawn to Matthew Sleeth; and those affiliated with the Sabbath Economics Collaborative, a group of theologians, clergy, and lay leaders interested in the message of "economic justice" in biblical passages relating to Sabbath and Jubilee. John Paul II has written a thoughtful pastoral letter, *Dies Domini* (1998), about Sunday, the "Lord's Day," which contributes to the conversation as well. From many corners of the Christian tradition, then, there is interest in, and observance of, some kind of Sabbath. I will briefly introduce these three major Sabbath-keeping Christian groups before discussing what Sabbath keeping entails.

Seventh-day Adventism arose from an earlier U.S. religious movement that became known as the Millerite movement after its founder, William Miller, a Baptist lay minister and farmer. Miller had predicted Christ's return in 1844, but his followers saw no such appearance. Nevertheless, a remnant of the movement rallied around an understanding that changes had indeed occurred in heaven, as Miller predicted, and that they would soon happen on earth. These faithful few developed into a group that, in the 1860s, became known as the Seventh-day Adventist Church.[15] Ellen G. White arose as a leader among this remnant of the Millerite movement, due to her charisma and proclivity for spiritual visions.

In 1846, for example, she had a vision "that the Millerites must begin keeping the 'true Sabbath' before Christ would come."[16] The idea of a Saturday Sabbath among this group did not originate with her, but her vision of its appropriateness served a confirmatory role. Many similar visions throughout her life guided the development of the Seventh-day Adventist Church.

Christian devotional writers, among them many evangelical authors or those affiliated with the "Emerging Church" movement, also value Sabbath keeping. Most of these Christians see the Sabbath primarily as a day of rest, to be taken preferably on Sunday but also—particularly for clergy and lay leaders—validly observed at other times of the week. Rob Bell, popular Christian author and pastor of Mars Hill Bible Church in Grand Rapids, Michigan, writes that his weekly Sabbath observance "has brought incredible healing," and that this practice helps diminish sins like pride, because the Sabbath is a day "to remind myself that I did not make the world and that it will continue to exist without my efforts."[17] Ethicist and author Marva J. Dawn holds that observing the Sabbath is profound and life altering; she names four transformative Sabbath-keeping practices: "ceasing, resting, embracing, and feasting."[18]

Finally, the Sabbath Economics Collaborative was founded in 2003 as a coalition of North American individuals and groups working in the area of "faith and economic justice." The Sabbath Economics Collaborative consists of a small group of religious leaders and scholars. They list several religious thinkers as their inspiration, including Ched Myers, Richard Lowery, and Wendell Berry. Theologian Norman Wirzba, a student of Berry's work, also belongs in this category, since his work is in conversation with the aims of the Sabbath Economics Collaborative.

The collaborative weaves together environmental concern and interest in justice for the economically marginalized, based upon an understanding of the Sabbath as a central symbol for Jews and Christians. "The Sabbath represents an ancient vision whose time has come again," they write, emphasizing themes such as suspending work, setting limits, and attending to those in need.[19] This perspective, they believe, should shape economic thought and practice. They summarize their beliefs as follows: "Sabbath Economics, then, concerns the theoretical, spiritual and practical tasks of imagining how we might *limit and shape our economic activity in order to keep the gifts of creation circulating justly among all living communities.*"[20]

While Sabbath Economics thinkers are interested in Sabbath keeping as a practice, their primary emphasis is on the Sabbath as a biblical and theological principle, as a source of spiritual insight into economic and lifestyle matters. Bible scholar Richard Lowery, for example, contends that observing the Sabbath does not entail following the biblical prescriptions to the letter ("moot or impossible") but does mean promoting certain values: "proportion, limits...and the need for rest, quiet reflection, and nonconsumptive recreation...[as well as] abundance, celebration, and social solidarity."[21] Though it may be more conceptual than practical, the Sabbath is not without power. Wirzba writes, it "is a teaching that has the potential to redirect and transform all our existence, bringing it into more faithful alignment with God's life-building and life-strengthening ways."[22]

WHAT DOES SABBATH KEEPING ENTAIL?

Observing the Sabbath means different things to different people, but its major characteristics are the same. Sabbath keeping means stopping one's everyday activities, in order to undertake

Sabbath-appropriate activities: rest, prayer, worship, and serving the community.

Abraham Joshua Heschel's writings on the Jewish Sabbath movingly describe the importance of the practice of Sabbath keeping. The day's beauty and splendor, he writes, is "expressed in terms of *abstentions*.... How else express glory in the presence of eternity, if not by the silence of abstaining from noisy acts?"[23] Heschel describes the Sabbath as a quiet day, free from "the profanity of clattering commerce, of being yoked to toil. He [the one observing the Sabbath] must go away from the screech of dissonant days, from the nervousness and fury of acquisitiveness and the betrayal in embezzling his own life."[24] Thus, economic life—marketplace consumption and production, buying and selling—has no place in the Sabbath.[25] Heschel describes the Sabbath as "a day of armistice in the economic struggle with our fellow men and the forces of nature," acknowledging the environmental, social, and spiritual damage wrought by market economics.[26] There is a connection, Heschel writes, between observing the Sabbath and being content with the possessions one already owns. Drawing a parallel between the fourth and tenth commandments, he writes: "Do not covet anything belonging to thy neighbor; I have given thee something that belongs to Me. What is that something? A day."[27]

Like Heschel, Pope John Paul II regards the Sabbath as a time to rest from human-centered pursuits and to focus on God's work. Rest is required on the Sabbath for many reasons: because it meets a natural human need, because rest from work allows time for worship and other activities that make the day holy, and because it enhances faith.[28] There is a sacred value to rest, as John Paul II writes: "the faithful are called to rest not only *as* God rested, but to rest *in* the Lord, bringing the entire creation to him, in praise and thanksgiving, intimate as a child and friendly as a spouse."[29]

In this way, Sabbath observance provides a powerful antidote to pride, much needed, according to John Paul II, because of humans' "prodigious power over creation," which can lead people "to forget that God is the Creator upon whom everything depends."[30] To rest from work and spend time contemplating creation is to acknowledge with humility humans' dependence on God and on creation.[31] In contemplating creation, according to John Paul II, humans experience a sympathetic "tremor of the Creator's joy when, after the creation, he saw that all he had made 'was very good'."[32]

On a more experiential level, many Christian devotional writers testify to the joy of Sabbath keeping. Congregationalist pastor and inspirational speaker Donna Schaper writes:

> Sabbath keeping is a spiritual strategy: it is a kind of judo. The world's commands are heavy; we respond with light moves. The world says work; we play. The world says go fast; we go slow. These light moves carry Sabbath into our days, and God into our lives.[33]

Evangelical environmentalist and physician Matthew Sleeth testifies, "I found God on my Saturday afternoons, or perhaps it simply got quiet enough for me to hear him once again. I found God by returning to the Sabbath, as did my son, daughter, and wife."[34] As a spiritual practice, Sabbath keeping has many supporters. But what does one actually *do* on the Sabbath, and why call it eschatological or visionary?

To Observe the Sabbath

Christian Sabbath observance is, to some degree, inspired by Jewish practice, particularly regarding consumption. In observant Jewish households, consumption of energy on the Sabbath is limited by restrictions on igniting or extinguishing fire (which includes electricity and internal combustion engines). Many observant Jews travel to Sabbath worship on foot because of this prohibition. Modern-day Jewish households often respond to the prohibition on electricity use by putting lights and appliances on timers, or by turning them on before the Sabbath and turning them off afterward. As Rabbi David A. Cooper recounts, on the Sabbath, "an electric urn is used to keep water hot all day for the preparation of coffee, tea, or instant soup. In addition, an electric hot plate is on all day to keep food warm. Sometimes an electric cooking pot is used to keep a ready supply of hot soup or stew."[35] Keeping a pot of water hot or a light burning all day may mean greater energy consumption. But these Sabbath rules can also be interpreted to require less energy—one may also keep all lights and appliances turned off rather than on, adjusting schedule and diet to the environmental conditions.

Sleeth fondly recalls the relaxed Sundays of his childhood, when having a day of rest meant "grown ups' attitudes mellowed."[36] Sleeth's current Sabbath observance amounts to avoiding work for a designated period, as he describes:

What qualifies as work for you? You get to decide. For me, driving is work, writing is work, and reading a newspaper is forced hard labor. Some of the things our family does on the Sabbath are resting, relaxing, listening to music alone and as a family (same for reading), meditating, talking, thinking, listening, walking, reading the Bible, sleeping with the Bible propped on chest, praying, going to church, and helping others. All of the Lord's activities can take precedence over rest.... Nancy [his wife] enjoys her long Sunday prayer walks. Emma and Clark [his children] avoid schoolwork; they will cram in work the day before in order to preserve their day of rest.[37]

Evangelical Christian psychologist and author Dan Allender asks his readers to consider the following question: "What would I do for a twenty-four hour period of time if the only criteria was [sic] to pursue my deepest joy?"[38] This pursuit of joy, he asserts, is the true meaning of Sabbath rest.

What Makes It Eschatological?

Be it Saturday or Sunday, there is something about the Sabbath that inspires reflection on the last days. John Paul II writes: "Sunday after Sunday, the Church moves towards the final 'Lord's Day,' that Sunday which knows no end."[39] The Sabbath, then, is "an invitation to look ahead."[40] According to the ancient rabbis, Heschel recounts, God created one final thing on the seventh day: *menuha*, a deep and harmonious peace and contentment. This is what Sabbath keepers are said to experience on the Sabbath. "In later times," Heschel adds, "*menuha* became a synonym for the life in the world to come, for eternal life."[41] Thus, observing the Sabbath is a way to touch eternity. In Heschel's words, "When the Sabbath is entering the world, man is touched by a moment of actual redemption; as if for a moment the spirit of the Messiah moved over the face of the earth."[42]

For Seventh-day Adventists, a Christian denomination with origins in the Millerite movement and its end-time prophecies, eschatology is important. The word *Adventist* in the denomination's title refers to the action of waiting for Christ's advent, his much-anticipated coming. For Seventh-day Adventists, there is a vital link between Sabbath observance and ultimate events, as Adventist biblical scholar Jacques Doukhan explains: "Marking the end of the week, the Sabbath functions as an *eschaton*, thereby pointing to the cosmic *eschaton*, the end of time."[43] Preparing for the end-times, according to White, meant preparing for the return of Christ by "doing only that which brought the self and others closer to a state prepared for redemption."[44] For White's followers, this preparation included observing the Sabbath and consuming carefully. Seventh-day Adventists today continue to follow their example in anticipation of Christ's return.

Popular Christian writers also make this connection between the Sabbath and the end-times. Dawn cheerfully refers to the Sabbath as "a weekly eschatological party...to emphasize our experience of both present Joy in our feasting and anticipation of the future, eternal consummation of Joy."[45] Allender writes, "The Sabbath is a day when the kingdom to come has come and is celebrated now rather than anticipated tomorrow. It is...a theater of divine comedy that practices eternity as a present reality rather than a future state."[46]

Wirzba, like Dawn, speaks of the Sabbath in terms of joy, in conversation with Heschel's *menuha*, the restful joy of God on the seventh day of creation in Genesis. This constitutes the fulfillment of creation: "Insofar as we genuinely experience Sabbath *menuha*, we catch a glimpse of eternity, a taste of heaven."[47] Sabbath teaching, then, offers "a concrete, practical vision that calls each of us to arrange our economic patterns and priorities so that they enable all members of creation to participate in the *menuha* of God."[48] In other words, the insight of Sabbath teaching and practice allows for humans (and all of creation) to glimpse eternity.

A foretaste of the world to come; a manifestation of the new creation; a sign of the coming kingdom—being in the Sabbath means living out the Christian vision for the future. This eschatological visioning is not separate from consumption practices.

HOW OBSERVING A SABBATH AFFECTS CONSUMPTION

The spiritual practice of Sabbath keeping engenders certain consumption habits through Sabbath keeping's personal impact: transformed people undertake new habits of consumption.

Transformed People

The Sabbath is a time set apart for communion with God, which takes the focus off of human striving and places it on God's purposes. Human striving is not necessarily at cross-purposes with God, of course; during the workweek Christians may find God working with them through their vocations. But there is a significant difference between the quotidian concerns of human lives and what Christians take to be God's greater agenda. By muting the hubbub of everyday human work, we may attend to the softer, deeper tones of the work that God does in the world, unaided by human hands. Without setting aside time to listen to God's quiet activity, we might see human work as the most important thing in the world; we might even start to idolize it. Sabbath keeping undercuts this potential for idolatry, inculcating humility as its altered perspective seems to assert the relative unimportance of human work, compared with that of God.

This does not mean that humans have no role to play in doing God's work. By taking on God's perspective on the Sabbath, humans come to appreciate what God wants from us. And God's agenda is far from empty. Adventist ethicist Miroslav Kis explains it this way: on the Sabbath, the presence of God attends believers, and continues throughout the week, so that "the priorities of Heaven, the divine sensitivity to injustice and oppression urge them to extend the Sabbath rest to those around them."[49] Adventists learn the value of justice and liberation by attending to God on the Sabbath. The Sabbath also teaches humility, according to Doukhan: it is a time for humans to remember their reliance on God, not their own works. "It teaches us the value of nonaction in relationship with God.... Refraining from working on the Sabbath is an indication of total dependence on God. What one *has* is not a result of work, but a free gift from God."[50]

The Sabbath Economics Collaborative also appreciates the altered perspective of the Sabbath, characterized by humility about the importance of human work by reference to God and creation. Wendell Berry contends that resting from work on the Sabbath instills the humble wisdom of "knowing when to stop" human work in deference to the workings of the "Great Economy"—which he defines as God's work through the total ecological system of material and energy exchange on the earth.[51] To observe the Sabbath is to set voluntary limits on human activity in honor of God's work. These limits are, in author and activist Ched Myers's understanding, essential to "disrupt" human hubris and reorient human priorities to mirror those of God.[52] Sabbath keepers maintain that this appreciation, this altered perspective, comes from the God-focus engendered by a day of ceasing from work, a day designed for prayer, worship, and rest. As Wirzba puts it, "Sabbath rest is thus a call to Sabbath trust, a call to visibly demonstrate in our daily living that we know ourselves to be upheld and maintained by the grace of God rather than the strength and craftiness of our own hands."[53]

Transformed Consumption

Observing a Sabbath, then, means more than simply slowing down the pace of activity and living simply one day out of seven; it also means trusting God's provision and humbly ceding the illusion of control over one's life. This personal transformation can mean altered consumption habits both on the Sabbath and throughout the rest of the week.

For Seventh-day Adventists, a Sabbath lifestyle means temperance and simplicity in the consumption of food. Thanks to White's interest in health, the Seventh-day Adventist church developed a set of hygienic and dietary rules, which are (with some modifications) still practiced today. White "saw that it was a religious duty for God's people to care for their health and not violate the laws of life. The Lord wanted them 'to come out against intemperance of every kind—intemperance in working, in eating, in drinking, and in drugging.'"[54] Inspired by her visions, White and her fellow Adventists gave up tobacco, alcohol, coffee, tea, and meat. They also worked on behalf of the prohibition of alcohol and became preachers of health, urging others to give up tobacco.[55]

The Adventist Dietetic Association (ADA) promotes a modernized version of White's dietary rules, remaining true to her vision of abstinence from alcohol, caffeine, tobacco, and meat, and promoting simple, whole foods over processed items. While the health advantages receive top billing in Adventist writing, there are other reasons given to support the dietary restrictions of Seventh-day Adventists. Adventist scholar Jack Provonsha promotes vegetarianism's ecological benefits, and the ADA touts the frugality and stewardship associated with less meat consumption: "Fruits, vegetables, grains, legumes, and nuts are often *less expensive* than meat. Plant foods use *fewer natural resources* from the environment."[56] Simpler, less processed foods cause less environmental degradation because they require, typically, less energy to process and less packaging. Consuming less meat is, often, advantageous for the environment because industrial meat production uses large amounts of energy and produces harmful waste; similar nutrition can be achieved through plant products with much lower levels of resource use and harm to natural systems.[57]

Adventists, like many Christian denominations, express concern for the environment in their official documents. The General Conference of Seventh-day Adventists Administrative Committee has, in their list of official church documents since 1980, six separate statements discussing creation and environmental problems.[58] Several of these make an explicit connection between environmental degradation and consumption choices. For example, their "Statement on Stewardship" concludes:

> Seventh-day Adventism advocates a simple, wholesome lifestyle, where people do not step on the treadmill of unbridled over-consumption, accumulation of goods, and production of waste. A reformation of lifestyle is called for, based on respect for nature, restraint in the use of the world's resources, reevaluation of one's needs, and reaffirmation of the dignity of created life.[59]

While the connection among the "simple, wholesome lifestyle," the simple, wholesome diet, and Sabbath observance is not explicitly drawn, it is clear that for Seventh-day Adventists their Sabbath beliefs—particularly as they link to their readiness to meet the returned Christ—continue to shape their consumption habits in ways that reduce their environmental impact.

Other Christian Sabbath keepers make a more explicit link between consumption and the Sabbath. Marva Dawn advocates making Sundays special by making the rest of the week mundane, and doing so through simplified, lessened consumption: "One way to increase our sense of the delight of the Sabbath day is by eating more simply during the week and saving favorite foods for our holy celebrations."[60] She suggests saving special

foods such as hot cocoa or special dishes such as heirloom china for Sabbath use, as a way to demarcate this set-apart, holy time. Dawn urges her readers to feast on the Sabbath and to live simply the rest of the week. She also recommends abstinence from shopping on the Sabbath: the day's purpose, she explains, is to focus on God and God's desires, not herself, her possessions, and her own desires.[61] Sleeth also explicitly forbids himself shopping on the Sabbath. "I find that I can pray or meditate for hours and have that peaceful glow taken away by ninety seconds spent in a retail establishment."[62]

Allender, like Dawn, sees the Sabbath as a day of feasting. He writes, "The Sabbath is the weekly entry into a taste of lavish, sensuous delight."[63] He narrates several Sabbath feasts with friends, concluding that enjoying food on the Sabbath offers "a taste of wonder that ushers us into the eternal party of God."[64] For Allender, the sensual delight of the Sabbath is one of the ways it is differentiated from the other days of the week. He writes, "The Sabbath is a day of sensuality when we say to one another, 'Taste and see that the LORD is good. Oh, the joys!'"[65] This sensual delight involves consumption, but it is careful and deliberate consumption, savored and cherished as gifts from God, pieces of "the feast of the coming kingdom."[66]

Wendell Berry concentrates less on the Sabbath as a day of rest, and more on the attitudes associated with Sabbath observance. In his poem "The Farm," Berry instructs a would-be farmer to let her land have a Sabbath rest ("The land must have its Sabbath/Or take it when we starve"), to grow her own food and make the things she needs herself ("Never buy at a store/What you can grow or find/At home"), to buy locally ("be/Faithful to local merchants/Too. Never buy far off/What you can buy near home"), and to give away her surplus to others.[67] This is Berry's vision of good participation in the Great Economy, the kingdom of God: to give to others, to work in cooperation with the land, to be locally rooted and self-sufficient. In discussing consumption, Berry also calls for good stewardship of resources in the form of quality work: "if we want our forests to last," he writes, "then we must make wood products that last, for our forests are more threatened by shoddy workmanship than by clear-cutting or by fire."[68] Throwaway products are unwise and therefore unworthy of those who have a Sabbath-formed outlook; Berry counsels his readers to steer clear of them.[69]

Wirzba, like Berry, discusses consumption and the Sabbath on a conceptual level, invoking Sabbath-endorsed habits of gratitude, sufficiency, and sharing, and creating a vision of how "Sabbath people" would consume. He advocates simplicity in terms of an uncluttered enjoyment of life free from overconsumption and the demands of the market. For Wirzba, eating food that comes from wholesome, well-known origins (ideally homegrown) can constitute a Sabbath-style encounter with God: "In the handling and consuming of the bodies of creation we come into direct contact with the love of God, and so experience again and again the divine, hospitable love that brought all creation into being."[70] Too often, however, this is not the case. "Our food industry," he writes, "bears all the marks of an anti-Sabbath mentality: sacrilege and ingratitude, obsessive control and profiteering, insensitivity and destruction."[71] Wirzba is concerned about the everyday ignorance of consumers, believing that this ignorance both leads to abuses and undermines efforts at praise and thanksgiving.[72] His remedy is to encourage consumer activism and the refusal "to be passive, ignorant consumers of products invisibly made": consumers should consume locally and lobby for transparency in production processes.[73] Wirzba bases this call to action not on political views as much as on his concept of the Sabbath and what it means to be a "Sabbath People": to effect a quiet revolution by making family meals composed of local, healthy foods a priority.[74] "If we are to become Sabbath people," he writes, "who take a humble stance within creation, who recognize creation as a gift of God given for all to enjoy, we simply have to realign and dramatically curtail our consumption habits."[75]

Wirzba does not delve into the more challenging aspects of his local-consumption vision, nor does he admit that genuine appreciation and holiness can exist around less-than-perfect meals.[76] But like Myers and other Sabbath Economics thinkers, Wirzba has a countercultural vision for those who truly observe the Sabbath, and he wants to persuade his readers to join him. He asks a lot of his readers, but he does not ask them to do it alone.[77] Observing the Sabbath; absorbing Sabbath values such as delight, self-restraint, and sharing; and becoming part of a Sabbath people are, for Wirzba, the ways to fulfill his eschatological vision of a renewed, redeemed humanity in harmony with creation.

A Transformed World

While observing the Sabbath is good for the individual, its influence extends beyond one person and one day. Sabbath keeping means reaching out to others, it means learning lessons that last throughout the week, and it means envisioning a better world.

Sharing is integral to many Christians' Sabbath practice. "The Sunday Eucharistic gathering is *an experience of brotherhood*," according to John Paul II.[78] The Sabbath is an appropriate time not only for rest and worship but also for acts of generosity, mercy, and compassion. Sister Mary Agnew, CPPS, in a pastoral commentary on *Dies Domini*, urges parish leaders to take on "the project of linking works of charity, justice, and peace to Sunday."[79] Lutheran ecotheologian Larry Rasmussen worries that much of the devotional literature on the Sabbath is too therapeutic and self-focused; in response, he writes, "Sabbath and its remembrances are a creation and projection not of ourselves, but of God. Keeping the Sabbath, then, means joining God as mystery that surpasses us and purpose that outstrips us."[80]

Seventh-day Adventists agree. The Sabbath, for Seventh-day Adventists, is not simply a time of personal reflection, but is a time to be shared with others, and spent in good works. There is, in Doukhan's words, a "social dimension of the Sabbath." He explains: "This holiness of the Sabbath, which sets the believers apart, should not however separate them from their neighbors. On the contrary, in the Sabbath the openness to the divine 'Other' is complemented with the openness to the human 'other.'"[81] The eschatological dimension of Adventist thought has led to an accusation of disregard for the concerns of this world. Adventist scholar Zdravko Plantak writes, "Human rights were not thought to be a believer's concern at a time when Christ's return was so near that they had to think about ultimate salvation from this corrupt and sinful world."[82] But many Seventh-day Adventists disagree with this assessment.[83] Seventh-day Adventists today, like many Christian denominations, engage in impressive charitable and missionary work; and Adventists in particular, because of their concern for health, have created hospitals and clinics around the world, especially at Loma Linda University and in the Washington, D.C., area, that engage in highly regarded medical research and outreach.[84]

Wirzba discusses the social dimension of the Sabbath when he notes that biblical descriptions of Sabbath rest are, explicitly, inclusive: all people, including women, strangers, and even animals, are commanded to rest on the Sabbath. "By proclaiming that everyone should rest together, we begin to see some of the revolutionary potential latent within a Sabbath sensibility. Put simply, *the rest of one person should not be at the expense of another's exhaustion or toil*."[85] Wirzba's notion that one person's rest should not come at another's expense echoes Woolman's views on luxury that is won by others' overwork. But for Wirzba, rest is no sinful luxury. Folded into the concept of the Sabbath is the understanding that rest is not only for the rich or those who can afford a day off: everyone has the right to a day of rest. Myers interprets biblical descriptions of Sabbath observance in terms of the poor and "the responsibility not to take too much."[86] Sabbath Economics, he writes, teaches "self-sufficiency through a practice of sharing available resources (what we today might call 'cooperative consumption')."[87] The emphasis is on justice and care for the needy, not on self-indulgent relaxation.

The Sabbath is also a particularly good time for works of mercy, according to the Sabbath Economics thinkers. For Methodist theologian L. Roger Owens it connects with Sabbath pedagogy: "Performing corporal works of mercy on Sunday retrains our desire, teaching us to relate ourselves to others in life-giving ways."[88] The Sabbath is an appropriate day to give money to those in need, as the early Christians did, according to Dawn's reading of Paul (1 Corinthians 16:1–2): money set aside to aid other congregations was collected in connection with worship, in response to the miraculous nature of the events commemorated by "the Lord's Day."[89]

John Paul II and most other Christian writers of the Sabbath emphasize the impact of one day's observance on the other days of the week. Sabbath observance, then, serves a pedagogical function.

> Sunday in a way becomes the soul of the other days, and in this sense we can recall the insight of Origen that the perfect Christian "is always in the Lord's Day, and is always cel-

ebrating Sunday." Sunday is a true school, an enduring program of Church pedagogy.[90]

The impact of its teaching endures throughout the rest of the week.

A countercultural movement like Sabbath Economics sees the everyday world of market idolatry and consumerism as a threat to individual, community, and planetary well-being. By contrast, an oasis like the Sabbath represents a safe haven, a time to prepare to face the onslaught of non-Sabbath society the other six days of the week. Owens calls Sabbath keeping "a counter pedagogy of desire...a Christian practice that frees our souls and our bodies from the evil age of consumption (and, correspondingly, teaches us to desire justice and peace)."[91] Dawn agrees, calling Sabbath keeping "a weekly counteroffensive" against "invasions" such as the commercialization of religious holidays.[92] Observing the Sabbath both inculcates and expresses values that serve to "vaccinate" Christians against market idolatry and consumerism; the lessons learned sustain those values throughout the week.

Ultimately, this is a comprehensive vision for a better world. According to Dawn, there is a link between observing the Sabbath and fulfilling a biblical vision of Jubilee justice: "Perhaps if God's people again observed the Sabbath, we would become more of a Jubilee people—setting free those oppressed by economic injustice, canceling debts, restoring the land, and thereby building peace."[93] When Sabbath Economics thinkers write of a better world, they include the natural environment, ascribing purpose and intentionality to the earth. Richard Lowery speaks of "earth's vocation of worship and generous hospitality," which may be undermined by human exploitation of nonhuman nature.[94] Jürgen Moltmann, writing on the topic of the Sabbath and the environment, urges human restraint, "so that nature too can celebrate its Sabbath."[95] Both of these writers understand nonhuman nature to have a purpose in God's plan, a vocation to celebrate, to worship, and to flourish. Their eschatological visions include the earth's redemption. In Wirzba's words, "Redemption of the land begins as we together with God undo the effects of sin. Practically speaking, this will involve the regular halting of human pressures and demands, a genuine Sabbath for the land."[96] This is in keeping with God's intentions for the Sabbath, in Moltmann's view. "The true intention," he writes, "is for us to stop intervening in nature on this day, to stop hurting it and instead to perceive it and esteem it as God's beloved creation. The true meaning of the Sabbath is ecological."[97]

Seventh-day Adventists, too, translate Sabbath caring into ecological concern. Because they honor nonhuman nature and human beings in their unity as God's creation, some Seventh-day Adventist theologians have articulated a "doctrine of wholeness" particularly focused on the unity of the human person (body and spirit are seamlessly united in Adventist belief), the belief in healthy living, and the importance of connections between humans and the rest of creation.[98] This "doctrine of wholeness" has distinct ethical implications. Adventist scholar Ginger Hanks-Harwood writes, "The doctrine of wholeness..., if it is applied consistently and conscientiously, has the potential of aiding ethical discernment by clarifying that behavior which is fitting to persons."[99] She sees the concept of wholeness as the motivation for "'advocacy ethics': speaking and acting on behalf of wholeness and healing wherever and whenever humanity or the creation is threatened."[100] This sort of advocacy is called for today, she argues, in situations of war, oppression, and environmental degradation that constitute a threat to health and life.

From all of these Christian voices, we learn this: Christians may prepare for, and even build, the world-to-come through proper consumption practices; and Sabbath-style consuming, with its slower pace and deeper connections, its healthful conscience and social awareness, and its eschewing of stress and excess, is the type of consumption that will characterize the world to come.

EUCHARIST

> For a biologist nutrition-consumption is a physiological function. For an economist, it expresses the struggle for existence.... For the theologian it is Eucharistic consumption, the anticipation of the banquet of the Kingdom (Mt 26:29). The Eucharistic bread and wine appear as a part of the age to come.[101]

The Eucharist[102] is foremost among the few instances of physical consumption that occur in a Christian ritual.[103] As the founding ritual of the church, it communicates the essence of the Christian story through sharing food and drink. One of the strengths of this ritual is its ability to convey multiple layers of mutually reinforcing meaning. The many gifts of the Eucharist include its power to shape Christian attitudes toward consumption.

In this book, Eucharist is broadly defined to include all Christian practices of ritually sharing bread and wine (or grape juice), in conscious imitation of Jesus' actions at the Last Supper and it includes practices known as the Lord's Supper or Communion. There is substantial disagreement among Christians on certain components of eucharistic belief (e.g., the debates on Christ's real or metaphorical presence in the bread and wine, or who should be included in the community sharing the food). The points I make here apply, to some degree, regardless of these disagreements, and in this discussion I use theological insights from many parts of the Christian tradition. I draw especially upon Eastern Orthodox eucharistic theology and emphasize the work of early twentieth-century Orthodox theologian Sergei Bulgakov because these sources particularly support an eschatological understanding of Christian consumption.

WHAT IT MEANS TO TAKE THE EUCHARIST

A Balance of Feasting and Fasting

One lesson to be gained from the Eucharist is its particular balance between feasting (sensuous enjoyment of festive food) and fasting (disciplined avoidance of some or all food). Both of these can be spiritual practices in Christianity, and both are, paradoxically, present in the Eucharist. Many Christians fast before taking Eucharist, for example, eating no breakfast before Sunday morning worship, allowing the eucharistic elements of bread and wine to break the fast in a holy way.[104] Some Christian eucharistic worship is followed by a larger meal, a potluck or other celebration after worship reminiscent of the agape meals that Paul describes in 1 Corinthians 11. Thus the Eucharist occupies a middle ground between the preparatory fasting and celebratory feasting surrounding it.

The Eucharist itself does resemble fasting, as it takes on elements of ascetic practice. The liturgy's emphasis on quiet reflection, its invocation of Jesus' sacrifice, and its slow, staid pace allow ample time to observe temperance and abstention before receiving the food. The food received, typically, is quite meager—a small piece of bread or a thin wafer, and a sip of wine (or grape juice), hardly a meal, and certainly a far cry from gluttony. (Indeed, some medieval saints have fasted on the sacrament, eating only the eucharistic elements and nothing else.[105])

Fasting and other forms of ascetic practice are integral to Orthodox Christianity. Such practices characterize Orthodox observation of Lent, but *askesis* also makes an appearance in Orthodox writings about the ecological crisis.[106] Notably, John Zizioulas, metropolitan of Pergamon, discusses "ecological asceticism" as a way to bring about greater care for the earth apart from self-serving motives.[107] As discussed in chapter 2, ascetic practice (refraining from consumption and renouncing certain pleasures for the sake of greater holiness) often lightens the burden that human consumption places on the earth's natural resources. Certainly, the Eucharist allows Christians to practice, in a limited way, the habit of *askesis*.

But the Eucharist also resembles a feast, as the community comes together, gives thanks, and celebrates Christ's role in their salvation. All are fed, and there is enough for everyone, often with food left over. The food is savored and gratefully tasted. The priest or pastor who raises the cup to heaven evokes Christ who offers his own flesh and blood as sustenance and medium of grace, and Christians rejoice in the liberating sacrifice of this "paschal lamb."[108] Though the quantity of food consumed is small, the joy and celebration correlate to a bountiful feast.

Practicing the Eucharist, then, demonstrates for Christians a deft negotiation between a contrite *askesis* and what theologian Marion Grau calls "strategic excess."[109] The Eucharist is an opportunity to derive lavish joy from a meager amount of physical consumption. This practice of richly embracing minor consumption fits with process theologian Catherine Keller's description of "sensuous asceticism": "enhancing the inexpensive joys of our senses—at the rhythm of day and night, the rising of sun and stars, the parade of seasons, the delight of fresh water, of wholesome food."[110] This is not self-denial for the sake of holiness, as described in chapter 2, nor is it self-denial for the sake of others, as described in chapter 4, but rather, this echoes and deepens the savored consumption described in chapter 3. This is "sensuous asceticism" and "strategic excess" in response to God's lavish provision: an abundant grace derived from a small morsel of bread and a sip of wine.

Theosis, Priesthood, and Consumption

In Orthodox theology, the aim of Christian life is described as theosis, or divinization. Boris Jakim, translator and Orthodox scholar, describes the Chalcedonian creed as a source for this teaching: the creed defines Christ's dual nature as human and divine, "and expresses the process whereby [humanity] cooperates with God, leading to the transfiguration of humanity and fusing the entire human community into a heavenly Church."[111] The transfiguration of humanity means theosis, in which humans share the divine nature, becoming, in a sense, God. Theosis is not limited to humans, however: all of creation is to be transfigured, rendered divine, and brought into the fullness of communion with God.[112] As ecotheologian Willis Jenkins understands it, "natural change and ecological processes ... [are] natural indicators of the way creation anticipates divinization," but humans can also play a role in creation's fulfillment.[113] He writes that Maximus the Confessor (ca. 580–662), a pivotal figure whose writings shaped the theology of the early Orthodox Church, "anticipates the peaceable kingdom of the ecclesial economy, where Christians reconcile the world as they dwell within it, transfiguring creation through worship, offering the world to God as they enter into the communion of the cosmos."[114]

Orthodox theologians refer to humans as "priests" of creation who play an intermediary role in relating nonhuman nature to

God. As Zizioulas writes, "The priest is the one who takes in his hands the world to refer it to God, and who, in return, brings God's blessing to what he refers to God. Through this act, creation is brought into communion with God himself."[115] Humans, then, are to use their ability to bring disparate elements into communion as a vehicle for creation's—and humanity's—theosis.[116] "Reversing its usual valence as a presumptively violative threat to nature," Jenkins writes, "transformative human action brings forth nature's essence, responding to its longing for liberation."[117] All creation longs for this transformation; it is through both natural processes and human action that creation moves closer to its final fulfillment.

Note, then, that Orthodox theology uses a metaphor from the liturgy—that of the priest—to describe how all humans ought to behave toward nature. This means that participating in the liturgy trains humans for all other realms of life. Jenkins, interpreting Orthodox theologian Dumitru Stăniloae, explains: "the Eucharistic liturgy contains the highest instance of personal communion [with nature and God], as humans fulfill the theurgic interval between God's offer and their own response with creative, reconciling, elevating uses of the world."[118] The liturgical celebration of the Eucharist, then, is the paradigm case for human use of the physical matter of creation.

All human work, in the eyes of Orthodox theologian Paul Evdokimov, should be "a priestly action, a sacrament transforming" the world "into a place of theophany."[119] Not only production but also consumption can summon nature's glory. In consumption, Sergei Bulgakov writes, "The boundary between the living and the dead, the animate and the inanimate, is lifted. In it nature receives assurance of the possibility of universal reanimation."[120] Universal reanimation means that something dead is incorporated into what is living through consumption, or that something nonhuman is incorporated into what is human through consumption. It is to effect nature's fulfillment in the form of a *"natural communion,"* a removal of the barrier between living and non-living.[121] Insofar as consuming something makes it become a part of the consumer, and the consumer is closer to God than the consumed, then consumption can contribute to the process of theosis. Bulgakov writes, "All of nature thirsts for the body and blood of Christ."[122] The work of human consumers, for Bulgakov, constitutes the intermediary step that is required to allow nature to taste the Eucharist.

Consumption brings humans into unity with the world and its historical development. Bulgakov writes:

> When I take in food, I am eating world matter in general, and in so doing, I truly and in reality find the world within me and myself in the world, I become a part of it. In the immediate sense, I eat this bread here. But dynamically, as a result of the unity and connectedness of the universe . . . , I take in the flesh of the world in general in the guise of this bread. For the history of this bread, as of every particle of matter, contains the history of the entire universe. . . . Food in this sense uncovers our essential metaphysical unity with the world.[123]

Bulgakov sees humans as microcosms of a larger macrocosm, and refers to "the entire universe" as "a living body."[124] Consumption, according to Bulgakov, enacts that cosmic connection by physically manifesting the unity of disparate elements for the sake of a greater purpose. When disparate elements are unified, when humans commune with the nonhuman world and with one another, then we fulfill our role as priests of creation and enact the transformation that is central to the Eucharist (and to all holy consumption).

Being Transformed by the Eucharist

As many Christians experience it, the Eucharist is a medium of God's transforming grace, a true sacrament that opens the community to receive holy help.[125] This help happens through Christ's presence. Jesus is, truly, host in both senses of the word: its liturgical meaning as "sacrifice" and its vernacular meaning as "one who offers hospitality."[126] His sacrifice is a hospitable one, and it feeds Christians, offering both physical and more-than-physical nourishment, like the "living water" that Jesus offered to the Samaritan woman at the well (see John 4:10–13). This nourishment (or nourishing sacrifice) is a recurring miracle of incarnation: Christ's presence in the Eucharist continually feeds those gathered together to receive it.

For those who believe that Christ is present in the bread and wine, taking communion means assimilating Christ into themselves. As Evdokimov sees it, "This sharing of nature between Christ and those who partake of his 'sacred flesh' constitutes the universal effect of the Eucharist."[127] By becoming one with Christ's nature, we become part of the universal body of Christ. By consuming Christ in the Eucharist, as William T. Cavanaugh points out, "the consumer of the Eucharist is taken up into a larger body, the body of Christ."[128] When Christians eat Christ's body, it becomes a part of their bodies, even as they are consumed by, and constitutive of, the larger body of Christ. Becoming part of the body of Christ is significant and demanding: it means being willing to endure what Christ's body endured, to serve, to be broken, and to "become food for others."[129] The transformation that occurs because of eucharistic practice can be subtle (we may not "feel" so different afterward) but Christian theologians insist it is real and significant. Orthodox theology teaches that as the Eucharist unifies us with Christ and Christ's body, we also become more godlike, closer to the ultimate goal of theosis.

WHAT MAKES THE EUCHARIST ESCHATOLOGICAL?

Just as Sabbath keepers describe their practice as a foretaste of the world to come, so Christian writers on the Eucharist say that participating in communion means experiencing God's fondest wish for the future. Some elements of eucharistic theology are backward-looking, invoking the creation of the world and the liberation of God's people, allowing participants to root their eating practices in a robust sense of history and creation. But the Eucharist also looks forward, offering a glimpse of a redeemed world. The elements, formerly living grapes and living wheat, have died, but this death—like Jesus' death on the cross—becomes life giving. A limited amount of bread can, in a eucharistic ritual, be fully nourishing to everyone, since it is a medium of God's fulfilling grace. From death to life, from limitation to abundance: the Eucharist articulates the profound paradox of God's provision and in so doing offers a foretaste of the world to come, an orientation to the new creation.

Bulgakov confirms the eschatological dimension of the Eucharist, referring to Christ's presence in the Eucharist as a transfiguration. He writes:

> This transfiguration of creation, corresponding to the Savior's second coming, is accomplished in the Divine Eucharist.... That which is accomplished in the sacrament will be accomplished, at the end of time, in the whole world, which is the body of humankind. And the latter is the Body of Christ.[130]

There is something about the Eucharist—its unified community of believers, the presence of Christ, the sharing and equality around the table—that Christians of all kinds identify with the reign of God. At the Eucharist, participants experience the future fulfillment that God intends for the whole world.

Often in Christianity, the life of the world to come is envisioned as a feast, which may resemble the feast of the Eucharist. Jesus describes God's reign as a wedding banquet to which the invited guests reject their invitations, but to which the people on the street are all invited (Matthew 22:1–14; Luke 14:15–24). Nuptial banquets figure prominently, from the beginning of Christ's ministry at Cana (John 2) to "the marriage supper of the lamb" in the book of Revelation (19:9). Feastlike consumption, then, figures prominently in Christian eschatological visions.

Bulgakov's is no exception. He envisions a fulfilled world, a world "transfigured and glorified":

> the earth is no longer accursed, and... the economic enslavement of man to the earth has passed. However, although immortal life does not depend here on food and the stomach, man maintains his good connection with the natural world by partaking of its fruits. By no means is man taken out of the natural world; rather, he is eternalized in it.[131]

Even in the new creation, Bulgakov sees a place for consumption, because it forms a "good connection with the natural world."[132]

WHAT THE EUCHARIST TEACHES ABOUT CONSUMPTION

Do insights about consumption in the Eucharist apply more broadly, to instances of everyday consumption? Yes. Holy Communion offers Christians a reminder of the potential holiness inherent in sharing food, of the ways that sharing this consumption offers both community and grace to believers seeking to encounter and embody Christ. The Eucharist represents a blessed middle ground between fast and feast, and anchors the ends of this spectrum with its dual nourishment of physical and spiritual food. Regular practice of the Eucharist helps Christians acquire the habit of seeing the holy dimensions of all eating, while everyday eating practices, such as sharing meals and saying grace, enhance and deepen an understanding of the Eucharist.

In an expansion of the spirit of the eucharistic meal, L. Shannon Jung asks, "Could it be that all eating is sacramental?"; he answers that yes, it can be: "Food itself is a means of revelation. Through eating together we taste the goodness of God."[133] All eating *can* be sacramental, but is it? Not necessarily. Paul, in his first letter to the Corinthians, condemns heedless, hedonistic eating ("Let us eat and drink, for tomorrow we die") that lacks the perspective offered by understanding God's imminent glory (1 Corinthians 15:32). True Christian consumption, by contrast, is laden with promise, manifesting the sacramental, revelatory dimension of everyday eating.

A passage from Wendell Berry, quoted in chapter 3, describes everyday eating as a potential sacrament ("To live we must daily break the body and shed the blood of creation"), but warns against the failure to observe its holiness ("When we do it ignorantly, greedily and destructively it is a desecration").[134] Whether food consumption points toward the sinful destruction of the earth's resources or toward a grace-filled communion depends on our attitudes and behaviors. What Jenkins writes of Bulgakov would be equally true of Berry: "Economy is now an eschatological craft."[135] To bring the weight of eschatology to economic transactions is not only to reveal new dimensions of the economy but also to provide new motivation to act on theological convictions. Using Bulgakov's perspective, Jenkins writes:

> Christian Jubilee campaigns become more than moralist; they creatively and correctively illuminate the ultimate purpose of economy. So too for patterns of consumption: within [Bulgakov's vision of the] economy, they become a "means of communion with the flesh of the world."[136]

Not all consumption is communion, or the means of the world's theosis. Surely some consumption is, in Berry's words, "ignorant, greedy, and destructive," not a means of grace. Orthodox voices counteract the sinful human tendency to apotheosize human striving with calls for wisdom and asceticism. As Jenkins writes of Stăniloae, "Asceticism . . . purifies our senses to see creation rightly and will to use it blessedly."[137] To use creation blessedly means right discernment of creation's true needs and the will to act on that wisdom. Orthodox ecotheologian Elizabeth Theokritoff declares, "We are in a position to realize or thwart a potential in the cosmos that cries out for fulfillment. Our task is not to redirect creation, but to *articulate* its 'wordless word revealing God' rather than 'exporting our fallenness' into it."[138]

The eucharistic discussion affirms, however, that consumption is necessary for spiritual transformation and the bringing about of God's kingdom. As Evdokimov writes, "Communion with Christ who is present [in the Eucharist] is not fulfilled except in the very act of eating and drinking."[139] Bulgakov describes consumption as essential for life, both for physical survival and for spiritual and intellectual life: to live is to commune with the world through consumption; to die is to cease consumption; and to be resurrected is to commune and consume in infinite ways.[140]

Theosis, Bulgakov writes, requires a balance between denial and creativity, between renouncing and saving the world.[141]

We acquire the sensitivity and habituation that are needed to maintain this balance by practicing it, as we repeatedly receive the Eucharist. As Stephen Webb, a Catholic theologian, writes, "Just as children learn to behave and act like adults at the dinner table, so Christians learn what it means to be a Christian at communion."[142] The Eucharist may instill simple habits such as sharing food with others or virtues such as humbly receiving what God gives. Or the eucharistic lessons may be more direct, as in Catholic theologian Monika Hellwig's conclusions that practicing the Eucharist should prompt Christians to support organizations that feed the hungry.[143]

The Eucharist may inspire such sacrifices and transformed consumption practices, but is that the typical Christian experience of it? Not necessarily. Some Christian writers believe the practice of communion needs reformation if it is to become a more effective tool of spiritual and moral transformation. Jung suggests that the communion elements should be both genuinely delicious and sourced locally if possible, and the ritual should be followed by a full meal, offering genuine physical sustenance (a revival of the agape meal, as practiced by early Christians).[144] Ecotheologian Michael Northcott agrees, suggesting that families from the congregation take turns baking the bread for the Eucharist, and offer "drinkable quantities of wine"; he, too, advocates rehabilitating the token meal into a full meal, and placing it at the center of the worship, rather than at the end.[145] These reforms, according to Jung and Northcott, would help the lessons of the Eucharist to take deeper root in participants, thereby influencing everyday Christian consumption habits.

For Lutheran liturgical scholar Gordon W. Lathrop, there are larger-scale economic insights to be gained from the practice of the Eucharist. Lathrop notes that eucharistic practice welcomes all and finds food enough for everybody gathered at the table. "There is enough food in the earth to feed us all," he concludes, "if we use it and the earth itself with care and reverence, and if we share it equitably."[146] This lesson is designed to influence not only other Christian meals but also the entire food economy. As Lathrop puts it, "The shared bread and cup, the body and blood of Christ poured out in this world, will always continue to propose a deeper, wider, more life-giving economics yet."[147]

BEYOND BREAD AND WINE

The way Christians consume in the Eucharist is the way God wants us to consume in the kingdom. So what does that mean for consumption—including nonfood consumption—in the here and now?

In the Eucharist, all who come are graciously fed, and even small consumption is richly embraced as a blessing from God. Similar consumption practices appear in the work of organizations such as Food Not Bombs, which enacts the parable of the wedding banquet by offering full meals to whomever they meet, in parks and public places; they do not turn water into wine, but they do turn discarded food into nourishing meals.[148] The graciousness and generosity involved in offering delicious free hot meals to anyone, rich and poor alike, is a striking example of Grau's notion of "strategic excess," and a fitting instantiation of Eucharist-like consumption.

In the Eucharist, a balance is struck between fasting and feasting. What might this look like with clothing, for example? Somewhere between minimal, plain clothing (religious habits, Anabaptist Plain dress, nudism) and extravagant, sumptuous garments (liturgical vestments, golden crosses, "Sunday best") lies a place of grace-filled thanksgiving and sharing. Christ's own garment was, in fact, shared (but not broken) at his crucifixion; he urged his followers to be willing to give up their clothing for others (Matthew 5:40; Luke 6:29). To break and share one's wardrobe, perhaps, constitutes a kind of Lord's Supper of clothing. A clothing Eucharist would also include practices of receiving clothing and giving thanks for it.[149]

In the Eucharist, the people of God consume in a way that enriches them but does not impoverish others. In fact, the consumption has strong positive effects: it strengthens the community, it establishes a connection with God, and it brings everything—human and nonhuman elements alike—closer to the vision of a fulfilled world. How might we do the same with, say, energy consumption? Methodist author Bill McKibben argues for a dispersed grid of energy production—a wind turbine here, a few solar panels there—such that all participate in the production of energy.[150] Most North American consumers have never visited a power plant, but when my neighbor puts up solar panels, I certainly take note, and probably walk over to investigate: this kind of energy production strengthens the community. In McKibben's vision, then, the solar panels and wind turbines in my neighborhood produce enough power not only to supply the houses where they're located but, collectively, they can (at least in part) support the entire neighborhood. So when I flip on the light switch, I'm neither ignorant of the source of that power, nor guiltily aware that my desire for light means ecological harm. Instead, I'm thanking God for the sun and wind. This form of energy production and consumption, then, shares many factors with the Eucharist: it comes from, and strengthens, the community; it is a vital resource that is distributed and accessible to many; it is an occasion for thanksgiving and closeness to God; and it brings the world that much closer to (one ecological version of) the vision of its fulfillment.

Of course, not all consumption brings about the vision of the new creation. As I write this, I consume both coal (which creates the electricity I use to power the computer) and plant matter (the vegetables and grains I had for lunch are powering my body). Potentially, in Bulgakov's view, I am contributing to the theosis of that coal and those carrots, and if this book serves God's purposes in the world, then their theosis will be served. But I could just as easily be using the same energy to compose a hateful screed against my enemies, or pursuing some self-centered amusement. In that case, the carrots may not have achieved much in the way of theosis.

To judge consumption by its conformity to a vision of the world's fulfillment is to bring an aesthetic element into ethics, because the vision of "a new heaven and a new earth" is by definition beautiful—"prepared as a bride adorned for her husband" (Revelation 21:1–2). As Evdokimov writes, "Orthodoxy has bequeathed a union of the ethical and the esthetic in an iconographic contemplation best expressed by the Greek word, *kalokagathia*, a symbiosis of the Good and the Beautiful."[151] Humans are called to be priests of creation, but also artists, seeking, in Stăniloae's words, "creative, reconciling, elevating uses of the world,"[152] that bring disparate elements into communion and model God's reconciling work in the Eucharist.

Christian consumption in the Eucharist makes the world a better place. It strengthens the body of Christ, it brings God and creation into communion with each other, and it inspires a vision of ultimate reconciliation. This is the goal of Christians who wish to envision the future as they consider consumption: to find ways of consuming that are more helpful than harmful, that contribute to the world as much as, or more than, they take away from it.

SABBATH, EUCHARIST, AND
VISIONS OF THE FUTURE

The Sabbath and the Eucharist are not the only practices in which Christians anticipate the world to come, but they are exemplary in how they connect Christian eschatology with conscientious consumption. This fourth and final consideration for Christian consumption shows, in response to the first consideration, that consumption need not simply avoid what is sinful but may actively participate in creating what is good. Even as consumption can embrace the richness of creation, as in the second consideration, it can point beyond created wonders, toward the new creation. Last, in conversation with the third consideration, it need not only incorporate neighbor-love but may also inspire neighbors to come together in aid of a common vision of the future.

This fourth consideration for conscientious consumption vitally deepens the first three, yet it cannot stand alone. Eschatological consumption can be both vague and idiosyncratic, since different Christians have radically different views of the eschaton. Noting that consumption should contribute to the world's fulfillment forms an insufficient normative agenda. As Jenkins writes,

> How do we know when technology, art, and construction express the glories of creation and when they fracture it, alienating us further? How do we know when our cultivation brings forth the saving beauty of the world? Within a world simultaneously imperfect, glorious, and corrupted, what does authentic transfiguration look like?[153]

In the "not yet" of a yearning world, we see this dimly at best.

Nevertheless, Christians, inspired by glimpses of the "already" of God's reign and susceptible to the lure of a fulfilled future, strive for authentic consumption that manifests "the glories of creation." This conscientious consumption requires four considerations, then: avoiding sin, embracing creation, loving the neighbor, and envisioning the future. Together, as the next chapter shall explain, these four considerations create a comprehensive Christian ethics of consumption.

Chapter 6

Conclusion

Considered Consumption

"Boycott BP!" my friend Janelle wrote in her Facebook status, a few months after the 2010 Deepwater Horizon oil spill in the Gulf of Mexico. The oil was still gushing months after the drilling rig had exploded, and the prospects for both human and environmental well-being in the region looked grim. I sympathized with Janelle's call for a boycott: many were angry with British Petroleum (BP), the company who owned and operated the rig that exploded, and wished to withdraw financial support in hopes of convincing the company to do more to mitigate the effects of the spill. In fact, BP had topped the Sierra Club's "pick your poison" list as one of the "least bad" oil companies to patronize, but now, it seemed, everything had changed and many environmental activists wished to boycott the company.[1]

The same morning I saw Janelle's plea for a boycott, I had also read an article about the impossibility of boycotting an oil company. The complex process of drilling oil and creating gasoline involves such mixing, it seems, that no consumer can be sure that by avoiding the BP gas stations she avoids either oil extracted by BP or avoids sending some portion of the revenue to them.[2] It is a discouraging thought, for those who wish to be conscientious in their consumption: we simply cannot avoid a company whose practices we wish to censure. And yet it highlights both the complexity of the problems that Christian consumers face and the necessity for creative solutions. The best way to avoid BP gasoline, of course, is to avoid using gas altogether. But this requires a much bigger effort than simply choosing one gas station over another. It requires completely rethinking the way we pattern our lives.

FOUR CONSIDERATIONS

This book began by seeking to understand consumption and situate it in Christian lives. This was followed by a tour of Christian thought about consumption, organized according to four major considerations that arise in Christian thought about consumption. Invoking considerations such as avoiding sin and embracing creation, loving the neighbor and envisioning the future, Christians have been thinking about consumption for centuries. Catholics and Quakers, Lutherans and Orthodox, Seventh-day Adventists and evangelicals—many voices have weighed in, adding their own considerations to the conversation.

A conversation, however, may not be the most apt metaphor for what we see here. It is more helpful to think of these four considerations as four melodies discernible within a vast cacophony of reflection about consumption. The preceding chapters have already offered glimpses of the ways that these four melodies interact with and echo one another, such that together—all four at once—they form an astonishing harmony, or perhaps polyphony. Together, they operate like another kind of chorus, a Greek chorus that offers commentary on the content of our shared lives. Together, they create rich insights that none of them could have offered alone, and do so in a strong voice, albeit one that is not often so readily heard as that of a Greek chorus, nor as homogenous.

For example, *avoiding sin*, all alone, is certainly a recipe for careful consumption, but the care is primarily self-focused; *loving the neighbor* balances this consideration with some other-regard. *Avoiding sin* by itself also seems too grim to be appealing for any but the most disciplined Christians; *embracing creation* adds a much-needed note of celebration, and indeed gratitude, which *avoiding sin* may miss. *Embracing creation* seems a delightful way to approach consumption, but as chapter 3 demonstrated, it can easily be abused and become justified self-indulgence; adding considerations such as *avoiding sin* and *loving the neighbor* add vital realism and other-awareness. *Embracing creation* also is much helped by *envisioning the future*: what may have been a shallow appreciation for "what is" acquires depth in light of a robust yearning for "what ought to be."

Loving the neighbor and *envisioning the future* are each insufficient in their own ways. A recognition of the human propensity to sin and an awareness of the world's fallenness are vital to a thorough Christian understanding of consumption. And the will to embrace God's gifts and to find gratitude and joy in the created world offers a much-needed source of renewal and grounding to those who primarily seek to love the neighbor or envision the future. *Loving the neighbor* and *envisioning the future*, in fact, also operate in synergy, as a fulfilled world is characterized by abundant neighbor-love, and the culmination of true neighborly communion cannot happen without the grace-filled future fulfillment of the new creation.

Consumption that is consistent with the Christian tradition, then, should consider all four; for a Christian to judge an act of consumption as fully good, it should avoid sin, embrace creation, love the neighbor, and live into a vision of the future. Having seen them separated into four chapters, it may be difficult to envision them working in concert, so in the following pages I offer three examples of contemporary Christian thinkers whose work expresses all four considerations. Next, I discuss an ethics of discernment by using concrete examples of some types of consumption encountered by many North Americans. Finally, I revisit consumerism, delivering fresh insights for dealing with the social situation of consumption today.

CONSIDERATIONS WORKING TOGETHER: THREE CONTEMPORARY AUTHORS

The four considerations of Christian consumption ethics are my own invention, a heuristic typology intended to elucidate major positions in a complex field. None of the three contemporary authors I describe below was intentionally applying these four considerations as such. Rather, and much like in earlier chapters on particular considerations, I identify the use of all four considerations here in order to demonstrate how one person may adopt all of them in his or her thought, and how powerful such a strategy can be.

L. Shannon Jung

Alert readers may have noticed that although Jung was introduced in chapter 3, he made appearances in chapters 4 and 5 as well. Jung's thorough treatment of food consumption amply includes all four considerations. He discusses the need to avoid sin, embrace creation, love the neighbor, and anticipate the future in our consumption decisions.

Jung addresses the need to avoid sin in consumption when he discusses "eating disorders," broadly understood: eating too much, and too little, and within a disordered, sinful system of food production and distribution.[3] Jung is particularly concerned about the sin of complicity, the moral taint that rubs off on consumers who reap benefits from a food system that is unjust to others (food workers, animals, the earth).[4] Complicity is a problem partly because "as long as people anywhere are hungry for food, true happiness and well-being will elude us."[5] And happiness, deep enjoyment, and profound well-being are Jung's true concerns.

As noted in chapter 3, Jung speaks movingly of the importance of enjoying and savoring food. He writes, "The message is this: Live joyously; don't cheat yourself! God intends that we take delight in and share food and eating."[6] When discussing delight in food, Jung nearly always mentions sharing food. This is because, for him, good consumption occurs in light of others' well-being. Sharing with needy neighbors expresses the neighbor-love that is at the basis of Christian ethics. Jung believes the practice of sharing to be vital to human happiness. As he repeatedly asserts, *We were created in such a way that caring for the neighbor is essential to our well-being.*[7]

Jung offers a vision of a fulfilled world to strengthen his points, arguing that "we are to eat here ('on earth') as though we were eating in heaven."[8] Jung's is an immanent eschatology, affirming that though we may not see it clearly now, creation properly understood is already living out the "biblical vision of *Shalom*, . . . that all of creation is one, every creature in community with every other, living in harmony and security toward the joy and well-being of every other creature."[9] The way to enter into this fulfilled world, for Jung, lies in Christian eating practices such as saying grace, sharing, offering hospitality, feasting, and fasting.[10]

Jung's works on food are well received because they are both thoughtful and joyful. He has articulated a workable balance between avoiding sinful consumption and enjoying the blessings of food, enjoining his readers to take delight in their food, while at the same time remembering the very real opportunities for sin in food consumption. Jung's use of neighbor-love and eschatology adds depth to his discussion, offering reasons for his positions and situating his balance of avoidance and embrace within the framework of a robust Christian theology.

Elizabeth Theokritoff

Greek Orthodox scholar Elizabeth Theokritoff addresses consumption in her essay collection *Living in God's Creation: Orthodox Perspectives on Ecology*.[11] With an elegant clarity, Theokritoff understands consumption to be a necessary human action that is both potentially holy and potentially disastrous. Theokritoff spends a significant amount of time on the concept of asceticism, but she understands it in a broad way that encompasses the first three considerations: the need to avoid sin in consumption; the need to embrace, and properly value, God's creation; and the need to love the neighbor. For Theokritoff, a certain amount of detachment (the fruit of ascetic practice) is the prerequisite for truly loving God's creation. She writes:

> If we give up all attachments for the sake of God's love, only then are we able to love all of his creation in freedom, without needing to possess it or be possessed by it.[12] ... The materialistic person values things in relation to his own desire and appetite for them; detachment, by contrast, enables one to value things for themselves, as parts of God's creation. ... Asceticism is not an individual matter of self-improvement, but something profoundly communal: it has to do with how we use gifts bestowed for the benefit of all.[13] ... The ascetic aspect indicates that we walk lightly on the earth as we learn to distinguish need from greed. But ... this differs from a joyless Puritanism: the emphasis is not on *giving up* but on *giving thanks*.[14]

Theokritoff tells the story of a wise monk who ate his food extremely slowly. After a long, deliberate meal, he was finally asked why he eats in such an unhurried way. In his response, he explained that with each bite he pauses "to give praise for [God's] bounty" and to pray "on behalf of those who labor and sweat and toil to supply my need."[15] Theokritoff uses this story to demonstrate the value of disciplined consumption that is grateful and attends to the well-being of others. Sometimes, she acknowledges, we must sacrifice our own desires for the sake of others' well-being. But "if we can truly see ourselves as members of one body, we may learn to see personal sacrifice as gain rather than loss: for in this way the whole body can truly 'win.'"[16] Like Dorothy Day and the other voices in chapter 4, Theokritoff envisions neighbor-love expanding the self and shaping consumption choices.

Like other Orthodox thinkers, Theokritoff has a keen sense of eschatology and the sacramental use of creation. However, "just because human products can have a sacramental use," she writes, does not mean that "anything that we might do with the world is thereby given blanket legitimacy."[17] On the contrary, "our use of the world and its materials must be in one way or another an offering for God's glory."[18] She uses the example of an icon: this work of art, created from the materials of the earth and the talent and creativity of the painter, is a devotional tool that serves as a "window" for God's presence. In creating an icon, humans are clearly using natural materials for the glory of God; how many other human products could also be said to exist for God's glory? A "truly Eucharistic and sacramental ethos," she writes, "would totally transform the way Christians handle material goods."[19]

Theokritoff's treatment of consumption is clear and well balanced, and she handles the topic of asceticism in a way that is both simple and profound. I detect in her treatment a preference for the first consideration, *to avoid sin*, above the others, but the other criteria for judging consumption are certainly present in her writings. These other considerations offer a refreshing counterbalance to the emphasis on renouncing consumption through asceticism, and a clearer picture of what Christian ethics requires of good consumption.

James A. Nash

In the introduction, I mentioned the modalities of virtue ethics that underlie the ethics of consumption described in this book. So it is fitting to end with an exemplary study of the virtue of frugality, by Methodist ecotheologian James Nash.

In "Toward the Revival and Reform of the Subversive Virtue: Frugality," Nash writes, "Solutions to major social and ecological problems depend on the revival of this virtue and its re-formation from a personal virtue into a social norm."[20] Frugality, in Nash's understanding, means the responsible control of human desires, free from the manipulations of advertising and other forces that foster consumerism.[21] "Frugality," he writes, "denotes moderation, temperance, thrift, cost-effectiveness, efficient usage, and a satisfaction with material sufficiency."[22] But it is not the same as grim austerity. Nash affirms enjoyment too: "surely there are a number of occasions for justifiable indulgence—perhaps a festive frugality."[23] Nash styles frugality as a creative, dynamic middle ground between utter austerity and hedonistic indulgence.

> From a Christian perspective, frugality is a grateful affirmation of the biophysical in fidelity to the God who, as Creator, lovingly made the biophysical, who, as incarnated Christ, united lovingly with the biophysical, and who, as sacramentally present Spirit, dwells lovingly in the biophysical.[24]

But Nash does not stop with this nuanced balance of asceticism and enjoyment. He grounds it in an understanding of frugality as loving the neighbor.

> Thus, the essence of frugality is sacrifice for the sake of higher ends—in fact, for Christians, sacrifice for the sake of Christ's cause of love. This sacrifice is real. Some comforts and pleasures, some lesser values...must be given up. Frugality cannot be made pretty by denying the values lost. Nevertheless, frugality is a form of sacrifice that promises to bring fullness of being in solidarity.[25]

Nash echoes many of the Christian authors of chapter 4, who see loving the neighbor as a guiding norm justifying sacrifice and solidarity.

Interestingly, Nash's notion of frugality includes concern for future generations; he discusses "an extension of the covenant of solidarity to the future."[26] He addresses "sustainability" as an essential component of frugality, and envisions a more just and sustainable world that would come about as a result of the widespread adoption of this virtue—in the long term. In the short term, he admits, "It is a formula for market depression."[27] But Nash defends his vision of a better, frugal, world. "The task of ethics is not to adapt reasonable norms to fit current practices, but rather to challenge and enable societies to adapt their practices to fit these norms."[28] This idealism has an eschatological ring to it, clearly less concerned with what works now than with what should be, ultimately.

Nash makes a persuasive case for the revival of frugality as a personal virtue and a social norm. He covers all four considerations of Christian consumption in his discussion, balancing asceticism and enjoyment with a grounding in love, sacrifice, and a vision of the future. "When freed from distortions," he writes, "frugality seems to be one of the cardinal virtues of our age. As an expression of love, frugality is an indispensable instrument of social and ecological justice and sustainability."[29]

Sunday Dinner with Jung, Theokritoff, and Nash

Though there is something messy and open-ended about consumption ethics—we rarely find the perfect product or ideal item to consume—that messiness can lead to creativity as well. Creativity, particularly the use of the imagination, is vital to ethical reflection. John Woolman, when determining whether to boycott silver, convinced himself of the gravity of the situation by envisioning the plight of the workers in the silver mine.[30] His ability to imagine it vividly evoked an emotional reaction in him that strengthened his resolve to avoid complicity in the abuses of silver miners. All of us, not just saints like Woolman, benefit from the use of imagination as we hypothetically "try on" ethical options.

On that note, let us imagine that we are inviting Jung, Theokritoff, and Nash to Sunday dinner.[31] In so doing, we can imagine ways to apply their ethical frameworks to practical decisions. What shall we serve? What would all three of these thinkers enjoy consuming together?

Given that it is Sunday dinner, perhaps we should serve food that can be prepared ahead of time, so that the Sabbath-like Sunday can be observed in relative peace: how about soup? Soup is simple, which would probably suit Nash's call for frugality, though he does not eschew some degree of festivity. Jung especially appreciates delicious food, so we had better choose a flavorful soup. Black bean lime chili, perhaps, or a rich, wintry borscht. All three authors care about the sourcing of our consumption, so a soup that can be made with produce from the garden or the farmer's market would be ideal. Bread complements soup well, but I am not much of a bread baker, and artisanal bakeries are scarce in this area; still, the bakery within walking distance does make delicious bread (though they ship the dough in from California)—maybe that will do. We can serve little tastes of this and that—all three would agree that quality trumps quantity in consumption. Perhaps my friend's violet jam could top the bread, and some of those strawberry preserves we kept from the summer.

What shall we drink? One of the less mature local wines? Tap water? Local milk may be our best bet—delicious and sustainable—but some water or wine may be appropriate as well. Perhaps even a wine from California, to acknowledge Jung's desire for good taste, although there is something to be said for seeking to appreciate this place, even if it does produce less interesting wine. Probably not a wine from Europe, as we are west of the geographical divide in the United States that makes the carbon footprint of wine from California smaller than that from Europe.[32] They all might approve of the top-shelf boxed wines that reduce the shipping footprint, even if there are only a few such varieties available in local stores.

Shall we serve dessert? Would Nash think it too indulgent? Would Jung find that its absence diminishes his holy joy? Perhaps Theokritoff can help us. She writes about consumption as communal, as taking into account the needs of all. What if we made a dessert with fair trade chocolate, fair trade sugar, fair trade vanilla, local flour, local milk, and local eggs? We'd be remembering the needs of our neighbors, near and far, while creating a joyful experience for ourselves. I believe even Nash would acquiesce to try our new recipe for neighbor-love chocolate cake.

The meal will begin with a prayer, of course—Jung and Theokritoff both write of the importance of giving thanks, and such dedication of the food may support Theokritoff's vision of sacramental consumption. We hope she will agree that our use of the world, in eating this meal, is "an offering for God's glory," an icon of sorts. Since this will be Sunday dinner, we may have already experienced the Eucharist, but perhaps our meal can prolong it, the way early Christians did with their agape meals. Jung would certainly approve, given his support for a fuller, more robust eucharistic experience and the sacramental dimension of everyday eating. The joy we have in sharing our food can remind us of the joy we feel in consuming, and being consumed by, Christ's body.

We will savor and enjoy our meal, discussing its contents and tastes. This entails a kind of extended thanksgiving: beyond the blessing before the meal, we show our gratitude by attending to the details of our meal and expressing our delight and wonder as we enjoy its flavor. Jung, Theokritoff, and Nash would all agree with the importance of savoring and giving thanks as we consume our food. We will show the guests we care about them by explaining our considerations as we chose the menu, and by being attentive to their needs (be sure to offer everyone seconds on soup!). Theokritoff may suggest that we enhance our gratitude by observing the meal in silence, while Jung would probably prefer the celebratory atmosphere of a fiesta, with music and other friends joining the meal. Perhaps Nash can help us achieve a balance between the two, and encourage us to find satisfaction in sufficiency.

I never know how much food to prepare, and usually make too much. These three probably do not eat great volumes, but it is better to have leftovers than to run out, because being hospitable means being generous, and if we have the ingredients on hand, it is usually more efficient to cook a larger meal, anyway. We could make extra for Sunday dinner, and take the remainder to church for the Wednesday meal. The leftover cake might create a good opportunity to ring the doorbells of others on our street whom we see mostly in passing in order to offer them some dessert.

Perhaps it is clear by now that there is more at stake here than menu planning. Such exercises of imagination are ethical practices. The fourth consideration, envisioning the future, derives its ethical salience from the moral power of hopeful imagination. We cast our nets forward into time, asking ourselves "what if...?" and we gather them in, sorting through the possibilities we've gathered. Imagination is a space in which to integrate the different considerations, including those that seem contradictory, and synthesize them into practice, similar to the way Nash treats frugality as a creative space between hedonism and austerity. Before we can consume differently, we must be able to visualize doing so, and use this practice to help us discern well.

AN ETHICS OF DISCERNMENT

As a species of stewardship ethics, consumption ethics is situated and holistic, asking Christians to examine their entire lives—all the ways in which the world's materials flow into and out of their purview—and evaluate them in ways that may entail changing long-term habits and modes of being. As an ethic that focuses on choice (if we have no choice, our consumption decisions are hardly subject to moral evaluation), consumption ethics is concerned with how we arrive at our decisions, offering guidelines for the discernment of proper consumption choices. Consumption begins with desire and ends with an action of consuming; in-between is the decision whether to honor the desire by acting on it and, if so, what form that action will take.

This way of doing ethics differs from the conventional modes of moral reasoning. Moral philosopher Margaret Urban Walker calls these modes (deontology, utilitarianism, and the like) the "*theoretical-juridical model* of morality and moral theory," which poses discrete conundrums that may be neatly solved by the application of rules and principles.[33] The ethics of consumption I propose, by contrast, unearths messy, complex problems and seeks open-ended solutions that may require systemic changes in habits and attitudes, while continually questing for better and more complete ways to address problems that may never be completely solved. Walker's preferred, feminist mode of moral reasoning, the "expressive-collaborative model," resembles the ethics of consumption I articulate here.[34] The emphasis on habits and dispositions to act in a certain way also resembles virtue ethics. I am less interested in naming particular virtues, as some virtue ethicists do, than I am in examining the habits of thought and patterns of behavior that underlie virtuous consumption.

Issues of ethical consumption bear a complexity and particularity that may be best treated in this messy, conversational way. Like the principles in Beauchamp and Childress's *Principles of Biomedical Ethics*, the four considerations described in this book aid discernment by naming major concepts to bear in mind or important ideas to mentally rehearse when choosing a course of action. In the ideal case, every consideration would be amply met: everything I consume would help me to be free of sin, would allow me to embrace creation, would express love of my neighbor, and would participate in the future glory of a fulfilled world. But this ideal is rarely the reality. Virtually every act of consumption leads me into some kind of sin, and I am more likely to take creation for granted than to consciously embrace it as a gift from God. In a complex society, I can hardly know all the neighbors impacted by my consumption, much less love them. And the glimpses of God's reign that may shine through as I consume may go unnoticed or unidentified, and may not flourish as they ought. With complex problems like the multiple ethical impacts of an act of consumption, the solutions will be, at best, partial.

"Almost daily," write Beauchamp and Childress, "we confront situations that force us to choose among conflicting values in our personal lives."[35] In these cases, as in most cases concerning consumption, we must pay careful attention to the situation at hand, recall the relevant considerations from Christian ethics, attempt to specify what each consideration requires, balance them against one another, and choose appropriate priorities among them.[36] Each of the four considerations has value. Though I have listed them in a particular order, this should not imply that the first, or the last, take priority. If they do conflict in a particular situation, and one consideration "wins" over another, this should not be taken as an indication that one is better than another. The ideal is to attend to all four.

The process of discernment is difficult. Beauchamp and Childress refer to discernment as a virtue that "brings sensitive insight, astute judgment, and understanding to action."[37] Discernment is the central task of all Christian ethics, as individuals integrate different, often conflicting, ethical viewpoints and priorities from a variety of Christian sources. The task is to arrive at satisfactory choices that honor, even as they may fail to completely fulfill, all of these moral influences. Beauchamp and Childress associate wise discernment with the virtue of prudence, the ability to make "fitting judgments," and act on those judgments.[38] Frameworks for judgment, such as the typology of four considerations described in this book, are aids to discernment that help support, and even form, habits of prudence. The task of navigating complex sets of ethical considerations is aided not only by prudence and typologies but also by the exercise of imagination, which brings us to another set of hypothetical examples.

SOME EXAMPLES: TRANSPORTATION AND MEAT

Suppose that I have agreed to meet a friend downtown for lunch, and I live a few miles away, closer to the edge of town. How shall I get there?

As a relatively affluent and healthy North American, I own a car, a bicycle, and good shoes, giving me three options that result from prior consumption decisions. If I use the car, I will be consuming gasoline to get there. I have a fourth option—the bus—which also implies the consumption of gasoline. What is my thought process in determining how best to meet my friend?

My first thought is probably the third consideration: love of neighbor. What does love require in this situation? Because I love my friend, I have agreed to meet her. Because I love her, I hope to get there on time (excessive lateness would be disrespectful of her time and would strain our relationship). In this midwestern town, where traffic is not a problem but bus schedules are sparse, a car or a bike would be the surest way to get there on time. But there are others I also love, who figure into this decision: loving my family means respecting our tight budget. The least expensive ways to get downtown are human powered: walking and biking. Loving my family also means not taking undue risks on my bicycle (since an accident would cause anguish and expense), but in this place the streets are safe and the traffic sparse, so the risk seems low.

And then there is the community as a whole to consider. In my more generalized love of this community, I would prefer to travel in a way that allows me to meet and greet neighbors and strangers. The slow pace of walking is ideal for strengthening my relationship with this place. Additionally, I believe the bus system to be an important but underutilized mode of transport, a system that serves the community. Perhaps I should take the bus, to support the transit system and to express solidarity with those few who do ride the buses here. (Typically the bus patrons are neighbors who cannot afford a car, or who have disabilities that prevent them from driving.) Both walking and riding the bus put me in more contact with neighbors than driving does.

An important factor in transportation, however, is the weather. The second consideration of consumption prompts me to find ways to embrace creation, including my own needs as a creature and my own dignity as a child of God. Today, the temperature is fine, but while the skies are clear now, rain has been predicted for later. This means that if I travel by bicycle I need to be willing to get wet (since my bike has no fenders). Walking may also mean I'll get somewhat wet, but I usually enjoy a walk in the rain if I have remembered my umbrella. Valuing creation also prompts me to think about air pollution and good stewardship of natural resources; the car is not a good choice in this respect. My body is part of creation, and embracing its need for exercise—and anticipating the joy of eating lunch once I have worked up an appetite—makes walking or biking look like excellent options.

As someone who tries to observe a weekly Sabbath and partakes of the Eucharist regularly, I have a sense of readiness for the kingdom of God. For me, this means freedom from stress, worry, and hurrying; it means a sense of being part of a larger whole that is moving toward something better; and it means feeling in my bones the "already" potential in this "not-yet" world. As noted in chapter 5, the actual elaboration of this consideration can be idiosyncratic and vague, but nevertheless it is an important, guiding factor. How might my transporting myself downtown contribute to the world's fulfillment? If I am thinking of the fulfillment of nonhuman nature, avoiding pollution through fossil fuels is a good idea. But in addition, I believe that in the reign of God, none of us need to hurry; this helps me muster the patience required for the slower modes of transport such as walking or waiting for the bus. If I see the world's fulfillment as a beloved community of saints, I may seek ways to connect with my neighbors as I get downtown (which favors walking and bus riding).

But finally, I need to remember the first consideration and find ways to avoid sin. Eschewing fossil fuels may allow me to feel free of complicity in environmental evils, but there are other ways to sin in consumption. If I attach great pride to the fact that I avoided using my car, this is also a sin. I could equally seek to gain attention by showing off the excellent new bicycle I purchased, riding it ostentatiously by my neighbors' houses—this, too, courts sin. Ronald Sider might counsel me to transport myself in a way that saves money, by walking or bicycling, so I can give the excess to the poor. Woolman might wonder about the treatment of the bus drivers, and whether paying the fare (which is fairly cheap) might contribute to their underpayment (or, by contrast, whether avoiding the bus might mean layoffs).

These four considerations, as specified for this case, could lead me to any of these four modes of transportation. None is perfect. Walking risks my being late, getting wet, and taking too much time. Biking is more solitary and makes me more prone to getting wet. The bus costs money and fossil fuels (less than the car—at least, if the bus is fairly full), and risks my lateness and taking too much time. The car, of course, pollutes and is isolating. As with nearly every consumption decision, the dilemma is between the lesser of evils or, conversely, the greater of goods. For every option also contains some good. I can get exercise with walking and biking. I can meet my community with walking and bus riding. With the bike and the car, I can be timely in my arrival and flexible enough to run other errands while I'm out. On balance, in this situation, it looks like the car is the least ideal option and walking (if I can make the time for it) is the most ideal.

But even the above scenario, which seems quite complex, is over-simplified—there may be many other options available: perhaps another friend is going that direction and has offered me a ride; perhaps I also could use a motorcycle, a scooter, or a canoe; perhaps I intend to get groceries on my way home, which are too heavy for a bike or the bus; perhaps a genuine self-love indicates that I desperately need the peace and quiet I can get by driving alone; and so forth. With a different consumption scenario—for example, one that involves shopping for clothes, housewares, or food—such considerations become even more complex, in the choice among stores, producers, and products; quantities, sources, and destinations; and the responsible use of one's financial resources.

It is helpful to have a guide—to walk myself through all four considerations, mentally, as I make this decision. But by the time I have actually thought through all of the above, I may be late to meet my friend! As with nearly all consumption decisions, some options (typically the most environmentally sound ones) take more time than others. And this is why the true nature of this ethic of consumption is not to solve conundrums like the above but rather to address habits, structures, and choices that underlie the patterns of consumption in human lives. Many previous consumption decisions built up to this particular question about how to get myself downtown: if I had not already bought a car or a bike, those would not be available for my consideration. If I had chosen to live closer to downtown, the convenience of the non-car options would increase relative to the convenience of the car. I cannot, in the moment of need, decide that I should ride a bicycle if I do not already have one.

At another time, apart from any immediate need to transport myself, I should reflect on my typical transportation habits and my options in this regard. But the reflection should not end here.

To truly inculcate these habits, I will need the right environment: it is easier to drive less when living by a bus stop with frequent service; it is easier to bicycle when I own the proper equipment and keep it in good working order. Like a dieter stocking the kitchen with healthy foods, I need to set up my lifestyle in such a way that it is relatively easy and obvious to act on the consumption decisions I have determined to be right.

There are ways to make choices that "set up" the consumer for virtuous consumption. For example, Community-Supported Agriculture (CSA) is a subscription program allowing households to receive weekly food delivered directly from local farms. Consumers pay an up-front investment and receive their food in installments—thereby setting up a long-term consumption pattern (a continually stocked fridge full of produce) with an incentive to continue (the up-front investment). When my refrigerator is full of fresh fruit, and I know I will get more delivered shortly, I am less likely to reach for the candy bar: I may even feel some (salutary) pressure to eat the fruit before it spoils. The CSA model has many advantages consonant with the four considerations of consumption: the local, often organic food is good for the environment and healthful; it offers a rich opportunity for consumers to enjoy and celebrate the earth's bounty; it establishes a relationship with the farmers who grow the food; and the community and ecological harmony it entails may represent a foretaste of a fulfilled creation. But the key is the presence of a structure that inculcates certain consumption habits in a context of accountability to others.

An ethics of consumption, then, urges Christians to consume well, in part, by actively setting up our lives in such a way as to allow for consumption that loves neighbors, consumption that participates in God's reign, consumption that avoids sin and embraces creation. These are habits of thought and dispositions to action that can be cultivated in the general sense, rather than separate decisions to be made. If I live near the bus stop and have the schedule memorized, it is no great feat to avoid using my car—I am in the habit of taking the bus and I order my life accordingly. While sometimes Christian, ethical consumption simply requires choosing the "right" product off a shelf, it often speaks to longer-term habits and structures of daily life.

Here is another example, not of a specific consumption choice but a general policy in my life: should I make a habit of eating animals as food?

The fourth consideration would argue against it. As Andrew Linzey indicates in his book *Animal Gospel,* a fulfilled world emulates "the peaceable kingdom," in which interspecies violence has ceased: "The wolf shall live with the lamb, the leopard shall lie down with the kid, the calf and the lion and the fatling together, and a little child shall lead them" (Isaiah 11:6). "The truth is," writes Linzey, "human beings can now approximate the peaceable kingdom by living without killing sentients for food."[39] Since we can do so, Linzey argues, we should eschew animal protein in our diets. Linzey believes that humans, uniquely among creatures, can transcend the "natural" impulse to predation and live as God intends us to live, without harming other creatures.

But the third consideration adds a different dimension to this question. If I do consider nonhuman animals to be my neighbors, and accept the charge to love them, then it is almost inconceivable that killing them for food equates to loving them. And yet, as the bumper sticker says, "I love animals—they taste great!" Is it possible to love what we consume, and still consume it? Perhaps. Sergei Bulgakov would say that consuming something nonhuman is a way to answer its yearning to become more human, to become closer to God. Additionally, eating animals may play a role in loving other humans: it saves no animal lives if I reject the chicken potpie offered to me by my elderly aunt. In fact, it risks offending her. (If I'd told her in advance I didn't want chicken, of course, she might not have bought it, and this would save animal lives, but in this moment the deed has been done and the chicken is already on the table.) It certainly would offend my host in a visit to Haiti if I refused to eat the goat that he and his family had graciously, and at great cost to themselves, prepared for me. Human offense may be a more minor grievance than an animal's loss of life, but when it comes to establishing and maintaining loving relationships, it is significant.

Embracing creation entails a concern for proper stewardship, and most (but not all) meat production has egregious environmental ills associated with it.[40] Still, this consideration also entails sensuous enjoyment of nature's bounty—which for many people includes enjoying delicious meat dishes. The second consideration also includes an understanding of humans as "royal persons," blessed children of God, which may be interpreted to mean that our enjoyment of meat matters more than animals' lives. John Schneider, savoring his barbeque dinner on his back deck, was probably not eating veggie burgers. If undertaken in moderation and with proper gratitude, Jung would argue, there is no great sin in meat eating.

But the first consideration, avoiding sin, overwhelmingly comes down on the side of avoiding meat. Vegetarian eating was one form of fasting in Francis's time, and he almost never ate meat himself. Even Sider recommends "substituting vegetable protein for animal protein" as a way of diminishing the family food budget (to free up extra money, which can then be given to the poor).[41] For those concerned about complicity in environmental harm, avoiding meat is a good way to guarantee relatively clean hands.[42]

On balance, the arguments seem to indicate that I should make a habit of avoiding meat consumption, or at least being quite selective about the meat I do eat. But there are particular situations—health scenarios that require eating copious protein, contexts of poverty or hospitality where choices are constrained—in which this balance may be tipped. In effect, it comes down to the relative value of humans versus animals; if they do not count as neighbors to be loved, if my enjoyment outweighs their lives, then eating meat is solely an environmental concern, and I should simply restrict myself to relatively "green" meat options.

The discernment of ethical consumption choices may seem overwhelming, and even impossible, and it is hard to be satisfied with the often uncertain or provisional nature of the conclusions. Augustine holds that, in the realm of morality, God does not ask Christians to perform impossible tasks.[43] This is not to say that everything that Christian ethics exhorts is humanly attainable. Rather, Augustine holds that God actively helps believers to attain the levels of perfection demanded.[44] It is in this spirit of making a humble attempt, knowing that my efforts will be incomplete but trusting in God's help, that discernment of consumption decisions should occur. And such discernment cannot happen well without adequate time for reflection and exploration of different options.

This discernment also should not happen alone. In this book, I have primarily discussed individual consumption decisions, but I hope that this ethics of consumption can guide group decision making too. A congregation, for example, making decisions about electricity or paper consumption, can also be guided by the four considerations of avoiding sin, enjoying the earth's bounty and stewarding resources, heeding relationships, and aligning with God's ultimate plan. Many of the habits that ethical consumption requires can be better cultivated in communities than alone; we do well to consider these questions in groups and offer support to one another in the shifts of attitude and practice that are often required as we move toward virtuous consumption.

CONSUMERISM REVISITED

In chapter 1, I asserted that this is not a book about consumerism, but about consumption. While that is true, consumerism and the attendant problems of excess consumption form both my motivation for examining the topic and the context in which contemporary North American Christians operate. Consumerism complicates the task of considerate consumption in the contemporary context.

At its root, consumerism arises from a distorted view of human nature. This ethos teaches that our wants are insatiable (and the provocations of advertising help to make this so), that buying a new article of clothing or fancy gadget will answer our deepest longings, that we *are* what we *own*. Humans, then, are seen as greedy and lacking and shallow. To the degree that we believe this, we are under the thrall of consumerism, rather than following the teachings of Christianity.

The four considerations described in this book address this anthropology problem by offering a different view of humanity: we are prone to sin but called to renounce it; we are creatures who can and should delight in creation; we are neighbors who can love ourselves and one another; and we are denizens of the new creation, who can and should align our actions with those of a fulfilled world. We are not—or need not be—greedy, lacking, and shallow. We do not have to believe what consumerism tells us, because Christianity has an alternate view of human nature.

Theologian Vincent Miller has written about the interaction between religion and consumerism, articulating the concern that Christians who see themselves as consumers "encounter the elements of tradition in an abstract, fragmented form and are trained to engage them as passive consumers."[45] For those concerned that Christians are ignoring the depths of their own tradition, I offer this book as one example of the rich insights to be gained by those who seek it. Consumption may seem to be a topic best treated by other sources or other fields of study, but the Christian tradition offers robust insights into contemporary problems faced by consumers. Miller argues that, for religion, "the only way forward is through consumer culture, by embracing grassroots agency."[46] He wishes to "encourage and deepen religious agency, to give people the formation and responsibility necessary to engage their traditions creatively as mature practitioners."[47]

By offering readers in-depth analysis and multiple resources, I hope that this book can contribute to Miller's goal of deepening personal agency. I offer Christian consumers a journey into the depth of insight present in their own tradition and an education in the concepts and practices that can equip them to make conscientious choices in the midst of consumer culture.

The four considerations outlined in this book indicate that although consumption can be tricky and fraught, it is possible to consume in ways that honor God and generate delight and flourishing in ourselves and the rest of the world. Achieving this in a time and place substantially influenced by consumerism is a challenge, but we do not face it empty-handed. Equipped with resources from the Christian tradition, aids to discernment, and visions of virtue, with help from others and with grace from God, we can consume both Christianly and well.

NOTES

Introduction

1. Stephanie Kaza, "Penetrating the Tangle," in Kaza, ed., *Hooked! Buddhist Writings on Greed, Desire, and the Urge to Consume* (Boston: Shambhala, 2005), 139.
2. Ibid.
3. John F. Kavanaugh, *Following Christ in a Consumer Society: The Spirituality of Cultural Resistance, 25th Anniversary Edition* (Maryknoll, N.Y.: Orbis, 2006), 185.
4. The Episcopal Church, *1979 Book of Common Prayer, Economy Edition* (New York: Oxford University Press, 2008), Eucharistic Prayer C, 370.
5. Alan Aldridge outlines three ways of defining consumerism: as a social movement (activism on behalf of consumers), as a way of life ("living to consume"), and as an ideology (supporting free-market capitalism). My definition most resembles his second category (Alan Aldridge, *Consumption* [Cambridge: Polity Press, 2003], 6).

    Peter Stearns defines consumerism as characteristic of "a society in which many people formulate their goals in life partly through acquiring goods that they clearly do not need for subsistence or traditional display" (Peter N. Stearns, *Consumerism in World History: The Global Transformation of Desire* [New York: Routledge, 2006], vii). He also offers a thorough treatment of the ways that consumption can vary across different times and places, with an exemplary sensitivity to context.
6. See, notably, David Loy, "The Religion of the Market," *Journal of the American Academy of Religion* 65, no. 2 (1997): 275–90; W. Fred Graham,

"America's Other Religion," *Christian Century* (March 17, 1982): 306–8; Craig Bartholomew and Thorsten Moritz, eds., *Christ and Consumerism: Critical Reflections on the Spirit of Our Age* (Carlisle: Paternoster, 2000), 177.

7. See, for example, Vincent J. Miller, "Taking Consumer Culture Seriously," *Horizons* 27, no. 2 (2000): 276–95; and Jennifer Rycenga, "Dropping in for the Holidays: Christmas as Commercial Ritual at the Precious Moments Chapel," in *God in the Details: American Religion in Popular Culture*, ed. Eric Michael Mazur (New York: Routledge, 2001), 139–53.

8. See Rodney Clapp, "The Theology of Consumption and the Consumption of Theology: Toward a Christian Response to Consumerism," in *Consuming Passion: Christianity and the Consumer Culture*, ed. Rodney Clapp (Downers Grove, Ill.: InterVarsity, 1998), 188, 192; James A. Nash, "Toward the Revival and Reform of the Subversive Virtue: Frugality," *Annual of the Society of Christian Ethics* (1995): 140, 151–52; and Owens's treatment of the Sabbath as a "counter pedagogy of desire" in L. Roger Owens, "Sabbath-Keeping: Christian Sabbath-Keeping and the Desire for Justice," in *Vital Christianity: Spirituality, Justice, and Christian Practice*, eds. David L. Weaver-Zercher and William H. Willimon (New York: T&T Clark, 2005), 202, 209.

9. See Clifford A. Jones Sr., "How a Christian African-American Reflects on Stewardship in a Consumer-Oriented Society," in Clapp, *Consuming Passion*, 151–66; Robert A. Kelly, "Lutheranism as Counterculture? The Doctrine of Justification and Consumer Capitalism," *LWF Documentation*, no. 45 (March 2000): 209–12.

10. Sallie McFague, *Life Abundant: Rethinking Theology and Economy for a Planet in Peril* (Minneapolis: Fortress, 2001), 96.

11. Aldridge, *Consumption*, 14.

12. Lizabeth Cohen, *A Consumers' Republic: The Politics of Mass Consumption in Postwar America* (New York: Knopf, 2003), 8.

13. Jo Littler, *Radical Consumption: Shopping for Change in Contemporary Culture* (New York: Open University Press, 2009), 8.

14. See, for example, Charles Mathewes, "On Using the World," in *Having: Property and Possession in Religious and Social Life*, ed. William Schweiker and Charles Mathewes (Grand Rapids, Mich.: Eerdmans, 2004), 189–221. Mathewes addresses the Augustinian "use vs. enjoyment" contrast.

15. This book does not address the question of waste in any significant way. Readers interested in the topic would benefit from consulting Gay Hawkins's *The Ethics of Waste: How We Relate to Rubbish* (Lanham, Md.: Rowman & Littlefield, 2006).

16. See, for example, Herman E. Daly and Joshua Farley, *Ecological Economics: Principles and Applications* (Washington, D.C.: Island, 2003), 6.

17. Thorstein Veblen's *The Theory of the Leisure Class* (1899), which coined the phrase "conspicuous consumption," and Mary Douglas and Baron Isherwood's *The World of Goods* (1979) are two classic instances of this position.

18. Quoted in Adam Daniel Finnerty, *No More Plastic Jesus: Global Justice and Christian Lifestyle* (Maryknoll, N.Y.: Orbis, 1977), 167.

19. Mary Douglas and Baron Isherwood, *The World of Goods* (New York: Basic, 1979), 62.

20. Fred Pearce, *The Coming Population Crash and Our Planet's Surprising Future* (Boston: Beacon, 2010), 204.

21. Wendell Berry, "Getting Along with Nature," *Home Economics* (Berkeley, Calif.: Counterpoint, 1987), 15.

22. Some nonhuman animals do consume beyond their basic animal needs—the typical overweight housecat is a case in point. But usually these animals overconsume in captivity—they are in a human-ordained context. Without human influence, it is unclear whether animals would consume in excess—and indeed, whether an opportunity to do so would even be present. A situation of long-term excess and abundance, it seems, is something created exclusively by humans (and by God, in some Christian perspectives).

23. Aldridge notes that the "neutral, abstract usage" of consumption as a term for economic acquisition "passed into general use in the mid-twentieth century, and has since become dominant" (Aldridge, *Consumption*, 2).

24. Of the many good descriptions of the unique pressures and challenges of consuming in the contemporary world, Bauman's is particularly thorough (Zygmunt Bauman, *Work, Consumerism, and the New Poor* [Buckingham: Open University Press, 1998], 23–44).

25. See, for example, Stearns, *Consumerism in World History*; Bauman, *Work, Consumerism, and the New Poor*; Daniel Miller, ed., *Acknowledging Consumption: A Review of New Studies* (London: Routledge, 1995).

26. Kaza, *Hooked!* 6.

27. Ibid.

28. David T. Schwartz, *Consuming Choices: Ethics in a Global Consumer Age* (Lanham, Md.: Rowman & Littlefield, 2010), 4.

29. Ibid., 85.

30. Ibid., 86.

31. Ibid., 107.

32. Ibid.

33. Ibid., 111, 110.

34. Daniel Goleman, *Ecological Intelligence: How Knowing the Hidden Impacts of What We Buy Can Change Everything* (New York: Broadway, 2009), 14.

35. Ibid., 79–82.
36. Ibid., 113.
37. Christopher Decker, for example, advocates the virtue of chastity in a world whose economy seems dependent on the vice of lust. "Selling Desire: Would a Return to Christian Virtue Cause a Recession?" *Christianity Today* (April 4, 1994): 37–38.
38. Jay McDaniel, "Christianity and the Pursuit of Wealth," *Anglican Theological Review* 69, no. 4 (October 1987): 358.
39. Jaydee Hanson, "God's Vision of Abundant Living," *Christian Social Action* 12 (1999): 14.
40. Bill McKibben, "Returning God to the Center: Consumerism and the Environmental Threat," in Clapp, *Consuming Passion*, 44. McKibben's faith manifests in many of his writings, notably in his treatment of the book of Job (*The Comforting Whirlwind: God, Job, and the Scale of Creation* [Cambridge, Mass.: Cowley, 2005]).
41. Michael Schut, "The Great Economy/The Big Economy: Can We Make a Difference as We Confront the Global Economy, Poverty, and Ecological Degradation?" *Christian Social Action* 10 (June 1997): 36; William E. Gibson, "The Lifestyle of Christian Faithfulness," in *Beyond Survival: Bread and Justice in Christian Perspective*, ed. Dieter T. Hessel (New York: Friendship, 1977), 128; Michael Foley, "The Poverty of Enough: Reflections on a Moral Obligation," *Sojourners* 12, no. 8 (September 1983): 20–22; Nash, "Toward the Revival and Reform of the Subversive Virtue," 137–60.
42. David Schelhaas in Schut, "The Great Economy/The Big Economy," 12.
43. Tsvi Blanchard, "After Eden: The Search for the Holy in a Consumer Society," in Clapp, *Consuming Passion*, 106.
44. Wendell Berry, *Home Economics* (San Francisco: North Point, 1987), 144.
45. Erwin Wiens, "Christian Life-Style in an Affluent Society," in *The Believers' Church in Canada: Addresses and Papers from the Study Conference in Winnipeg, May 15–18, 1978*, ed. Jarold K. Zeman and Walter Klaasen, with John D. Rempel (Waterloo, Ont.: Waterloo, 1979), 307–8.
46. William Gibson writes, "Because consumerism is a phony substitute for, and therefore a barrier to, community, a reaffirmation of community helps to free us from consumerism, just as a reduction of consumption helps to free us for community" (Gibson, "The Lifestyle of Christian Faithfulness," 138).
47. William T. Cavanaugh, *Being Consumed: Economics and Christian Desire* (Grand Rapids: Eerdmans, 2008), 57.
48. I am not speaking of typological biblical interpretation, but rather a typology that groups or classifies diverse ideas into broad categories in order to better understand them.

49. James M. Gustafson, *Christ and the Moral Life* (New York: Harper & Row, 1968), 5.
50. Ibid.
51. John Howard Yoder, "How H. Richard Niebuhr Reasoned: A Critique of *Christ and Culture*," in *Authentic Transformation: A New Vision of Christ and Culture*, ed. Glen H. Stassen, D. M. Yeager, and John Howard Yoder (Nashville: Abingdon, 1996), 48.
52. Tom L. Beauchamp and James F. Childress, *Principles of Biomedical Ethics*, 6th ed. (New York: Oxford University Press, 2009).
53. See www.newdream.org.

Chapter 2

1. *What Would Jesus Buy?* a documentary about Reverend Billy and the Church of Life After Shopping, formerly the Church of Stop Shopping, was released in 2007. See http://www.wwjbmovie.com/and http://www.revbilly.com/.
2. He writes in a manual for others who seek to follow his example, "The key is: perform ANYWHERE YOU CAN. We have sung in Planning Commission meetings, precinct station houses, at gas pumps, in cemeteries, and generally anywhere there are too many cars or cash registers" (Reverend Billy, *What Would Jesus Buy?: Fabulous Prayers in the Face of the Shopocalypse* [New York: PublicAffairs, 2006], 83).
3. Brad Tytel, "Changeallujah: The Reluctant Religion of Reverend Billy," *The Revealer*, November 28, 2005, accessed May 5, 2006, http://www.therevealer.org/archives/timeless_002248.php (no longer present on the Web site).
4. There is, in fact, an interesting proto-theology behind this practice:

    When we back away—literally reach out for, even hold, pause, and then retreat—from a product, or an advertisement, or a cash register, then the magic happens. The soul and the body do a double take as the addiction is lifted. That's when all the stuck stuff can move. Consumerism congeals our insides, imprisons our godsightings [*sic*].... When the signal comes in that the way is clear, all sorts of experiences—dreams and traumas and glories—rise up. (Reverend Billy, *What Would Jesus Buy?* 87)

5. Bill Talen, "Beatitudes of Buylessness," *Reverend Billy and the Church of Life After Shopping*, December 2007, accessed Nov. 2, 2010, http://www.revbilly.com/work/music/songs/beatitudes-of-buylessness.

6. Talen prays to the "God That Is Not A Product," rails against "a culture led by Consumerism and apocalyptic Christianity—the twin fundamentalisms that overwhelm governments, silence creative culture or any noncommercial Life, and make routine the crying out of a world of victims," and recites, "We believe in the God that people who don't believe in God believe in" (Reverend Billy, *What Would Jesus Buy?* 18, 56, 58).

7. In addition to the thinkers profiled in this chapter, this attitude can be seen in the work of Basil of Caesarea, Ambrose of Milan, Augustine of Hippo, Anthony and the other desert fathers of monasticism, Bernard of Clairvaux and other Cistercian reformers, Menno Simons and other Anabaptist reformers, John Wesley, Jonathan Edwards, Søren Kierkegaard, Karl Barth, and many contemporary theologians. In fact, this attitude of renunciation and censure is not absent from many Christian thinkers whose work is featured in later chapters, as exemplars of other themes: Thomas Aquinas, Martin Luther, Dorothy Day, Sallie McFague, and Norman Wirzba.

8. Maria Antonaccio, "Asceticism and the Ethics of Consumption," *Journal of the Society of Christian Ethics* 26, no. 1 (2006): 80.

9. Francis was probably influenced by these movements, seeing them firsthand on his travels with his father's business (Donald Spoto, *Reluctant Saint: The Life of Francis of Assisi* [New York: Viking Compass, 2002], 22, 24). See also James M. Powell, "Francis of Assisi," in *Encyclopedia of Monasticism*, ed. William M. Johnston (London: Fitzroy Dearborn, 2000), 497–98.

10. See, for example, the story of the rich man and Lazarus (Luke 16:9–31) or the beatitudes about the poor (Luke 6:20).

11. As Rob Foot explains, "Voluntary poverty, despite the widespread admiration and official sanction that Francis attracted to himself and his order, was from the very beginning an ambiguous performance (as poverty was, itself, an ambiguous condition)" (Rob Foot, "The Poverty of Francis of Assisi: Historical Actions and Mythologized Meanings," in *No Gods Except Me: Orthodoxy and Religious Practice in Europe, 1200–1600*, ed. Charles Zika, Melbourne University History Monograph Series 14 (Parkville, Victoria: History Dept., University of Melbourne, 1991), 48.

12. "The doctrine of evangelical poverty was not new even in his own lifetime, and Francis added nothing to it that seemed on its surface heretical or dangerous," according to Foot, "but the debate about its meaning was to rage for a hundred years before its central tenet—that Christ and the apostles possessed no property—was declared heretical by Pope John XXII in 1323" (ibid., 37–38).

13. Spoto, *Reluctant Saint*, 68.

14. Francis of Assisi, *Rule of 1221*, trans. Benen Fahy, OFM, in *St. Francis of Assisi: Writings and Early Biographies; English Omnibus of the Sources for*

the Life of St. Francis, ed. Marion Alphonse Habig (Chicago: Franciscan Herald Press, 1973), 33.

15. Foot, "The Poverty of Francis of Assisi," 45.

16. Michael Allen Heller, "John Woolman," in *Historical Dictionary of the Friends (Quakers)*, by Margery Post Abbott, Mary Ellen Chijioke, Pink Dandelion, and John William Oliver Jr. Historical Dictionaries of Religions, Philosophies, and Movements Series 44 (Lanham, Md.: Scarecrow, 2003), 306–7. "The Society of Friends is significant in world history for becoming the first religious group publicly to denounce slavery and the first to require all members to free blacks held in bondage" (Hugh Barbour and J. William Frost, *The Quakers* [New York: Greenwood, 1988], 3:119).

17. Concerning the credibility of Woolman's account of his life, Barbour says, "All that we have been able to discover indicates a congruence between the persona in the Journal and the man his countrymen knew" (ibid., 131).

18. Thomas P. Slaughter, *The Beautiful Soul of John Woolman, Apostle of Abolition* (New York: Hill & Wang, 2008), 279–80, 297.

19. Ibid., 4.

20. Craig Blomberg, *Neither Poverty nor Riches: A Biblical Theology of Material Possessions* (Grand Rapids, Mich.: Eerdmans, 1999), 23. I use the term "evangelical" to denote a movement among North American Christians beginning in the 1940s, which distinguished itself both from liberal Christianity and from Fundamentalist Christianity, tending toward a conservative theology but without the fractious debates associated with Fundamentalism. Evangelicals have largely been characterized as politically right leaning, but Sider and others have certain left-leaning agendas, as well (third-world debt relief, environmental conservation, critiques of capitalism).

21. Ronald J. Sider, *Rich Christians in an Age of Hunger: Moving from Affluence to Generosity*, 5th ed. (Nashville: W Publishing Group, 2005), 335.

22. More information about Evangelicals for Social Action is available on their Web site, http://esa-online.org. Sider himself is a member of the Mennonite Church.

23. Sider, *Rich Christians*, 192–94.

24. Ibid., 206–7.

25. Søren Kierkegaard, "To Need God," in *Eighteen Upbuilding Discourses*, trans. Howard V. Hong (Princeton: Princeton University Press, 1992), 303.

26. Spoto, *Reluctant Saint*, 72.

27. *First Life of St. Francis*, trans. Placid Hermann, OFM, in Habig, *St. Francis of Assisi*, 272.

28. Spoto, *Reluctant Saint*, 64.

29. Leonardo Boff, *Saint Francis: A Model for Human Liberation* (New York: Crossroad, 1982), 21.

30. Francis of Assisi, *Rule of 1221*, in Habig, *St. Francis of Assisi*, 39.

31. Ibid., 32.

32. Francis of Assisi, *Rule of 1223*, trans. Benen Fahy, OFM, in ibid., 61.

33. Philip Peacock notes that the increase in trade and commerce during Francis's time also increased the use of money, a convention still new enough to make his radical renunciation of money reflect nostalgia for an earlier, simpler time (Philip Peacock, "The Relevance of St. Francis in an Age of Globalization," *Indian Journal of Theology* 44, nos. 1–2 [2002]: 62–78).

34. *The Legend of Perugia*, trans. Paul Oligny, in Habig, *St. Francis of Assisi*, 1087. The worldview implied in this statement sees all creation as a gift from God, ideally available for everyone's needs; thus to have more than one needs, more than one's fair share, is to have "stolen" from those who do not have enough. This has been a common Christian worldview throughout history, perhaps most clearly explained in Thomas Aquinas, *Summa Theologia*, II.II.66.

35. Thomas of Celano, *Second Life of St. Francis*, trans. Placid Hermann, OFM, in ibid., 434.

36. Boff, *Saint Francis*, 39.

37. Wilmer A. Cooper, *A Living Faith: Historical and Comparative Study of Quaker Beliefs*, 2nd ed. (Richmond, Ind.: Friends United Press), 2001, 133. "A testimony is an outward expression of an inward leading of the Spirit, or an outward sign of what Friends believe to be an inward revelation of truth" (ibid., 128). Testimonies today represent basic principles of Quakerism. Common listings today include Integrity, Simplicity, Peace, and Equality Testimonies (ibid., 132–40).

38. Ross Martinie Eiler, "Luxury, Capitalism, and the Quaker Reformation, 1737–1798," *Quaker History* 9, no. 1 (Spring 2008): 14.

39. Phillips Moulton, "John Woolman's Approach to Social Action—as Exemplified in Relation to Slavery," *Church History* 35 (December 1966): 400.

40. John Woolman, *The Journal and Major Essays of John Woolman* (New York: Oxford University Press, 1971), Phillips Moulton, ed., 226, 54.

41. Ibid., 54.

42. Ibid., 247.

43. Ibid., 240. Note that he includes animals here. Woolman was concerned about overworking animals as well as humans. But, as Slaughter mentions (*The Beautiful Soul of John Woolman*, 240–41), he did not mind eating meat or wearing fur or leather; his concern with animals was limited to their well-being while alive, not their use once killed.

44. Woolman, *Journal*, 120.
45. Sider, *Rich Christians*, 48.
46. Ibid., 56.
47. Ronald J. Sider, *Rich Christians in an Age of Hunger: A Biblical Study*, rev. and exp. ed. (Downers Grove, Ill.: InterVarsity, 1984), 29–30. In the 2005 edition, his rhetoric is somewhat softened. He leaves out the word *liberal* and does not speak of demonic justification for heresy.
48. Sider, *Rich Christians* (2005), 97. All subsequent citations are from the 2005 edition, unless otherwise noted.
49. Ibid., 177.
50. Blomberg, *Neither Poverty nor Riches*, 23. Most evangelicals at the time did not confront structural sin, and Sider faults them for this: "In the twentieth century, evangelicals have become imbalanced in their stand against sin, expressing concern and moral outrage about individual sinful acts while ignoring, perhaps even participating in, evil social structures. But the Bible condemns both" (Sider, *Rich Christians*, 108).
51. Sider, *Rich Christians*, 113.
52. Michelle Gonzalez, *Shopping* (Minneapolis: Fortress, 2010), 23.
53. Sider, *Rich Christians*, 177.
54. Ibid., 113.
55. Ibid., 121ff.
56. Ibid., 178.
57. Woolman, *Journal*, 129.
58. See Sallie McFague, *Life Abundant: Rethinking Theology and Economy for a Planet in Peril* (Minneapolis: Fortress, 2001), 188–90.
59. Woolman, *Journal*, 157.
60. Ibid.
61. Moulton, "John Woolman's Approach to Social Action," 403. Moulton approves: "Today, even in Christian circles, a widespread prejudice prevails against such attempts at non-involvement in rather remote ramifications of evil. The purity of one's own soul is likely to be considered too trivial a matter to warrant serious attention. Woolman thought otherwise" (ibid.).
62. McFague notes: "he also chose to sail steerage to Europe: so he could experience—and hence empathize with—the misery of the poorest and most oppressed" (McFague, *Life Abundant*, 90).
63. Slaughter, *The Beautiful Soul of John Woolman*, 4.
64. Woolman, *Journal*, 156.
65. Moulton, "John Woolman's Approach to Social Action," 401.
66. Woolman, *Journal*, 59–60. Moulton notes that Woolman's visits to slaveholding Friends were singularly effective in his crusade against slavery. "Over a period of 30 years he systematically visited leading slaveholders,

urging them to consider the unethical aspects of the system in which they were involved" ("John Woolman's Approach to Social Action," 404). Woolman lived to see the Friends Annual Meeting declare unequivocally the unrighteousness of slaveholding in 1754.

67. Sider, *Rich Christians*, 79.

68. Ibid., 87.

69. Ibid., 187–90.

70. Ibid., 188–90.

71. Ibid., 190.

72. Ibid., 194. While acknowledging the usefulness of charities and foreign aid, Sider is much more enthusiastic about micro-loan programs in developing countries and other programs that empower the poor to produce their own wealth (ibid., 231).

73. Ibid., 202.

74. Adam Daniel Finnerty, *No More Plastic Jesus: Global Justice and Christian Lifestyle* (Maryknoll, N.Y.: Orbis, 1977), 110.

75. Sider, *Rich Christians*, 74.

76. *Sacrum Commercium*, in *St. Francis of Assisi*, ed. Habig, 1550.

77. Francis of Assisi, *Rule of 1223*, in ibid., 60–61.

78. Thomas of Celano, *Second Life of Saint Francis*, in ibid., 422.

79. Saint Bonaventure, *Major Life of St. Francis*, in ibid., 686. For a contrasting perspective on the act of Christian giving and receiving, which nonetheless also acknowledges God as the primary giver, see John Milbank, "Can a Gift Be Given? Prolegomena to a Future Trinitarian Metaphysic," in *Rethinking Metaphysics*, ed. L. Gregory Jones and Stephen E. Fowl (Oxford: Blackwell, 1995), 119–61.

80. Antonaccio, "Asceticism and the Ethics of Consumption," 90.

81. Kenneth Baxter Wolf, *The Poverty of Riches: St. Francis of Assisi Reconsidered* (New York: Oxford University Press, 2003), 23.

82. Ibid., 88. Because beggars were seen in two ways, as holy or as thieves, those who were most clearly holy had an advantage. "Francis's extreme love of poverty, pursued for the sake of his own spiritual progress, did surprisingly little to elevate anyone's opinion of the other kind of poverty" (ibid., 4).

83. Ibid., 86. Francis's kind of holiness, on Wolf's reading, only appealed to or benefited the richer classes who wished to give up their riches; and indeed most of the brothers in his order fell into this category. Presumably, a poor person could join Francis's order, thereby gaining some of the social benefits enjoyed by Francis and his brothers. But Wolf correctly notes that no record exists for poor people joining the order. The poorest on record was "John the Simple," who was from a peasant farming family, but even he had some livestock to renounce (86).

84. "Francis would not let any form of material accumulation interfere with his pursuit of holy poverty, even if the goal of such accumulation was poor relief" (ibid., 24). Lady Poverty is quoted as approving this ideal in the *Sacrum Commercium*.
85. Ibid., 25.
86. Martin Luther King Jr., *Stride Toward Freedom: The Montgomery Story* (Boston: Beacon, 2010), 82.
87. Antonaccio, "Asceticism and the Ethics of Consumption," 90.

Chapter 3

1. L. Shannon Jung, "Taste and See: As We Experience God's Bounty, We Also Delight and Share," *The Lutheran: The Magazine of the Evangelical Lutheran Church in America*, August 2004, accessed Nov. 2, 2010, http://www.thelutheran.org/article/article.cfm?article_id=2125.
2. John R. Schneider, *Godly Materialism: Rethinking Money and Possessions* (Downers Grove, Ill.: InterVarsity, 1994), 55.
3. Ibid.
4. L. Shannon Jung, *Sharing Food: Christian Practices for Enjoyment* (Minneapolis: Fortress, 2006), 144.
5. "We do not know much about celebrating.... We simply do not delight very well ... [but] food offers us the possibility of relearning how to feast" (Jung, ibid., 57). Jung seeks to teach his readers to celebrate their food, and truly feast. To this end, he suggests practices such as saying grace, offering hospitality, feasting, preparing food, fasting, honoring the body, and participating in the Eucharist. It should be noted, however, that not everyone needs to be taught to feast; in some cultures, feasting traditions, including Spanish and Hispanic fiesta traditions and the Mardi Gras celebrations of French and Cajun cultures, are strong.
6. Ibid., 6.
7. "The Pleasures of Eating," in *The Art of the Common-Place: The Agrarian Essays of Wendell Berry*, by Wendell Berry and Norman Wirzba (Washington, D.C.: Counterpoint, 2002), 326.
8. Jung, *Sharing Food*, 146.
9. George D. Chryssides, *Historical Dictionary of New Religious Movements* (Lanham, Md.: Scarecrow, 2001), 42:257. Positive confession and seed-faith are defined below.
10. "About Creflo Dollar," *Creflo Dollar Ministries*, 2008–2011, accessed Jan. 15, 2011, http://www.creflodollarministries.org/About/CrefloDollar.aspx.
11. Yonat Shimron, "Popular Preacher Rouses RBC Center: Some Theologians Skeptical of Message," *Raleigh (N.C.) News & Observer*, June 24, 2006.

12. "About Creflo Dollar." Dollar, by his own admission, has had no formal theological training, just a lot of experience with prayer, which he calls "kneeology," in contrast with theology (Creflo A. Dollar, *Total Life Prosperity: Fourteen Practical Steps to Receiving God's Full Blessing* [Nashville: Thomas Nelson, 1999], 17). His training came primarily from his mentor in the Word of Faith movement, Kenneth Copeland (Jonathan L. Walton, *Watch This! The Ethics and Aesthetics of Black Televangelism* [New York: New York University Press: 2009], 147).

13. Kim S. Nash and Mel Duvall, "Know Thy Customer," *Baseline* (December 6, 2005), 1.

14. Walton, *Watch This!* 150. On the congressional investigation, see "Response to Senators," *Creflo Dollar Ministries*, March 2008, accessed Jan. 15, 2011, http://www.creflodollarministries.org/About/ResponseToSenator.aspx.

15. Dollar, *Total Life Prosperity*, ix. Prosperity, on Dollar's interpretation, does not seem to include humility, patience, or other less achievement-oriented spiritual gifts.

16. Ibid., x.

17. Abigail Rayner, "Preaching the Path to the Riches of the Lord—a Dollar at a Time," *London Times*, Dec. 11, 2004, 71.

18. Walton, *Watch This!* 149.

19. Rayner, "Preaching the Path to the Riches of the Lord."

20. David Hazard, *You Set My Spirit Free: A Forty-Day Journey in the Company of John of the Cross* (Grand Rapids, Mich.: Bethany, 1994), 43.

21. Thomas Aquinas, *Summa Theologica*, trans. Fathers of the English Dominican Province (1269–73; repr., New York: Benziger Brothers, 1947–48), I.97.3, http://www.ccel.org/ccel/aquinas/summa.toc.html. Subsequent references to the *Summa* will appear as parenthetical citations in the text.

22. Aquinas delineates several ways a person's desires may be twisted into gluttony: by desiring food that is too costly ("sumptuous") or too prepared ("dainty"), or by eating too quickly ("hastily") or without proper decorum ("greedily") (II–II.148.4).

Aquinas himself, as legend has it, enjoyed eating. G. K. Chesterton writes in his biography of Aquinas:

It may be that he . . . was responsible for the sublime exaggeration that a crescent was cut out of the dinner-table to allow him to sit down. It is quite certain that it was an exaggeration; and that his stature was more remarked than his stoutness; but, above all, that his head was quite powerful enough to dominate his body (G. K. Chesterton, "St. Thomas Aquinas," *The Catholic Primer*, accessed Jan. 15, 2011, http://www.catholicprimer.org/chester-ton/st_thomas.pdf).

23. "For imperfect happiness, such as can be had in this life, external goods are necessary, not as belonging to the essence of happiness, but by serving as instruments to happiness, which consists in an operation of virtue" (I–II.4.7). For "perfect happiness," which is incorporeal knowledge of God, no consumption is necessary.

24. John R. Schneider, *The Good of Affluence: Seeking God in a Culture of Wealth* (Grand Rapids, Mich.: Eerdmans, 2002), 39.

25. Ibid., 43.

26. L. Shannon Jung, *Food for Life: The Spirituality and Ethics of Eating* (Minneapolis: Augsburg Fortress, 2004), 13, 21.

27. Stephanie Y. Mitchem, *Name It and Claim It? Prosperity Preaching in the Black Church* (Cleveland: Pilgrim, 2007), 21. Prosperity theology is particularly influential in African American Christianity, but it originated with white churches; many prosperity congregations are currently very mixed in terms of race and ethnicity.

28. Ibid.

29. "The nature of our desires, and our potential self-deception about them, gets very little attention," notes Jason Byassee ("Be Happy: The Health and Wealth Gospel," *Christian Century* 122, no. 14 [July 12, 2005]: 22).

30. Schneider, *Godly Materialism*, 15–16.

31. Ibid., 16.

32. Jung, *Sharing Food*, 29.

33. Ibid., 37.

34. Ibid., 31.

35. Ibid., 33.

36. Matthew Fox, *Original Blessing: A Primer in Creation Spirituality Presented in Four Paths, Twenty-Six Themes and Two Questions* (Santa Fe, N.M.: Bear, 1983), 52.

37. Brian MacLaren, *A Generous Orthodoxy* (Grand Rapids, Mich.: Zondervan, 2004), 200.

38. Jung, *Sharing Food*, 113.

39. Ibid., 34–35.

40. Schneider, *Godly Materialism*, 79.

41. John Avanzini, "Believer's Voice of Victory," January 20, 1991. Quoted in *Christianity in Crisis*, by Hank Hanegraaff (Eugene, Ore.: Harvest House, 1993), 381n34.

42. John Avanzini, "Praise the Lord," January 20, 1991. Quoted in Hanegraaff, *Christianity in Crisis*, 381n35.

43. John Avanzini, "Believer's Voice of Victory," January 20, 1991. Quoted in Hanegraaff, *Christianity in Crisis*, 381–82n. 36.
44. Frederick K. C. Price, "Ever Increasing Faith," Dec. 9, 1990. Quoted in Hanegraaff, *Christianity in Crisis*, 383n. 55.
45. Schneider, *Godly Materialism*, 111, 113. These and other turns of phrase show, I believe, a distinctly American middle-class interpretation at work here.
46. Ibid., 112. Schneider is not explicitly saying so, but he assumes a connection between health and a certain level of affluence.
47. Ibid., 185.
48. Craig Blomberg, *Neither Poverty nor Riches: A Biblical Theology of Material Possessions* (Grand Rapids, Mich.: Eerdmans, 1999), 24. Blomberg discusses charitable giving on 19–20.
49. Clement of Alexandria, "Who Is the Rich Man That Shall Be Saved?" in *The Ante-Nicene Fathers: Translations of the Writings of the Fathers Down to A.D. 325*, by Alexander Roberts and Others (Grand Rapids, Mich.: Eerdmans, 1980), 1. Hereafter, references to Clement's "Rich Man" will be cited parenthetically within the text.
50. Clement's openness to Greek philosophy influences his interpretation here: "Clement's own understanding...is clearly derived from Stoic and other notions of the need to rid the soul of its passions" (Justo L. González, *Faith and Wealth: A History of Early Christian Ideas on the Origin, Significance, and Use of Money* [San Francisco: Harper & Row, 1990], 113).
51. Clement of Alexandria, *Instructor*, in *The Ante-Nicene Fathers: Translations of the Writings of the Fathers Down to A.D. 325*, by Alexander Roberts and Others (Grand Rapids, Mich.: Eerdmans, 1980), 3.6. Hereafter, references to Clement's *Instructor* will appear as parenthetical citations in the text.
52. Walter H. Wagner, "Lubricating the Camel: Clement of Alexandria on Wealth and the Wealthy," *Festschrift: A Tribute to Dr. William Hordern*, ed. Walter Freitag (Saskatoon: University of Saskatchewan, 1985), 72. Ernst Troeltsch describes Clement's treatise as "most favorable towards wealth," though he adds, "at the same time it is one of the most sensible works from the economic point of view, and it is also filled with a spirit of very fine and tender piety" (Troeltsch, *The Social Teaching of the Christian Churches*, trans. Olive Wyon [Chicago: University of Chicago Press, 1981], 184n57).
53. Schneider, *Godly Materialism*, 88–89.
54. Fox, *Original Blessing*, 99–100.
55. Schneider writes, "Whatever human dominion is in Genesis, then, it ennobles us for the purpose of ennobling everyone and everything else. We, too, are servants in royal form" (*Godly Materialism*, 53).
56. Ibid., 56.

57. Ibid., 163.
58. Schneider, *Good of Affluence*, 192.
59. Walton, *Watch This!* 153.
60. Dollar, *Total Life Prosperity*, 44–50.
61. Quoted in Walton, *Watch This!* 150–51.
62. David Pilgrim, "Egoism or Altruism: A Social Psychological Critique of the Prosperity Gospel of Televangelist Robert Tilton," *Journal of Religious Studies* 18, nos. 1–2 (1992): 3–4.
63. Dollar, *Total Life Prosperity*, 38.
64. John Blake, "Dollar and the Gospel: Pastor Revered by Many, Criticized by Some," *Atlanta Journal-Constitution*, March 5, 2000.
65. Barbara Ehrenreich and Dedrick Muhammad, "The Recession's Racial Divide," *New York Times*, Sept. 12, 2009.
66. Dollar, *Total Life Prosperity*, 90. It should be noted that Dollar does not condone irresponsible spending, but rather he counsels his readers to buy high-quality items in small quantity or on sale, if they cannot afford it otherwise. Buy a nice car used, he suggests, and fix it up so it looks like new (ibid).
67. Walton, *Watch This!* 160.
68. Ibid., 161.
69. Dollar, *Total Life Prosperity*, 89.
70. Ibid., 103. Note the interesting phrasing: "believing God for something"— not "believing in God." Dollar uses this phrase frequently, as do other prosperity preachers (see Pilgrim, "Egoism or Altruism," 3, 4).
71. James R. Goff Jr., "The Faith That Claims," *Christianity Today* 34, no. 3 (Feb. 19, 1990): 21.
72. Byassee, "Be Happy," 21.
73. Ken L. Sarles, "A Theological Evaluation of the Prosperity Gospel," *Bibliotheca Sacra* 143 (Oct.–Dec. 1986): 343.
74. Geoffrey Grogan, "Liberation and Prosperity Theologies," *Scottish Bulletin of Evangelical Theology* 9, no. 2 (Autumn 1991): 121. His article makes a number of excellent points in comparing liberation and prosperity theologies, particularly with regard to their reliance on the Old Testament and their focus on the physical aspects of well-being.
75. Milmon Harrison represents the former view, writing that prosperity theology "might be seen (at least in part) as a type of 'poor people's movement.' The people who are its followers are primarily those whose experience has produced the *desire* for, if not the actualization of, upward socioeconomic mobility" (Milmon F. Harrison, *Righteous Riches: The Word of Faith Movement in Contemporary African American Religion* [Oxford: Oxford University Press, 2005], 148). Mitchem disagrees: "However, I contend that middle-class black people are also drawn to prosperity preaching.... Prosperity churches

provide answers for black middle-class social anguish about solidifying and growing personal assets, while justifying an often new social position. These answers become enticements to participate in prosperity churches" (Mitchem, *Name It and Claim It?* 40–41).

76. On unfittingness, see Jame Schaefer, "Valuing Earth Intrinsically and Instrumentally: A Theological Framework for Environmental Ethics," *Theological Studies* 66, no. 4 (December 2005): 792n41.

77. Ibid., 792n38.

78. Diana Fritz Cates, "The Virtue of Temperance (IIa IIae, qq.141–70)," in *The Ethics of Aquinas*, by Stephen J. Pope (Washington, D.C.: Georgetown University Press, 2002), 322.

79. Ibid.

80. Barry Gordon, *The Economic Problem in Biblical and Patristic Thought* (Leiden; New York: Brill, 1989), 9:87.

81. Ibid.

82. Ibid., 85.

83. David W. Jones, "The Bankruptcy of the Prosperity Gospel: An Exercise in Biblical and Theological Ethics," *Faith and Mission* 16 (Fall 1998): 82.

84. Walton, *Watch This!* 155.

85. Dollar, *Total Life Prosperity*, 65.

86. Robert Tilton, *God's Laws of Success* (Tulsa: Harrison House, 1986), 137, quoted in Sarles, "A Theological Evaluation of the Prosperity Gospel," 333. His passive phrasing in the acquisition of the shoes and watch is notable.

87. Dollar, *Total Life Prosperity*, 86.

88. Ibid., 82.

89. Mitchem, *Name It and Claim It?* 120.

90. Nash and Duvall, "Know Thy Customer," 1.

91. Rayner, "Preaching the Path to the Riches of the Lord," 71.

92. Jones, "The Bankruptcy of the Prosperity Gospel," 82 (emphasis mine). Jones is quoting Luke 6:35.

93. Mitchem, *Name It and Claim It?* 83, 110.

94. Walton, *Watch This!* 159.

95. Harrison, 69 (emphasis mine).

96. Ibid., 69.

97. For example: "James Harmon, 37, an investor, has been a Dr. Dollar follower for two years. He gives 50 per cent of his annual income to World Changers. 'You are looking at a multimillionaire in my heavenly bank account,' he says" (ibid).

98. Jung declares, "I am convinced that we have a need to share. We experience real joy in sharing.... God created us with the instincts to seek not only our own well-being but that of others as well" (Jung, *Sharing Food*, 5).

99. Ibid., 43 (emphasis mine).
100. Ibid., 45.
101. Ibid., 161.
102. Ibid., iv.
103. Jung, *Food for Life*, 98.
104. Ibid., 100–101, 111–12.
105. Ibid., 107.
106. Joanna is referred to in Luke 8:3, along with Susanna, as one of the women who "provided for them [Jesus and the apostles] out of their resources."
107. Schneider, *Godly Materialism*, 155. As an example, Schneider interprets the parable of Lazarus and the rich man: the rich man's reward is the torment of hell, not because he failed to engage with the structural evils of poverty, but because he failed with regard to one particular man, Lazarus, whose name he knew and who was right there, outside his house. The judgment is bound by the limits of his direct interaction and knowledge.
108. Schneider, *Good of Affluence*, 88.
109. This principle of proximity is endorsed by some ethicists. See, for example, Margaret Urban Walker, *Moral Understandings: A Feminist Study in Ethics* (New York: Routledge, 1998), 80–86.
110. Schneider, *Good of Affluence*, 89.
111. Schneider, *Godly Materialism*, 186.
112. Wendell Berry, *The Gift of Good Land* (San Francisco: North Point, 1981), 281.
113. Jung, *Food for Life*, 26, 43.
114. Berry and Wirzba, *The Art of the Common-Place*, 326.
115. Jung, *Food for Life*, 60, 76.
116. Jung discusses the Eucharist as a "master practice" offering insights for ways to make all eating sacramental: "The Eucharist is an exemplar of who we really are and what our eating and drinking really are at their (and our) best." Eating, guided by the Eucharist, should be joyful, in communion with God and others, a source of faith revival, and a reminder of both human connections with the material world and the mission to connect with others in God's love (Jung, *Sharing Food*, 131).
117. Jean Porter, *The Recovery of Virtue: The Relevance of Aquinas for Christian Ethics* (Louisville: Westminster/John Knox, 1990), 178.
118. Jung, *Food for Life*, 5. Jung's source for this phrasing is the Westminster Catechism.
119. Not all Christians would agree. While Augustine affirms God as the one thing worthy of enjoyment, nothing else should be enjoyed. Augustine thought that only God could be desired and enjoyed without sin; other,

lesser goods should simply be "used" as instruments to attain closeness to God (Augustine of Hippo, *On Christian Doctrine*, trans. D. W. Robertson Jr. [Upper Saddle River, N.J.: Prentice-Hall, 1997], 9 [IV]). "For him even the pleasure involved in eating and drinking is 'an evil which we put to good use'" (John Mahoney, *The Making of Moral Theology: A Study of the Roman Catholic Tradition* [Oxford: Clarendon, 1987], 65).

120. Schneider, *Good of Affluence*, 141ff.

121. For a fuller treatment of this question, see my "Consuming Christ: The Role of Jesus in Christian Food Ethics," *Journal of the Society of Christian Ethics* 30, no. 1 (Spring/Summer 2010): 45–62.

122. Nash, "Ethics and the Economics-Ecology Dilemma: Toward a Just, Sustainable, and Frugal Future," *Theology and Public Policy* 6, no. 1 (Summer 1994): 53.

123. Ibid., 55.

Chapter 4

1. Dorothy Day, *Writings from Commonweal*, ed. Patrick Jordan (Collegeville, Minn.: Liturgical, 2002), 81.

2. Dorothy Day, *The Long Loneliness: The Autobiography of Dorothy Day* (San Francisco: HarperSanFrancisco, 1997), 235. She continues: "'Nothing is too good for the poor,' our editor Tom Sullivan says, and he likes that aphorism especially when he is helping himself to something extra good" (ibid.).

3. Day, *Long Loneliness*, 172. The first issue of *The Catholic Worker* was created in May 1933, in New York City (James H. Forest, *Love Is the Measure: A Biography of Dorothy Day* [Mahwah, N.J.: Paulist, 1986], 63–81). It sold for one penny per copy—"to make it so cheap that anyone could afford to buy," Day explained (ibid., 80). That price did not cover the costs of its production: "The Paulist Press was willing to set type and print 2,500 copies of an eight page tabloid paper for $57. Dorothy calculated she could pay this with recent income from her writing and research work and by delaying the payment of her utility bills" (ibid). It still sells for a penny per copy.

4. The corporal works of mercy are to feed the hungry, give drink to the thirsty, clothe the naked, shelter the homeless, visit the sick, visit the imprisoned (some say "ransom the captive"), and bury the dead (primarily derived from Isaiah 58:6–10 and Matthew 25:35–40). The spiritual works of mercy are to instruct the ignorant, to counsel the doubtful, to admonish sinners, to bear wrongs patiently, to forgive

offenses willingly, to comfort the afflicted, and to pray for the living and the dead. *The Catholic Worker* historically has focused primarily on the corporal works of mercy, but Day exhorted her fellow workers to the spiritual works of mercy as well.

5. Mel Piehl, "The Politics of Free Obedience," in *A Revolution of the Heart: Essays on the Catholic Worker*, ed. Patrick G. Coy (Philadelphia: Temple University Press, 1988), 212.

6. Rosalie Riegle, "A Long Loneliness: Metaphors of Conversion within the Catholic Worker Movement," in *Dorothy Day and the Catholic Worker Movement: Centenary Essays*, ed. William J. Thorn, Phillip M. Runkel, and Susan Mountin (Milwaukee: Marquette University Press, 2001), 568.

7. James H. Forest, "Dorothy Day: Saint and Troublemaker," in Thorn et al., *Dorothy Day and the Catholic Worker Movement*, 578. Ammon Hennacy, a radical anarchist who joined the Catholic Worker despite his deep suspicion of institutional religion, spoke of the "love which radiates from Dorothy and true CW's [Catholic Workers]" (Eileen Egan, "Dorothy Day: Pilgrim of Peace," in Coy, *A Revolution of the Heart*, 161). Hennecy did join the Catholic Church in 1952, after being associated with The Catholic Worker for sixteen years.

8. Day, *Long Loneliness*, 249; James H. Forest, *Love Is the Measure: A Biography of Dorothy Day* (Mahwah, N.J.: Paulist, 1986), 112, 212; and Roger A. Statnick, "Dorothy Day: Citizen of the Kingdom," in Thorn et al., *Dorothy Day and the Catholic Worker Movement*, 377. A shortened version of this statement, "love is the measure," forms the title of a section of Day's autobiography, *The Long Loneliness* (167), as well as the title of a biography by James H. Forest.

9. Arthur J. Dyck, "Referent-Models of Loving: A Philosophical and Theological Analysis of Love in Ethical Theory and Moral Practice," *Harvard Theological Review* 61, no. 4 (October 1968): 531.

10. Deirdre McCloskey, *The Bourgeois Virtues: Ethics for an Age of Commerce* (Chicago: University of Chicago Press, 2006), 91.

11. This is similar to Gene Outka's position in his influential book *Agape: An Ethical Analysis* (New Haven, Conn.: Yale University Press, 1972).

12. Benedict XVI, *Caritas in Veritate*, encyclical letter on integral human development in charity and truth, 6, accessed Nov. 13, 2010, http://www.vatican.va/holy_father/benedict_xvi/encyclicals/documents/hf_ben-xvi_enc_20090629_caritas-in-veritate_en.html.

13. Matthew 22:37, 39.

14. See Søren Kierkegaard, *Works of Love*, trans. Howard Hong and Edna Hong (New York: Harper & Row, 1962), 40–57.

15. As the U.S. Catholic Bishops write, "Jesus taught us to love God and one another and that the concept of neighbor is without limit" (U.S. Catholic

Bishops, "Economic Justice for All," in *Catholic Social Thought: The Documentary Heritage*, ed. David J. O'Brien and Thomas A. Shannon (Maryknoll, N.Y.: Orbis, 2001), 664 [§365]). The bishops are probably referring to the story of the good Samaritan (Luke 10:29–37) and Jesus' command to "love your enemies" (Matthew 5:44; Luke 6:27, etc.).

16. U.S. Catholic Bishops, "Economic Justice for All," 594 (§64).

17. Kathryn Tanner, "The Care that Does Justice: Recent Writings in Feminist Ethics and Theology," *Journal of Religious Ethics* 24, no. 1 (Spring 1996): 171–91 (emphasis mine).

18. Linda Woodhead, "Love and Justice," *Studies in Christian Ethics* 5, no. 1 (1992): 50.

19. Paul Tillich, for example, thought it was impossible literally, but could be used as a metaphor; others equate self-love with selfishness and decry it as ethically odious (Paul Tillich, *Love, Power and Justice* [Oxford: Oxford University Press, 1954], 6). Kierkegaard acknowledges its necessity, but emphasizes the strength of the temptation to selfishness in self-love; he advocates instead self-sacrificial love of others (Kierkegaard, *Works of Love*, 34–39).

20. Gene Outka defends self-love as neither nefarious, nor prudent, nor simply justifiable, but as a definite obligation; in its enlightened form, self-love correlates to and bolsters neighbor-love (Outka, *Agape*, 73). Many Christian thinkers have defended self-love, including Augustine: "it is impossible for one who loves God not to love himself" (Augustine of Hippo, "Of the Morals of the Catholic Church," trans. Richard Stothert, *New Advent*, accessed Nov. 12, 2010, http://www.newadvent.org/fathers/1401.htm). See also Darlene Fozard Weaver, *Self Love and Christian Ethics* (Cambridge: Cambridge University Press, 2002).

21. Augustine, *Confessions*, trans. Maria Boulding (New York: Random House, 1998, X. 31, 44).

22. John B. Cobb, *Postmodernism and Public Policy: Reframing Religion, Culture, Education, Sexuality, Class, Race, Politics, and the Economy* (Albany: State University of New York Press, 2002), 121.

23. Sallie McFague, *Life Abundant: Rethinking Theology and Economy for a Planet in Peril* (Minneapolis: Fortress, 2001), 12. M. Douglas Meeks, making a similar argument for the value of human community, describes its exemplar in the Trinitarian perichoresis: "God is not a radical individual but rather a community of diverse persons that finds unity in self-giving love rather than in substantialist or subjectivist principles of identity" (M. Douglas Meeks, *God the Economist: The Doctrine of God and Political Economy* [Minneapolis: Fortress, 1989], 11).

24. McFague, *Life Abundant*, 138.

25. John B. Cobb and Herman Daly, *For the Common Good: Redirecting the Economy Toward Community, the Environment, and a Sustainable Future* (Boston: Beacon, 1989), 7. See also John B. Cobb, "Christianity, Economics, and Ecology," in *Christianity and Ecology: Seeking the Well-being of Earth and Humans*, ed. Dieter T. Hessel and Rosemary Radford Ruether (Cambridge, Mass.: Harvard University Press, 2000), 507.

26. L. Shannon Jung, *Food for Life: The Spirituality and Ethics of Eating* (Minneapolis: Fortress, 2004), 45.

27. Jung writes, "all [connections] are enhanced when these relationships are undertaken with a good meal" (ibid., 41).

28. Ibid., 75–76.

29. Ibid., 76.

30. Day, *Long Loneliness*, 263.

31. Forest, "Dorothy Day: Saint and Troublemaker,"580; Day, *Writings*, 132.

32. Michelle Gonzalez, *Shopping* (Minneapolis: Fortress, 2010), 80.

33. McCloskey, *Bourgeois Virtues*, 110.

34. Shirlyn Toppin, "'Soul Food' Theology: Pastoral Care and Practice through the Sharing of Meals: A Womanist Reflection," *Black Theology: An International Journal* 4, no. 1 (2006): 56.

35. Ibid., 57.

36. Mary Hinton, "Saying Grace: Praying over the Loss of African-American Religious and Food Culture (and How They Are Related)," *Religious Education* 103, no. 4 (July–Sept. 2008): 472.

37. Ibid., 473.

38. Ibid., 474.

39. Ibid., 476–77.

40. Day's consumption choices had an impact on her fellow Catholic Workers. As Forest testifies, "Every time I defeat the impulse to buy something I can get along without, Dorothy Day's examples of voluntary poverty have had renewed impact" (Forest, "Dorothy Day: Saint and Troublemaker," 586).

41. Ibid., 580.

42. Day, *Writings*, 132.

43. Forest, *Love Is the Measure*, 195. Day also smoked cigarettes for much of her life, a consumption decision she was unable to shake until prayer cured her of the habit (ibid., 581).

44. According to scholar George Forell, Luther's social ethics are grounded in concerns for relationships and neighbor-love, and he discusses the economic world in terms of these norms (George W. Forell, *Faith Active in Love: An Investigation of the Principles Underlying Luther's Social Ethics* [Minneapolis: Augsburg, 1954, 63).

It should be noted, however, that Luther's thought is complex and relatively unsystematic, and has been interpreted in many ways. "Luther, whose theological and ethical aim was to describe and interpret the relationship of man to God and God's creation, cared little whether the result was systematic or not, as long as he felt that it described the actual human situation" (ibid., 47). The positions I attribute to Luther, then, do not preclude other somewhat contradictory statements he has also made.

For example, though he grounds his ethics and political views in love and the Christian gospel, according to many interpreters, Luther has also declared in *Trade and Usury*, "I have often taught thus, that the world ought not and cannot be ruled according to the gospel and Christian love, but by strict laws and with sword and force, because the world is evil" (Martin Luther, *Luther's Works*, ed. Walther I. Brandt, Jaroslav Pelikan, and Helmut T. Lehmann; trans. Charles M. Jacobs [Philadelphia: Muhlenberg, 1962], 45:264).

I include Luther in this chapter because of the novel interpretations of feminist scholar Cynthia Moe-Lobeda, whose book, *Healing a Broken World: Globalization and God*, daringly invokes Luther and his anticapitalist, pro-neighbor-love writing to address the complex problems of globalization (Cynthia Moe-Lobeda, *Healing a Broken World: Globalization and God* [Minneapolis: Fortress, 2002], 7).

45. Luther, *Trade and Usury*, 247–48. Luther catalogs many different forms of questionable market dealings—many of which are common practice today—and condemns the sinful lack of neighbor-love in all of them.

46. Ibid., 249–51.

47. Jung, *Sharing Food*, 42, 39.

48. Many Catholic orders, for example, name hospitality as central to their charism, a specific calling supported by, and gifted from, the Holy Spirit (this includes the order of St. Benedict and the Order of St. John of God, among others).

49. Forest, *Love Is the Measure*, 92.

50. Daniel DiDomizio, "The Prophetic Spirituality of the Catholic Worker," in Coy, *A Revolution of the Heart*, 222.

51. Luther, *Trade and Usury*, 259.

52. Martin Luther, "Large Catechism (Seventh Commandment)," *Christian Classics Etherial Library*, accessed Nov. 12, 2010, http://www.ccel.org/ccel/luther/large_cat/files/large_catechism.html#Heading9.

53. "The obligation to evaluate social and economic activity from the viewpoint of the poor and the powerless arises from the radical command to love one's neighbor as one's self.... Volunteering time, talent, and money to work for greater justice is a fundamental expression of

Christian love and social solidarity. All who have more than they need must come to the aid of the poor" (U.S. Catholic Bishops, 599 [§87], 607 [§119]).

54. "Aims and Means of the Catholic Worker Movement," in Coy, *A Revolution of the Heart*, 366.

55. Day, *Writings*, 62.

56. Ibid., 111.

57. Forest, "Dorothy Day: Saint and Troublemaker," 578. Reserving as many resources as possible for the poor was not the only criterion for the Catholic Worker's financial conduct. They also refused to pay federal taxes, because the Catholic Worker's strong pacifist position meant a desire to avoid contributing money to any war (see Forest, *Love Is the Measure*, 180).

58. U.S. Catholic Bishops, 574 (§14).

59. Ibid., 594 (64).

60. Ibid., 594 (66).

61. She writes, "It is not true that simply because an individual is part of the public, it is to the individual's own benefit to contribute to that public. In cases where no one can be excluded from the benefits of the public good, it is to each individual's benefit to 'free ride' on the contributions of others" (Jane Mansbridge, "Pluralism and the Common Good: A Response," in *American Catholics and Civic Engagement: A Distinctive Voice*, ed. Margaret O'Brien Steinfels [Lanham, Md.: Rowman & Littlefield, 2004], 21).

62. Ibid., 22.

63. Cobb, *Postmodernism*, 137.

64. Cobb and Daly, *For the Common Good*, 202; Cobb, "Christianity, Economics, and Ecology," 507–8. Cobb also envisions a community that extends into the future, including future generations (ibid., 508).

65. Cobb and Daly, *For the Common Good*, 377.

66. McFague, *Life Abundant*, 167.

67. Ibid., 31.

68. U.S. Catholic Bishops, 574 (§14).

69. Cobb and Daly, *For the Common Good*, 269.

70. Cobb, "Christianity, Economics, and Ecology," 209; Cobb and Daly, *For the Common Good*, 177.

71. The bishops define subsidiarity as follows: "This principle states that, in order to protect basic justice, government should undertake only those initiatives which exceed the capacity of individuals or private groups acting independently. Government should not replace or destroy smaller communities and individual initiative" (U.S. Catholic Bishops, 608 [§124]). Cobb acknowledges the relation between Catholic subsidiarity

and his vision of "communities of communities." See Cobb and Daly, *For the Common Good*, 17; and Cobb, *Postmodernism*, 139.

72. Toyohiko Kagawa, *Brotherhood Economics* (New York: Harper & Brothers, 1936), 36.

73. Ibid., 37. Like Tanner, he directs gratitude to God into work on behalf of others rather than a futile attempt at mutual giving between humans and God.

74. Kathryn Tanner, *Economy of Grace* (Minneapolis: Fortress, 2005), 68–69.

75. Ibid., 74–75.

76. Kagawa, *Brotherhood Economics*, 101.

77. Ibid., 195–96.

78. Ibid., ix.

79. He writes, "The most important problem facing economics is, therefore, how to harmonize these two, freedom and brotherly love. Here enters the cooperative movement" (ibid., 93).

80. Kagawa exhorts dissatisfied cooperative members to "loyalty" and the need for "education," for example (ibid., 112). But of course, dissatisfied members of a cooperative, by virtue of the cooperative governing structure, would be empowered to change it if something needed to be changed. One of the Rochdale Principles stipulates that each member has one vote, regardless of their economic or social status. Thus, dissatisfied members of a consumers' cooperative ought to be able to reform it, rather than simply submit to Kagawa's exhortations to be loyal.

81. Tanner, *Economy of Grace*, 73.

82. Ibid., 76.

83. Ibid., 79. Mansbridge's discussion of the "free rider" problem above is in agreement with Tanner about the relation between identifying with, and wanting to sacrifice on behalf of, the community.

84. Ibid., 82. Tanner assuages the fears raised by the concept of allowing oneself to be owned by others in this way: others, she says, "own you only insofar as, respecting your differences from them, they give you to yourself in ways that advantage you. If they don't . . . they void their ownership of you" (ibid.).

85. Ibid., 58.

86. Kagawa, *Brotherhood Economics*, 150.

87. Ibid., 117.

88. Day, *Long Loneliness*, 227–28. She is referencing Luke 10:8 ("Whenever you enter a town and its people welcome you, eat what is set before you").

89. Hinton, "Saying Grace," 472.

90. John B. Cobb, *Sustaining the Common Good: A Christian Perspective on the Global Economy* (Cleveland: Pilgrim, 1994), 8–9.

91. Cobb, "Christianity, Economics, and Ecology," 505.

92. Ibid., 504, 502.

93. McFague, *Life Abundant*, 22-23.

94. Ibid., 14.

95. Ibid., 168.

96. Day, *Writings*, 68.

97. U.S. Catholic Bishops, 600 (§90); 596 (§75). As J. Philip Wogaman explains, "There is no necessary conflict between an affirmation of the common good and a preferential option for the poor since the latter is an inescapable condition of the former" (J. Philip Wogaman, "The Common Good and Economic Life: A Protestant Perspective," in *The Common Good and U.S. Capitalism*, ed. Oliver F. Williams and John W. Houck [Lanham, Md.: University Press of America, 1987], 96).

98. Ronald J. Sider, *Rich Christians in an Age of Hunger: Moving from Affluence to Generosity*, 5th ed. (Nashville: W Publishing Group, 2005), 202.

99. Larry L. Rasmussen, *Earth Community, Earth Ethics* (Maryknoll, N.Y.: Orbis, 1996), 261.

100. John Ruskin, *Unto This Last and Other Writings* (London: Penguin, 1997), 227-28 (emphasis mine).

101. Second Vatican Council, "Gaudium et Spes," in *Catholic Social Thought: The Documentary Heritage*, ed. David J. O'Brien and Thomas A. Shannon (Maryknoll, N.Y.: Orbis, 2001), 181 (§26). The fact that it needs to be defined, rather than being assumed, shows the concept's diminishing currency in Catholic thought, according to Ernest Bartell (Ernest Bartell, CSC, "Private Goods, Public Goods, and the Common Good: Another Look at Economics and Ethics in Catholic Social Teaching," in Williams and Houck, *The Common Good and U.S. Capitalism*, 189).

102. U.S. Catholic Bishops, 574 (§14).

103. DiDomizio, "The Prophetic Spirituality of the Catholic Worker," 227.

104. "Aims and Means of the Catholic Worker Movement," 364.

105. Drew Christiansen, "Ecology and the Common Good: Catholic Social Teaching and Environmental Responsibility," in *And God Saw that It Was Good: Catholic Theology and the Environment*, ed. Drew Christiansen and Walter Grazer (Washington, D.C.: United States Catholic Conference, 1996), 190.

106. William French, "Catholicism and the Common Good of the Biosphere," in *An Ecology of the Spirit*, ed. Michael Barnes (Lanham, Md.: University Press of America, 1993), 192. While not dismissing the anthropocentric principles of Aquinas's thought, French pushes past this, to embrace the ecological aspects of Aquinas. "Our emerging ecological concerns...provide the hermeneutical impetus to discern a second organizing principle in Thomas' ethics, namely his stress on the good of the

order of the universe, the common good, that is, of the community of creation" (193).

107. Christiansen, "Ecology and the Common Good," 188.

108. Wendell Berry, "Word and Flesh," in *Simpler Living, Compassionate Life*, ed. Michael Shut (New York: Morehouse, 2009), 102.

109. Cobb and Daly, *For the Common Good*, 164. See also Cobb, *Postmodernism*, 123.

110. David Klemm, "Material Grace: The Paradox of Property and Possession," in *Having: Property and Possession in Religious and Social Life*, ed. William Schweiker and Charles Mathewes (Grand Rapids, Mich.: Eerdmans, 2004), 224.

111. Augustine, *Confessions*, 223 (X. 29, 40).

112. Ibid., 227 (X. 31, 45).

113. Augustine, *Confessions*, trans. Edward Bouverie Pusey ("Augustine's Confessions, translated by E. B. Pusey," accessed Jan. 22, 2011, http://www9.georgetown.edu/faculty/jod/augustine/Pusey/book13, XIII. 8, 9).

114. Patrick Coy, introduction to *A Revolution of the Heart*, 3.

115. Cobb, *Sustaining the Common Good*, 12, 14. Cobb and Daly, *For the Common Good*, 297.

116. McFague, *Life Abundant*, 198.

117. Kagawa, *Brotherhood Economics*, 113.

118. Tanner, *Economy of Grace*, 142.

119. U.S. Catholic Bishops, 594 (§67).

Chapter 5

1. Glenn Scherer, "The Godly Must Be Crazy: Christian-Right Views Are Swaying Politicians and Threatening the Environment," *Grist Magazine*, Oct. 27, 2004, accessed Nov. 14, 2010, http://www.grist.org/article/scherer-christian.

2. He may, however, be quite right about end-time prophecies' influence on other political matters, such as foreign policy in the Middle East.

3. Scherer, "The Godly Must Be Crazy." The falsely attributed Watt quote comes from Austin Miles's *Setting the Captives Free: Victims of the Church Tell Their Stories* (Amherst, N.Y.: Prometheus, 1990), 229.

4. James G. Watt, "The Religious Left's Lies," *The Washington Post*, May 21, 2005, accessed Nov. 14, 2010, http://www.washingtonpost.com/wp-dyn/content/article/2005/05/20/AR2005052001333.html.

5. Wendell Berry, *Life Is a Miracle: An Essay against Modern Superstition* (Berkeley, Calif.: Counterpoint, 2000), 101.

6. Alice Walker, *In Search of Our Mothers' Gardens* (Orlando, Fla.: Harcourt, 1983), 351.

7. Portions of this section are drawn from my "Sabbath-Keeping as an Environmental Practice," *Worldviews: Global Religions, Culture, and Ecology* 15, no. 1 (March 2011).

8. In the Catholic and Anglican traditions, this commandment is interpreted as the third commandment; most Protestants and Jews refer to it as the fourth commandment. In deference to its Jewish origin, I will refer to it as the fourth commandment.

9. The dispute between Saturday and Sunday Sabbaths is especially important to Saturday-observing Christians, such as Seventh-day Adventists. As Roger Beckwith and Wilfrid Stott observe, "It is a striking fact that the Jewish Sabbath almost disappears from recorded Christian practice after Christ's resurrection.... [It is] never mentioned except as a tolerated option for Jewish Christians" (Roger T. Beckwith and Wilfrid Stott, *This Is the Day: The Biblical Doctrine of the Christian Sunday in Its Jewish and Early Church Setting* [Greenwood, S.C.: Attic, 1978], 30). On this day, Gentile Christians made time for worship and the agape meal before and after the workday; it was not a day of rest. "Christians kept no day as a rest day, neither Saturday nor Sunday, until the civil legislation of Constantine in the fourth century made Sunday a legal holiday for many occupations" (Everett Ferguson, *Early Christians Speak: Faith and Life in the First Three Centuries*, 3rd ed. [Abilene, Tex.: ACU, 1999], 69). One of the factors contributing to this development includes a desire to differentiate themselves from the Jews. Craig Blomberg writes, in response to those who blame anti-Semitism for the Sunday switch, "To be sure, growing anti-Semitism enabled such views to be held comfortably, but I am not persuaded that anti-Semitism can fully account for this earliest Christian theology of the Sabbath" (Craig Blomberg, "The Sabbath as Fulfilled in Christ: A Response to S. Bacchiocchi and J. Primus," in *The Sabbath in Jewish and Christian Traditions*, ed. Tamara C. Eskenazi, Daniel J. Harrington, and William H. Shea [New York: Crossroad, 1991], 128).

10. Specifically, they ruled that "the saving of life supersedes the Sabbath"; but healing, including most of the healing Jesus performed on the Sabbath, is generally forbidden, "unless there is danger to life" (B. Shabbath 132a, 18a [note 10]; Rabbi Isidore Epstein, *The Babylonian Talmud*, trans. Rabbi Isidore Epstein, vol. 3, *Shabbath* (London: Soncino, 1938), 660, 74). Arguably, Jesus could have healed these less urgent cases another day, rather than violate the Sabbath.

11. Romans 14:5–6: "Some judge one day to be better than another, while others judge all days to be alike. Let all be fully convinced in their own minds. Those who observe the day, observe it in honor of the Lord."

Some Christians take this to mean that there is no need to observe a Sabbath; others maintain that the fourth commandment was never explicitly abrogated, and still stands as a Christian duty.

12. For an enlightening interpretation of the connection between Puritans, the Sabbath, and American theology, see Herbert W. Richardson, *Toward an American Theology* (New York: Harper & Row, 1967), 112–13.

13. See, for example, Dan Allender, *Sabbath* (Nashville: Thomas Nelson, 2009); Lynn M. Baab, *Sabbath Keeping: Finding Freedom in the Rhythms of Rest* (Downers Grove, Ill.: InterVarsity, 2005); Mark Buchanan, *The Rest of God: Restoring Your Soul by Restoring Sabbath* (Nashville: W Publishing Group, 2006); Keri Wyatt Kent, *Rest: Living in Sabbath Simplicity* (Grand Rapids, Mich.: Zondervan, 2009); Wayne Muller, *Sabbath: Finding Rest, Renewal, and Delight in Our Busy Lives* (New York: Bantam, 2000); Norman Wirzba, *Living the Sabbath: Discovering the Rhythms of Rest and Delight* (Grand Rapids, Mich.: Brazos, 2006).

14. Seventh-day Adventists are the largest and best known of these denominations, but there are also Seventh-day Baptists and several smaller denominations descending from the Sabbatarian movements of the mid-1800s. These denominations base their Saturday observance on their interpretation of the Decalogue, which they say was not abrogated by Jesus.

15. Jonathan M. Butler, Ronald L. Numbers, and Gary G. Land, "Seventh-Day Adventism," in *Encyclopedia of Religion*, 2nd ed., ed. Lindsay Jones (New York: Thompson-Gale, 2005), 12:8235.

16. Ronald L. Numbers, *Prophetess of Health: Ellen G. White and the Origins of Seventh-day Adventist Health Reform* (Knoxville: University of Tennessee Press, 1992), 15.

17. Rob Bell, *Velvet Elvis: Repainting the Christian Faith* (Grand Rapids, Mich.: Zondervan, 2006), 117.

18. Marva J. Dawn, *Keeping the Sabbath Wholly: Ceasing, Resting, Embracing, Feasting* (Grand Rapids, Mich.: Eerdmans, 1989).

19. Sabbath Economics Collaborative, "About Us: What Do We Mean by 'Sabbath Economics'?" accessed Nov. 14, 2010, http://www.sabbatheconomics .org/content/page.php?section=4&content_id=6.

20. Ibid.

21. Richard H. Lowery, *Sabbath and Jubilee* (St. Louis: Chalice, 2000), 4, 149.

22. Wirzba, *Living the Sabbath*, 20.

23. Abraham Joshua Heschel, *The Sabbath: Its Meaning for Modern Man* (New York: Farrar, Straus and Young, 1952), 15.

24. Ibid., 13.

25. See Nehemiah 10:31: "and if the peoples of the land bring in merchandise or any grain on the sabbath day to sell, we will not buy it from them on the sabbath or on a holy day; and we will forgo the crops of the seventh year and the exaction of every debt."

26. Heschel, *The Sabbath*, 28.

27. Ibid., 90. (The tenth commandment prohibits covetousness.)

28. John Paul II, "Dies Domini," accessed Nov. 14, 2010, http://www.vatican. va/holy_father/john_paul_ii/apost_letters/documents/hf_jp-ii_apl_05071998_dies-domini_en.html, 13, 64.

29. Ibid., 16.

30. Ibid., 65.

31. Karl Barth's *Church Dogmatics* contains a discussion of human surrender to God on the Sabbath, in the same vein as John Paul II's discussion, but with an even greater emphasis on human dependence on God's grace. Barth writes, "The aim of the Sabbath commandment is that man shall give and allow the omnipotent grace of God to have the first and the last word at every point; that he shall surrender to it completely, in the last as well as in the greatest things; that he shall place himself, with his knowing, willing, and doing, unconditionally at its disposal" (Karl Barth, *Church Dogmatics* 3 [Edinburgh: T&T Clark, 1958], part 4, chapter 12, §53.1, 54).

32. John Paul II, "Dies Domini," 17 (the reference is to Genesis 1:31).

33. Donna Schaper, *Sabbath Keeping* (Boston: Cowley, 1999), xii.

34. J. Matthew Sleeth, *Serve God, Save the Planet: A Christian Call to Action* (White River Junction, Vt.: Chelsea Green, 2006), 85.

35. David A. Cooper, *Renewing Your Soul: A Guided Retreat for the Sabbath and Other Days of Rest* (San Francisco: HarperSanFrancisco, 1995), 76.

36. Sleeth, *Serve God, Save the Planet*, 84.

37. Ibid., 86.

38. Allender, *Sabbath*, 15.

39. John Paul II, "Dies Domini," 37.

40. Ibid., 84.

41. Heschel, *The Sabbath*, 23.

42. Ibid., 68.

43. Jacques B. Doukhan, "Loving the Sabbath as a Christian: A Seventh-Day Adventist Perspective," *The Sabbath in Jewish and Christian Traditions*, ed. Tamara C. Eskenazi, Daniel J. Harrington, and William H. Shea (New York: Crossroad, 1991), 152.

44. Ginger Hanks-Harwood, "Wholeness," in *Remnant and Republic: Adventist Themes for Personal and Social Ethics*, ed. Charles W. Teel Jr. (Loma Linda, Calif.: Loma Linda University Center for Christian Bioethics, 1995), 134.

45. Dawn, *Keeping the Sabbath Wholly*, 151.

46. Allender, *Sabbath*, 12.
47. Wirzba, *Living the Sabbath*, 34.
48. Ibid., 41.
49. Miroslav M. Kis, "Sabbath," in *Remnant and Republic: Adventist Themes for Personal and Social Ethics*, ed. Charles W. Teel Jr. (Loma Linda, Calif.: Loma Linda University Center for Christian Bioethics, 1995), 99.
50. Doukhan, "Loving the Sabbath as a Christian," 156.
51. Wendell Berry, *Home Economics* (San Francisco: North Point, 1987), 66.
52. Ched Myers, *The Biblical Vision of Sabbath Economics* (Washington, D.C.: Tell the Word, Church of the Saviour, 2002), 13.
53. Wirzba, *Living the Sabbath*, 38.
54. Ronald L. Numbers, *Prophetess of Health: Ellen G. White and the Origins of Seventh-Day Adventist Health Reform* (Knoxville: University of Tennessee Press, 1992), 81.
55. Joseph Bates, an early church leader, reported from a missionary trip to Maine that tobacco use was on the wane. He related this news with an eschatological spin, as Numbers observes: "With the Second coming so close, it seemed to him that nothing was 'to[o] dear or precious to let go in end of the cause now'" (ibid., 39).
56. Seventh-day Adventist Dietetic Association, "Position Statement on the Vegetarian Diet," accessed Nov. 14, 2010, http://www.sdada.org/position.htm.
57. These assertions are often accepted as truisms among environmentalists; those wishing to research the matter further may find resources at sites such as http://www.chooseveg.com/environment.asp.
58. See http://www.adventist.org/beliefs/statements/index.html. Other topics are treated much as would be expected from a more conservative Protestant denomination: Adventists are against homosexuality, against abortion, against euthanasia, and in support of creationism over evolution.
59. General Conference of Seventh-day Adventists Administrative Committee, "Statement on Stewardship of the Environment," Office of the President, General Conference of Seventh-day Adventists, accessed Nov. 14, 2010, http://adventist.org/beliefs/statements/main-stat10.html.
60. Dawn, *Keeping the Sabbath Wholly*, 183.
61. Ibid., 38.
62. Sleeth, *Serve God, Save the Planet*, 85.
63. Allender, *Sabbath*, 79.
64. Ibid., 78.
65. Ibid., 65. He is quoting Psalm 34:8.
66. Ibid., 79.

67. Wendell Berry, "The Farm," in *A Timbered Choir: The Sabbath Poems, 1979–1997* (Washington, D.C.: Counterpoint, 1998), 139–40.
68. Berry, *Home Economics*, 143.
69. Berry, according to Wirzba, has provocatively compared this pattern of buying something, using it briefly, and throwing it away to a "one-night stand": "we enjoy the good time associated with our consumption but prefer not to know the many details or histories of our products for fear that we might be ashamed of what we are doing" (Wirzba, *Living the Sabbath*, 112).
70. Ibid., 24–25.
71. Ibid., 25.
72. Ibid., 72, 125–27.
73. Ibid., 127.
74. Ibid., 112. Additionally, Sabbath people ought to lead the fight against "big box" chain stores by supporting small, local businesses (ibid., 126).
75. Ibid., 151.
76. Wirzba does not address the deprivations that exclusively local consumption entails—no olive oil, no almonds, and no bananas for him and his neighbors in Kentucky, where he wrote the book. And he perhaps hastily discounts the "shallow thanksgiving" offered over food of unknown origin, failing to recognize the genuine appreciation, enjoyment, and fellowship that can exist even over less-than-ideal meals (ibid., 112).
77. "Sabbath practices," he notes, "are corporate in nature, which means that we will need to enlist the help of others....As worshiping communities, we have to do a better job of reminding each other how shopping is of great religious significance" (Wirzba, *Living the Sabbath*, 151).
78. John Paul II, "Dies Domini," 44.
79. Mary Barbara Agnew, CPPS, "Sunday: Synthesis of Christian Life," *Liturgical Ministry* 12 (Spring 2003): 90. Agnew notes (p. 98) that there has been little popular or scholarly response to *Dies Domini* beyond her own article and one other.
80. Larry Rasmussen, "Chase's Sabbath," *The Living Pulpit* (April–June 1998): 21.
81. Doukhan, "Loving the Sabbath as a Christian," 157.
82. Zdravko Plantak, *The Silent Church: Human Rights and Adventist Social Ethics* (New York: St. Martin's, 1998), 39. For example, Joseph Bates, an early leader in the Seventh-day Adventist church, was an active abolitionist before he came to believe in the imminent return of Christ; afterward he came to see human sin in general as a larger and more pressing concern than slavery, and he stopped his abolition work in order to preach the gospel (ibid.).

83. See Francis D. Nichol, *Reasons for Our Faith: A Discussion of Questions Vital to the Proper Understanding and Effective Presentation of Certain Seventh-Day Adventist Teachings* (Takoma Park, Washington, D.C.: Review and Herald Publishing Association, 1947), 110–11. Nichol refers to early Christians' belief in Christ's imminent return and their record of charitable help within and among churches.

84. In the United States, Adventist Health has a chain of well-regarded hospitals (see http://www.adventisthealth.org/) and a medical research facility at Loma Linda University in California (see http://www.llu.edu/). International health efforts are coordinated by Adventist Health International (see http://www.adventisthealthinternational.org/).

85. Wirzba, *Living the Sabbath*, 38–39.

86. Myers, *The Biblical Vision of Sabbath Economics*, 5.

87. Ibid., 49.

88. L. Roger Owens, "Sabbath-Keeping: Christian Sabbath-Keeping and the Desire for Justice," *Vital Christianity: Spirituality, Justice, and Christian Practice*, ed. David L. Weaver-Zercher and William H. Willimon (New York: T&T Clark, 2005), 210.

89. Dawn, *Keeping the Sabbath Wholly*, 125.

90. John Paul II, "Dies Domini," 83.

91. Owens, "Sabbath-Keeping," 202.

92. Marva J. Dawn, "A Systematic, Biblical Theology of Sabbath Keeping," in *The Sabbath in Jewish and Christian Traditions*, ed. Tamara C. Eskanzi, Daniel J. Harrington, and William H. Shea (New York: Crossroad, 1991), 185.

93. Ibid., 94.

94. Lowery, *Sabbath and Jubilee*, 151.

95. Jürgen Moltmann, *God in Creation: A New Theology of Creation and the Spirit of God* (San Francisco: Harper & Row, 1985), 296.

96. Wirzba, *Living the Sabbath*, 152. Regular halting of human pressures would indeed make a significant difference for ecological health. As Michael Northcott writes, with an eye to reducing the effects of global warming, observing an abstinent Sabbath might be ecologically salutary: "if all industrial devices and consumption and transportation activities were stopped one day in seven this would immediately represent a more than 10 per cent cut in human use of energy" (Michael S. Northcott, *A Moral Climate: The Ethics of Global Warming* [London: Darton, Longman and Todd, 2007], 187). He draws a biblical parallel invoking the perils of noncompliance with this commandment: "the Prophets interpret the long exile in Babylon not only as judgment on Israel for neglecting the Sabbath but to help the land recover from hundreds of neglected Sabbaths" (ibid., 262).

97. Moltmann, "Sabbath: Finishing and Beginning," *The Living Pulpit* (April–June 1998): 5.

98. See Hanks-Harwood, "Wholeness," 127–44.; also Doukhan, "Loving the Sabbath as a Christian," 151.

99. Hanks-Harwood, "Wholeness," 141.

100. Ibid., 142. "Advocacy ethics" is Hanks-Harwood's term. I take it to mean a method of putting one's ethical convictions to work by advocating for certain things or on behalf of certain people.

101. Paul Evdokimov, "The Church and Society: The Social Dimension of Orthodox Ecclesiology," in *In the World, of the Church: A Paul Evdokimov Reader*, ed. and trans. Michael Plekon and Alexis Vinogradov (Crestwood, N.Y.: St. Vladimir's Seminary Press, 2001), 76.

102. Portions of this section are derived from my "Consuming Christ: The Role of Jesus in Christian Food Ethics," *Journal of the Society of Christian Ethics* 30, no. 1 (Spring/Summer 2010).

103. Other instances include burning incense and candles, anointing with oil, and the historic practice of a Christian love feast (which is still practiced by some Protestant denominations). Baptism and foot washing also can be classified as consumption, since they use water. For a more detailed look at the material culture of Christianity, see Colleen McDannell, *Material Christianity: Religion and Popular Culture in America* (New Haven, Conn.: Yale University Press, 1998).

104. Fasting, associated with penance, is one way Christians may ready themselves to receive Christ's presence in the Eucharist. This practice is primarily associated with the Roman Catholic tradition. The Catholic Code of Canon Law reads, "A person who is to receive the Most Holy Eucharist is to abstain for at least one hour before holy communion from any food and drink, except for only water and medicine" (*Code of Canon Law*, can. 919, accessed Nov. 14, 2010, http://www.vatican.va/archive/ENG1104/__P39.HTM.

105. See Caroline Walker Bynum, *Holy Feast and Holy Fast* (Berkeley and Los Angeles: University of California Press, 1988), 92.

106. See Bishop Kallistos of Diokleia, "Lent and the Consumer Society," in *Living Orthodoxy in the Modern World: Orthodox Christianity and Society*, ed. Andrew Walker and Costa Carras (Crestwood, N.Y.: St. Vladimir's Seminary Press, 1996), 64–84.

107. Metropolitan John Zizioulas, "Ecological Asceticism: A Cultural Revolution," *Sourozh* 67 (Fall 1997): 22–25. John Chryssavgis also writes eloquently on the link between asceticism and ecology; see John Chryssavgis, ed., *Cosmic Grace, Humble Prayer: The Ecological Vision of the Green Patriarch Bartholomew I* (Grand Rapids, Mich: Eerdmans, 2003), 29–33.

108. Though a priest or pastor may be the one saying the words, Christians understand Jesus to be the origin, and therefore the host, of the Eucharistic meal (Matthew 26:17–29; Mark 14:22–25; and Luke 22:7–23). Paul refers to Christ as the "paschal lamb" in 1 Corinthians 5:7.

109. Marion Grau, *Of Divine Economy: Refinancing Redemption* (New York: T&T Clark, 2004), 208.

110. Catherine Keller, "A Christian Response to the Population Apocalypse," *Population, Consumption, and the Environment: Religious and Secular Responses*, ed. Howard Coward (Albany, N.Y.: State University of New York Press, 1995), 119.

111. Boris Jakim, introduction to *The Bride of the Lamb*, by Sergei Bulgakov, trans. Boris Jakim (Grand Rapids, Mich.: Eerdmans, 2002), xii.

112. Orthodox theologians draw on the Gospel stories of Christ's transfiguration (Matthew 17 and Mark 9): since Christ's clothes, in addition to his face, glow with supernatural glory, so nonhuman creation, including human artifacts, may be transfigured (Elizabeth Theokritoff, "Embodied Word and New Creation: Some Modern Orthodox Insights Concerning the Material World," in *Abba: The Tradition of Orthodoxy in the West*, ed. John Behr, Andrew Louth, and Dimitri Conomos [Crestwood, N.Y.: St. Vladimir's Seminary Press, 2003], 227).

113. Willis Jenkins, *Ecologies of Grace: Environmental Ethics and Christian Theology* (Oxford: Oxford University Press, 2008), 194.

114. Ibid., 195–96.

115. Metropolitan John Zizioulas, "Man the Priest of Creation: A Response to the Ecological Problem," in *Living Orthodoxy in the Modern World: Orthodox Christianity and Society*, ed. Andrew Walker and Costa Carras (Crestwood, N.Y.: St. Vladimir's Seminary Press, 1996), 183.

116. For Zizioulas, this is where the *imago Dei* resides: in the human ability "to collect what is diversified and even fragmented in this world and make a unified and harmonious world (cosmos) out of that.... Man has the capacity to unite the world" (Zizioulas, "Man the Priest of Creation," 182).

117. Jenkins, *Ecologies of Grace*, 213.

118. Ibid., 200.

119. Evdokimov, "The Church and Society," 213.

120. Sergei Bulgakov, *Philosophy of Economy: The World as Household*, trans. Catherine Evtuhov (New Haven, Conn.: Yale University Press, 2000), 106.

121. Ibid., 103.

122. Sergei Bulgakov, *The Holy Grail and the Eucharist*, trans. Boris Jakim (Hudson, N.Y.: Lindisfarne, 1997), 34.

123. Ibid., 103.

124. Ibid., 105.
125. One example of this belief arises in the Catholic catechism: "The sacraments [including Eucharist] are efficacious signs of grace, instituted by Christ and entrusted to the Church, by which divine life is dispensed to us. The visible rites by which the sacraments are celebrated signify and make present the graces proper to each sacrament. They bear fruit in those who receive them with the required dispositions" (*Catechism of the Catholic Church*, 1131, accessed Nov. 14, 2010, http://www.vatican. va/archive/ccc_css/archive/catechism/p2s1c1a2.htm).
126. The *host* of Christian liturgy derives from Latin, *hostia*, meaning victim or sacrifice. The word *host* relating to *hospitality* derives from a different Latin word, *hospit*. It is simply a linguistic convergence that these words may both be rendered *host* in English; but the connection between the two concepts in the person of Jesus makes for an interesting double entendre.
127. Evdokimov, "The Church and Society," 268.
128. William T. Cavanaugh, *Being Consumed: Economics and Christian Desire* (Grand Rapids, Mich.: Eerdmans, 2008), 54.
129. Ibid., 55.
130. Bulgakov, *Holy Grail and the Eucharist*, 137–38.
131. Bulgakov, *Philosophy of Economy*, 523. The passage is Bulgakov's interpretation of Revelation 22:1–2.
132. Rosenthal notes that "Bulgakov's eschatology was gentle and bloodless, for its agent, Sophia, is a mediator, bringing people together with one another, the created world, and the Logos" (Bernice Glatzer Rosenthal, "The Nature and Function of Sophia in Sergei Bulgakov's Prerevolutionary Thought," in *Russian Religious Thought*, ed. Judith Deutsch Kornblatt and Richard F. Gustafson [Madison: University of Wisconsin Press], 163). Rosenthal eloquently describes this as "transfiguration without catastrophe, the sophianization of the world" (ibid., 172).
133. L. Shannon Jung, *Food for Life: The Spirituality and Ethics of Eating* (Minneapolis: Fortress, 2004), 26, 43. (Originally, all was italicized.)
134. Wendell Berry, *The Gift of Good Land* (San Francisco: North Point, 1981), 281.
135. Jenkins, *Ecologies of Grace*, 221.
136. Bulgakov, *Philosophy of Economy*, 102, quoted in ibid.
137. Ibid., 200.
138. Bishop Basil, *Speaking of the Kingdom* (Oxford: St. Stephen's Press, 1993), 53, quoted in Theokritoff, "Embodied Word and New Creation," 231.
139. Evdokimov, "The Church and Society," 254.

140. He writes:

> The world enters us through all the windows and doors of our sense and, having entered, is apprehended and assimilated by us. In its totality this consumption of the world, this ontological communication with it, this communism of being, lies at the foundation of all of our life processes. Life is in this sense the capacity to consume the world, whereas death is an exodus out of this world, the loss of capacity to communicate with it; finally, resurrection is a return into the world with a restoration of this capacity, though to an infinitely expanded degree. (Bulgakov, *Philosophy of Economy*, 102)

141. Sergei Bulgakov, *Sophia: The Wisdom of God*, trans. Patrick Thompson, O. Fielding Clarke, and Xenia Braikevitc (Hudson, N.Y.: Lindisfarne, 1993), 17.

142. Stephen H. Webb, *Good Eating* (Grand Rapids, Mich.: Brazos, 2001), 144.

143. Monika K. Hellwig, *The Eucharist and the Hunger of the World* (New York: Paulist, 1976), 39. She also asserts that efforts to avoid consuming products that participate in the oppression of workers "is to become oneself in some measure bread for the life of the world…in tune with the life and spirit of Jesus" (ibid.).

144. L. Shannon Jung, *Sharing Food: Christian Practices for Enjoyment* (Minneapolis: Fortress, 2006), 132, 135, 138.

145. Northcott, *A Moral Climate*, 265–66.

146. Gordon W. Lathrop, *Holy Ground: A Liturgical Cosmology* (Minneapolis: Fortress, 2003), 150.

147. Ibid., 151.

148. Food Not Bombs is a loosely organized movement of activists who cook vegetarian and vegan meals using discarded or donated food and serve it in public places "to anyone without restriction" ("The Story of Food Not Bombs," *Food Not Bombs*, accessed Nov. 14, 2010, http://www.foodnotbombs.net/story.html. See also http://www.foodnotbombs.net.

149. Though to my knowledge no churches have done this, I believe Palm Sunday would be an especially appropriate time for a Eucharist of clothing. The people celebrated Jesus' entry into Jerusalem not simply by laying down palm leaves but also by laying down their clothing (Mark 11:8). Also, the passion story that is often narrated on Palm Sunday features (in the version from Mark) "a certain young man" who was "wearing nothing but a linen cloth"; when apprehended he leaves the cloth and runs away, naked (14:51–52). Further, the soldiers mock Jesus by giving him purple robes, taking them away again, and casting lots for

his clothing (Mark 15:17, 24). With these passages in mind, perhaps congregants could bring extra clothing to offer to Christ along with the palm leaves, orchestrating a clothing swap and donation as a way to break and share this often-overconsumed resource.

150. Bill McKibben, *Deep Economy: The Wealth of Communities and the Durable Future* (New York: Times Books, 2007), 145–46.
151. Evdokimov, "The Church and Society," 75.
152. Quoted in Jenkins, 200.
153. Ibid., 208.

Chapter 6

1. The Sierra Club has since changed its list, and BP rates a "dishonorable mention." See Sarah Ives and Robynne Boyd, "Pick Your Poison: An Updated Environmentalist's Guide to Gasoline," *Sierra Club*, accessed Nov. 14, 2010, http://www.sierraclub.org/sierra/pickyourpoison/.
2. Ron Lieber, "Punishing BP Is Harder than Boycotting Stations," *New York Times*, June 11, 2010, accessed Nov. 14, 2010, http://www.nytimes.com/2010/06/12/your-money/12money.html.
3. L. Shannon Jung, *Food for Life: The Spirituality and Ethics of Eating* (Minneapolis: Fortress, 2004), 60ff.
4. Ibid., 89; and Jung, *Hunger and Happiness: Feeding the Hungry, Nourishing Our Souls* (Minneapolis: Augsburg, 2009), 21ff.
5. Jung, *Hunger and Happiness*, 7.
6. Jung, *Sharing Food*, 144.
7. Jung, *Hunger and Happiness*, 111.
8. Jung, *Sharing Food*, 31.
9. Jung, *Hunger and Happiness*, 69.
10. See Jung, *Sharing Food*.
11. *Living in God's Creation: Orthodox Perspectives on Ecology* (Crestwood, N.Y.: St. Vladimir's Seminary Press, 2009).
12. Ibid., 94.
13. Ibid., 105.
14. Ibid., 190.
15. Ibid., 191–92.
16. Ibid., 209.
17. Ibid., 196.
18. Ibid.
19. Ibid., 200.
20. James A. Nash, "Toward the Revival and Reform of the Subversive Virtue: Frugality," *Annual of the Society of Christian Ethics* (1995): 139–40.

21. Ibid., 140–42.
22. Ibid., 144.
23. Ibid., 148.
24. Ibid., 152.
25. Ibid., 153.
26. Ibid., 156.
27. Ibid., 158.
28. Ibid.
29. Ibid., 159.
30. Thomas P. Slaughter, *The Beautiful Soul of John Woolman, Apostle of Abolition* (New York: Hill & Wang, 2008), 279–80.
31. James Nash died in November 2008, so, sadly, this thought experiment cannot be realized.
32. For details about relative impacts of wine shipping, see Andrea Thompson, "The Carbon Footprint of Wine," *LiveScience*, Nov. 10, 2008, accessed Dec. 21, 2010, http://www.livescience.com/environment/081110-wine-carbon-footprint.html.
33. Margaret Urban Walker, *Moral Understandings: A Feminist Study in Ethics* (New York: Routledge, 1998), 7.
34. Ibid., 9. Walker believes that moral norms are expressive of a community, generated as the community collaborates in their creation. My work here extends that model to include another community, the gathering of historic voices that constitute a religious tradition. In collaboration with those voices—not excluding any of them—I seek to articulate an ethics that expresses the collective wisdom of this intertemporal religious community.
35. Tom L. Beauchamp and James F. Childress, *Principles of Biomedical Ethics*, 6th ed. (New York: Oxford University Press, 2009), 15.
36. Ibid., 16–23.
37. Ibid., 40.
38. Ibid.
39. Andrew Linzey, *Animal Gospel* (Louisville: Westminster John Knox, 2000), 31–32.
40. The intensive energy and water usage and inefficient land usage associated with meat production make it less environmentally favorable than production of plant crops. For more details see http://www.chooseveg.com/environment.asp.
41. Ronald J. Sider, *Rich Christians in an Age of Hunger: Moving from Affluence to Generosity*, 5th ed. (Nashville: W Publishing Group, 2005), 193.
42. See the related discussion in David T. Schwartz, *Consuming Choices: Ethics in a Global Consumer Age* (Lanham, Md.: Rowman & Littlefield, 2010), 97–102.

43. This would, in fact "be tantamount to admitting that in some circumstances God compels man to sin by demanding of him what he is unable to do, and such action would argue injustice in God himself" (John Mahoney, *The Making of Moral Theology* [Oxford: Clarendon, 1989], 56).

44. Hence his controversial statement addressed to God: "give what you command, and then command whatever you will" (Augustine of Hippo, *Confessions*, trans. Maria Boulding [New York: Vintage, 1997], 223 [29, 40]).

45. Vincent J. Miller, *Consuming Religion: Christian Faith and Practice in a Consumer Culture* (New York: Continuum, 2005), 9.

46. Ibid., 9.

47. Ibid., 10.

INDEX

Nash, James A. (*continued*)
  natural communion, 157
  neighbor-love. *See* love
New American Dream, Center
  for a, 28
Nichol, Francis D., 226n83
Niebuhr, H. Richard, 26
norms, 13–14, 177, 215n44,
  232n34
Northcott, Michael, 163, 226n96
Numbers, Ronald L., 224n55

oppression, 42, 45, 141, 150–51,
  203n62, 230n143. *See also*
  exploitation; sin, structural
Origen, 149
Outka, Gene, 213n11, 214n20
Owens, L. Roger, 149–50

Palm Sunday, 230–31n149
Paul the Apostle, Saint, 41, 47,
  100, 132, 228n108
Paulist Press, 212n3
peaceable kingdom, 155, 189.
  See also God, reign of;
  kingdom of God
Peacock, Philip, 202n33
Pearce, Fred, 13
Piehl, Mel, 84
Pilgrim, David, 68
Plantak, Zdravko, 148, 225n82
positive confession, 57, 67. *See
  also* prosperity theology
possessions. *See also*
  materialism; poverty;
  prosperity theology; wealth
  common right of, 106–110

contemplation and, 62
creation and, 174
detachment and, 38–39, 51, 66,
  73, 101
dissatisfaction and, 15
hospitality and, 101
Jesus and, 33, 36, 65–66,
  200n12
prosperity theology and, 64, 68
relationships and, 123
renunciation of, 33, 37, 51, 65
Sabbath and, 136, 145
spiritual effect of, 22
poverty. *See also* asceticism;
  Catholic Worker Movement;
  Francis of Assisi, Saint;
  frugality; possessions;
  preferential option for the
  poor; prosperity theology;
  simplicity
  as measurement for other
  lifestyles, 47, 116
  as refusal of dominion, 38
  asceticism, simplicity, and,
  36–42
  Biblical position on, 41, 78
  Christian concern for
  involuntary, 22, 35–36, 38,
  42, 48, 65, 79–80, 116, 186,
  190, 203n62
  consumption of meat and, 191
  criticism of voluntary, 50–53,
  200nn11–12,
  204–205nn82–84
  hunger and, 77
  Jesus as representative of, 33,
  37, 64, 82
  Lady, 36–37, 205n84
  neighbor-love and, 88, 102